How Countries Compete

How Countries Compete

STRATEGY, STRUCTURE,

AND GOVERNMENT IN

THE GLOBAL ECONOMY

Richard H. K. Vietor

Harvard Business School Press
Boston, Massachusetts

Library of Congress Cataloging-in-Publication Data
Vietor, Richard H. K., 1945–
    How countries compete: strategy, structure, and government in the global economy /
Richard H. K. Vietor
      p.   cm.
    ISBN-13: 978-1-4221-1035-5 (hardcover: alk. paper)
    1. Competition, International. I. Title.
    HF1414.V54   2006
    382'.1—dc22

                                                                        2006034452

The paper used in this publication meets the minimum requirements of the American National Standard for Information Sciences—Permanence of Paper for Printed Library Materials, ANSI Z39.48-1992.

CONTENTS

Introduction

COUNTRIES COMPETE

COUNTRIES COMPETE to develop. This is one result of globalization. They compete for markets, for technology, for skills and investment. They compete to grow and raise their standards of living. In this competitive environment, it is government, invariably, that provides distinctive advantages to firms: high savings and low interest rates for investment, sound property rights and good governance, a technologically motivated and committed workforce, a low rate of inflation, and a rapidly expanding domestic market.

"Preparing our nation to compete," said President George W. Bush in his State of the Union message from January 31, 2006, "is a goal that all of us can share." In a dynamic world economy, "we are seeing new competitors, like China and India, and this creates uncertainty." The subject of this book is how government helps countries compete.

For twenty-five years, I have taught Business, Government, and the International Economy (BGIE) at the Harvard Business School. More recently, I taught this course in the school's Advanced Management Program—an eight-week program for executives. To date, I've had more than twenty-four hundred executive students, two-thirds of whom are non-American. Because of them, I have traveled extensively to do research. I've enjoyed incredible opportunities to meet presidents and prime ministers, business executives and economists, labor leaders, politicians, and soldiers.

These experiences convinced me that countries compete—implicitly, and sometimes explicitly. By "compete" I mean that countries contend for market share in the world economy, contesting foreign investment and export sales through their businesses. The global economy today is about $44 trillion. While it has grown at a healthy rate since the late 1940s, total exports

1

have grown even faster—more than twice as fast. This has stimulated consumption in rich countries and investment in developing countries—helping both grow faster. Accordingly, countries also compete for foreign direct investment, and for the managerial skills, technology, and distribution channels that accompany it. The purpose of this competition is growth and development—to reduce poverty, accommodate urbanization, increase living standards, and create jobs.

This competition is led by government in a score of fundamental ways. As the next chapter will explain, government is responsible for providing security, ensuring contracts, assuming risk, managing the macroeconomy, and shaping industrial policy. Government does this by creating and sustaining a variety of institutions—political, social, and economic—through which its people function, interact, and compete.

The American business executives I know particularly dislike government and generally think it incompetent. And yet, they vest it with huge responsibilities—not only fiscal and monetary policy, which shapes their macroeconomic performance, but resources for housing, education, health, research and development, and defense. To do this, they spend more than $2.7 trillion annually. And yet, too many business executives (as well as government bureaucrats and other well-meaning, educated citizens) know too little about the world economy—although they'd like to. They read in the news about China's growth, outsourcing to India, Putin's rule in Russia, and AIDS in South Africa, but they have no real context for appreciating those facts. Nor do they seem to understand the role of government.

Nowhere have I found well-informed citizens playing an adequate role in affecting their government's strategy—not in Russia, China, or South Africa, and certainly not in the United States. (Only Singapore comes close.) The reason, in part, is lack of knowledge. When I teach the BGIE course to executives, they see the degree to which economic performance is indeed a function of government policy. Firms obviously benefit from healthy economies with growing markets. They benefit from wage growth that is slower than productivity growth, from the availability of an educated workforce, and from relatively liberal work rules. Firms also benefit from low real interest rates that encourage investment, and relatively few regulatory barriers to invest. Firms need competitive exchange rates, secure property rights, reasonable income distribution, as little corruption as possible, and few trade barriers. And they need macroeconomic policies that control inflation and maintain long-term economic growth.

All of these conditions are delivered by effective government policies, in which executives indeed have a vested interest. Thus, I have written this book to convince readers that government strategy matters, and that they are personally responsible for effecting good government policy in their home countries.

To approach a usable understanding of the world economy, this book offers a three-part analytical framework. First, to understand current conditions, business managers must be able to analyze the strategy and organizational structure of nation-states, in terms of how they fit the sociopolitical context and how they affect economic performance. This approach to country analysis is the subject of chapter 1.

But second, managers are invariably more interested in where countries are going, rather than where they are today. So to think about the future, I've found it useful to consider a country's *trajectory*—its developmental pathway, cutting through time with a lot of momentum. Each country is developing in a particular direction, based on its current strategy, organizational structure, and context. This trajectory generally carries a country or region forward for years or even decades.

True, trajectories can sometimes change abruptly—with war, shortages (food or energy), political upheaval, or economic shocks. But in the absence of such radical change, an informed observer who understands the trajectory can make reasonable deductions about the near-term future: about fiscal balances and debt; about exchange rates and interest rates; about savings, investment, and growth; and about the sustainability of the country's political and economic institutions. Obviously, these pathways affect us all.

Third, with a reasonable sense of a country's trajectory, one can construct simple scenarios to think carefully about the near-term future. Looking at both optimistic and pessimistic futures, reasonably likely in either case, a manager can assess the economic conditions he or she will most likely experience. Is a market for direct investment likely to grow or maintain competitive costs for reexport? Should one expect worsening inflation or an appreciating currency? Will a country be forced to reduce fiscal deficits and thus slow its domestic growth? Or will increasing debt drive up interest rates?

After a discussion of country analysis in chapter 1, this book is organized broadly according to developmental trajectories that I find useful for thinking about the global economy. In part I, we will explore today's most important trajectory, which is Asian high growth. Japan, between 1954 and 1971, created the model and set a standard for high growth—10.1 percent annually for seventeen years! And since the late 1970s, China, Korea, Taiwan, Hong Kong, Singapore, Malaysia, and Thailand have been growing at 6–8 percent annually, and after 1992, they were joined by India. Taken together, this amounts to nearly half the world's population.

In Asia, we see strategies dependent on high savings and investment, including significant foreign direct investment. Wages are low, inflation controlled, and government, which is small, plays an active role in planning and implementing development strategy. (Of course, there are exceptions, like Hong Kong—which grew fast with little government direction, although with an exceptionally solid institutional structure.) The cultural values of Asians, moreover, support good primary and secondary education, high savings, and hard work. These are absolutely crucial in explaining high growth. Chapters 2–5 of this book explore the high-growth development strategies of Japan, Singapore, China, and India. Here we see extraordinary strategies of export-led growth and liberalization of previously closed systems of import substitution.

Part II (chapters 6–9) explores development trajectories that entail deep structural adjustment of institutions. Thus far, these trajectories have proved less successful. By examining Mexico, chapter 6 elucidates Latin America's recovery from debt crisis and its subsequent economic and political liberalization. Under the pressure of excessive foreign debt, generally closed right-wing or left-wing governments were forced to adjust structurally, usually under the guidance of and pressure from the International Monetary Fund. Notwithstanding Mexico's oil-rich endowment, two debt crises forced macroeconomic correction, liberalization of trade, investment, privatization, and finally, political reform. However, here too we will see the other aspects of Latin America—continuing problems of poverty, education, rigid labor markets, and lousy income distribution. What come into stark relief are the institutional and policy differences that distinguish Latin American performance from that of Asia.

Chapter 7 considers the African renaissance—the return of economic growth to sub-Saharan Africa after a century of colonial and postcolonial stagnation. It focuses on South Africa, where horrific apartheid finally gave way, peacefully, to majority black rule in 1994. While still in the process of rebuilding human and social institutions, South Africa is beginning to make real progress.

Chapter 8 deals with Islamic resurgence in the Middle East, trying to understand how Islamic culture copes with modernization and westernization. To do this, the chapter focuses on Saudi Arabia—by far the region's most important country given its oil wealth. Yet as the chapter shows, oil wealth is hard to translate into economic growth and a sustainable polity.

Chapter 9 focuses on Eastern European disintegration with the collapse of the Soviet Union and subsequent structural adjustment. Since 1989, this abrupt collapse has severely affected more than 400 million people. Two entire generations have been upended. We look at Russia—the biggest and most salient of some twenty-seven countries—to understand how simultaneous political and economic liberalization failed and to consider what its prospects are in the twenty-first century.

In part III, we turn to deficits, debt, and stagnation in the developed world of Europe, Japan, and the United States. Together these three account for two-thirds of world output.

In chapter 10, the trajectory is European integration—moving from separate states to a single European Union. This is a long process, beginning in 1946, with a very long way to go. We will see how Europeans first integrated trade, then exchange rates, then markets, and *finally*, a single currency. But through a focus on Italy we will also explore the significant problems that Europe still faces with growth and productivity, with aging and deficits, and above all, with economic competitiveness.

Chapter 11 examines Japan, now fallen into postbubble stagnation plagued by issues with deficits, debt, and demography. Here the problem is clearly institutional change. It has been very, very difficult for the Japanese to reform and modernize their institutions. After fourteen years of slow growth (1 percent) and halting reform, Japan is nearing either recovery or collapse.

And chapter 12 turns to the United States, which has similar problems—particularly deficits and debt—as well as excessive consumption and a massive current account deficit. But here, because the United States is politically and economically dominant and has a younger, more entrepreneurial population, its substantial problems are masked by continuing economic growth. Of course, such success makes it all the more difficult to confront those problems.

A final chapter draws some conclusions about ten elements of effective government policy that every country needs to develop. From these, we can examine the likely scenarios for each of these trajectories—the environments that businesspeople can expect, at least for the remainder of this decade. We can speculate, with care, about India's future growth, about Russia's institutional recovery, and about the likelihood that Japan and the United States will avoid economic crisis.

Business executives, politicians, and informed citizens need a clear picture of the forces that engender global competition. They need to think about what their governments are doing, effectively and ineffectively, and what improvements can be drawn from the examples of others. Which institutions help stimulate savings and investment? What prevents corruption? How can inflation be reduced while exchange rates move toward market values? Where, in government's array of policies, does productivity come from? Citizens need to understand these things if they are to have any effect on positive outcomes in their own policy environments.

The book is written to be understood. It uses simple graphs and tables to illustrate key points and limits endnotes to a bare minimum. It mixes my first-person interactions with business executives and government officials together with histories, scholarly economic analyses, and data.

Riyadh and Mumbai are no longer very far from New York and Brussels—just a few hours by plane, and instantaneously by Internet. Readers should realize that this is now their environment—a single global economy with increasingly integrated markets, political problems, and social issues.

—ᴍ—

Development Strategy and Structure

EVERY COUNTRY has a strategy for economic development. It may be explicit—carefully formulated and discussed as such by senior government officials. Or it may be entirely implicit—a loose collection of goals and policies that merely appears as strategy after the fact. Of course, strategy alone is not enough. Countries must have an organizational structure that can effectively implement their strategy. A mismatch between strategy and structure—or worse, with failing institutions—invariably leads to slow growth or no growth at all.

The strategy and structure must fit each country's *context*—the national and international conditions in which the country operates. In business, context would be analogous to the market. The country's culture, level of corruption, natural resources, education, income distribution, and international security are key among these contextual factors. A colonial legacy in India, for example, explains part of the country's post-1947 political choices, the effectiveness of its legal system, and its English language and democratic government. A similar legacy in South Africa, however, underlay the apartheid system that prevailed for too many decades.[1]

Strategy

National goals may consist of loose generalities, such as "economic growth" or "political stability." These, for example, appeared to be the goals for China articulated by pragmatist Deng Xiaoping in 1978. On the other hand, goals can be identified more precisely. In 1981, President Ronald Reagan listed four objectives of his supply-side revolution: (1) reduce inflation, (2) get the economy growing again, (3) reduce the size and role of government, and (4) strengthen national security.

To implement such goals, every government needs to adopt certain policies. At the very least, these must include macroeconomic choices. *Fiscal policy* is the government's budgetary stance—either a surplus, balanced budget, or a deficit. Moreover, these balances can be achieved through expanding or reducing various spending policies (e.g., defense, research, infrastructure investment, or social entitlements) that all have differing effects on output. Alternatively, they can be achieved by diverse choices of taxation, affecting business, investment, or consumer spending.

Monetary policy is the crucial flip side of the fiscal coin. Each country's central bank allows the supply of money to grow at a certain rate. It does this using several tools, including interest rates, reserve requirements, and *open market operations*—the buying and selling of treasury bills to the public. The purposes of monetary policy are to create enough money to finance healthy economic growth without inflation and to sustain adequate reserves of foreign exchange.

A related macroeconomic policy involves control of exchange rates. While some countries allow their currency to float freely at market rates, many others fix the price (in some other currency) or carefully manage its appreciation or depreciation. Countries that do manage their currencies generally employ a variety of controls on their *capital accounts*—the flows of capital into and out of the country.

A fourth macroeconomic tool, rarely used successfully, is *income policy*—direct control over wages and prices. This policy is mostly used in emergencies to deal with inflation when monetary policy has proved impractical or ineffective. In 1971, for example, President Nixon imposed wage and price controls in the United States. They didn't work very well, and it took nearly four years to get rid of them. Even then, control of gasoline prices hung on for six more years.

In addition to these macroeconomic choices, most countries deploy a range of microeconomic policies to affect economic growth. Six are especially important.

Trade policy—the use of tariffs, quotas, and various restrictive agreements (e.g., voluntary export restrictions) is perhaps the most common. Until recently, most countries employed a variety of taxes (or other controls) on imports. While these could range up to 100 percent or 200 percent of the price, they generally fell between 2 percent and 30 percent. Some countries also tax exports, although this is far less common. Eight rounds of negotiations under the General Agreement on Tariffs and Trade (GATT, the predecessor to the World Trade Organization), between 1947 and 1995, have substantially lowered these barriers to trade.

Restriction or promotion of foreign direct investment (FDI) is another policy tool. Restrictions are designed to protect domestic firms from foreign ownership or from foreign competition (through greenfield investment in the domestic market). While import substitution was still a popular development strategy, countries like Mexico and India virtually prohibited foreign direct investment. Today, most countries have significantly lowered the barriers to FDI, following more successful strategies of Singapore, China, and Canada. In fact, many countries eagerly encourage FDI by offering tax remissions and creating industrial parks or business clusters, modeled after China's successful policies.

Nationalization and privatization are mirror policies deployed by countries wishing to affect the ownership of firms. After World War II, strong socialist impulses in many countries led to the nationalization of firms that had previously been privately owned. These generally included utilities (oil, gas, electricity, railroads, airlines, and telecommunications), banking, and important heavy industries (steel, shipbuilding, and automobiles). Beginning in the 1970s, as many such firms suffered widening losses, a wave of privatization commenced that continues today. Often, when wholesale privatization remains politically unpalatable, governments privatize parts of firms (by selling, or distributing equity) and retain a majority or "golden share" minority interest for themselves.

Today, virtually all firms in the United States, England, and Australia are private. Most have been privatized in Japan, Italy, Canada, Chile, and Mexico. Some firms have been privatized in France, Germany, China, India, Russia, and Singapore, although many of the most important remain controlled by government. Relatively less privatization has occurred in Saudi Arabia, Turkey, and Brazil.

Economic regulation, which is usually implemented to correct some perceived economic flaw (such as a natural monopoly, a moral hazard, or externalities), has a major impact on development. Economic regulation has been applied to a host of vital industries, including transportation, energy, telecommunications, and financial services. Together, these sectors can amount to 25 percent of an economy and affect infrastructure vital to overall performance.

A related tool is competition policy, which certainly affects national output. Such policy can range from strong antitrust provisions designed to encourage competition, as in the United States and Europe, to cartel policies and monopoly pricing, as in Japan before the 1970s.

Provision of subsidy is the sixth microeconomic policy used to affect industry or sectoral growth. There is a wide range of subsidies, varying from direct grants, to tax remission, to help with inputs (e.g., land, trained workers, acquired technology), to defense contracting and government purchasing. When such policies are coordinated with a broad developmental rationale, they are generally referred to as "industrial policy."

Structure

By itself, strategy is useless without an organizational structure capable of implementing it. This is as true for countries as it is for companies. Indeed, it is far easier to devise a sound strategy than it is to create an organization that can effectively conduct strategy over time.

There are a variety of elements to structure that will differ sharply across national borders. Foremost is political structure. It might be democratic, autocratic, or Communist. Within these, moreover, are wide variations. In Japan, for example, a single party, the Liberal Democratic Party (LDP), has generally ruled since 1949 (except for eighteen months in 1993 and 1994). While this provided long-term stability, the five or six factions within the LDP have guaranteed gridlock during much of the past decade. Conversely, the democracy may be fragmented into dozens of political parties, like in India or Italy. The resulting coalitions make it inherently difficult to carry out broad changes in policy. Finally, democracy can be of the two-party variety, like in the United States and England, where an election can result in a sharp change in policy—sometimes detrimental to long-run objectives.

Economic structure is, of course, vital to the conduct of business. At a macrolevel, this applies to the relative weights of consumption, investment, government, and trade. In the United States, for example, consumption absorbs 70 percent of the gross domestic product (GDP). In Singapore, by contrast, consumption is as low as 42 percent, while trade (exports and imports) are more than 300 percent of GDP. In Europe, government may absorb 40 or even 50 percent of GDP. At a more microlevel, structure varies sharply in terms of private versus public ownership, concentrated versus fragmented incomes, and manufacturing versus agriculture versus services.

A country's institutional structure is absolutely vital to its economic development. Here too there is wide variance. The structure of its banking system, court systems, police and military, and rule of law—particularly property rights—are critical. In Russia, by way of example, these institutions collapsed in the mid-1990s, resulting in the failure of government's capacity to perform its minimal responsibilities. And there are many other institutional arrangements that must work effectively if the country is to develop. These include labor management arrangements, savings systems, the nature of bureaucracies, the separation of power between legislative and executive branches, and differential powers of the federal government and states. Consider Singapore, for example, where the Central Provident Fund has guaranteed a high enough savings rate to fund domestic investment, medical expenditures, and social security. In the United States, where no similar institution exists, savings rates are among the lowest in the world.

Developing Resources

To grow, every country must make choices about the use of scarce resources. Crucial among these are natural resources, human resources, technology, and capital resources. If economic growth is to occur, these not only must be increased but also must be used efficiently.

Consider natural resources. Some countries are blessed with an abundance of arable land, energy fuels, and vital minerals. These resources need to be developed effectively, however, avoiding excessive environmental damage, waste, and collateral economic damage. In China, for example, there is a limited amount of arable land for more than 1 billion people. However, if this land is deforested, overfertilized, or allowed to erode, it will adversely affect the country's future. Likewise, China has relied heavily on domestic coal to power its industry and electric utilities. Little, however, has been spent on environmental safeguards, leading to severe problems with air pollution and public health.

In the United States, by contrast, abundance of almost every resource has been immensely beneficial to economic growth. Fossil fuels, in particular, have been so readily available that the United States has underpriced and overused them. As a consequence, its domestic petroleum reserves are now declining sharply, forcing significantly higher prices and greater reliance on imports. Its carbon emissions, moreover, are the most inefficient (per capita) in the world.

In Saudi Arabia, oil has been extraordinarily abundant since the 1930s. Its daily production in 2004 was almost 10 million barrels, with reserves estimated at 259 billion barrels. As a consequence, an absolute monarchy has used oil revenues to sustain itself, by subsidizing critics and most potential opposition groups (such as militant Islam), and by buying a strong international defense (from the United States). But has this resource really helped economic growth? In 1983, Saudi Arabia's GDP per capita topped $18,000. Since then, it has fallen by more than half, because Saudi Arabia's weak GDP growth of 1.8 percent annually was exceeded by vigorous population growth of 3.2 percent.

South Africa too has had such an abundance of natural resources that it has become overly dependent on raw materials exports. It also suffered from the "Dutch disease" back in the early 1980s. Gold prices rose, forcing South Africa's currency, the rand, to appreciate. This overvalued currency undermined competitiveness. More recently, minerals exports have shrunk as a portion of GDP, but South Africans still aspire to do more value-added beautification at home.

Still other countries, such as the United Kingdom and Singapore, have relatively scarce, or no, natural resources. Indeed, both are islands with relatively little land. Yet both have found strategies that compensate for these inadequacies. The United Kingdom has abandoned its coal, automobile, and other heavy industries, relying instead on intellectual resources and a powerful financial services industry. Singapore, by contrast, has constructed artificial land on which to build petrochemical complexes and is now developing biotechnology, an industry whose only input is brainpower.

Development of human resources is absolutely critical to economic progress. Both the quantity and quality can be important. In China, the immense quantity of potential unskilled workers applies continuing downward pressure on wages. In Germany during the 1980s, and in Singapore more recently, workers needed to be imported to keep the economy growing. And in the face of declining birthrates, both Japan and Italy will be faced with similar challenges in the near future.

Quality, however, has usually been a more demanding challenge. Education is the most important component of labor quality. Countries with good educational systems have generally benefited from higher economic growth. Japan, where the primary and secondary school systems are excellent, has long enjoyed a literate and skilled workforce. In France, the United Kingdom, and the United States, where higher education is well developed, great advances in sciences have sparked whole new industries. In Italy and Germany, where skill development has been facilitated by technical schools and systems of apprenticeship, high-quality engineering has contributed substantially to economic success.

India, of late, is perhaps the best example of an economy aided by educationally led human resources. With its national universities and hundreds of colleges, India produces more than 5 million college graduates annually. Skills in computer programming have underpinned India's booming revolution in information technology. Other educated Indians contribute to the country's huge market for outsourced services—call centers, tax accounting, credit card processing, and the like.

Human resources can be augmented by informal education as well. In China, foreign direct investment by thousands of western firms has transferred technology, know-how, and managerial skills to thousands of Chinese workers who might otherwise not have had those opportunities for learning.

Technological resources are similarly vital. Educational institutions are an important source of technology but so are corporate research laboratories. Some countries, like France and the United States, have basically developed their own technology through strong institutions, including their patent offices. Other countries, such as Japan, initially chose a strategy of buying technology and then improving it. However, with the successful growth of its firms, Japan too has become a leading technological innovator. Finally, absorbing technological know-how through foreign direct investment has been another path, most notably followed by China.

Even with these various resources, no countries have successfully accelerated their economic growth without capital. In other words, if consumption and imports absorb all available resources, countries have too little surplus capital to invest in growth. From the historical record, there appear to have been five pathways for accumulating capital.

The first is debt from domestic banks. Asians are savers. Households save their income, rather than consuming it, to assure their survival in old age and to help their children build a stronger future. In this book, we will see prime examples of this savings behavior in Japan, Singapore, and China, where savings resides, *perforce*, in domestic banks. In these countries, savings rates have sometimes exceeded 30 percent, or even 40 percent, of GDP. These high savings rates are not just the result of cultural factors. Domestic policies and institutions also contribute. So in Japan, for example, a significant portion of household savings is exempted from taxes—as are capital gains. Conversely, household mortgages require as much as 40 percent down payments, forcing young would-be homeowners to save heavily for years. In Singapore, by contrast, the Central Provident Fund was established early on to force savings. Workers are required to save as much as 50 percent of their gross income—half contributed by employers and half by workers—and this before payment of income taxes!

The structure of institutions is thus crucial. If equity markets are weak (as they were in Japan) or nonexistent (as in China), and if capital controls prevent foreign investment, then savings flow to domestic banks, even at low interest rates. With a limited number of banks and nationwide branching, it is possible for government to channel savings to banks and then bank loans to the firms and industries targeted for success.

Domestic equity is a second institutional approach to making capital available for investment. The United States has long maintained well-developed equity markets with widespread access through investment banks, discount brokerages, and more recently, direct purchasing online. Combined with a healthy venture capital market, raising funds through equity has been far easier than in any other country. Both domestic and foreign savers have provided ample capital to these markets until quite recently, when domestic savings shrank significantly as a source. This equity channel benefits from competitive efficiency. Capital generally flows to successful firms, except perhaps during something like the dot-com bubble. But even this eventually corrects itself, albeit painfully.

Foreign direct investment has been a third source of capital. Most FDI comes from and goes to developed countries. Since the early 1980s, however, FDI has increasingly flowed from developed to developing countries—especially as those developing countries opened domestic ownership to foreigners and privatized. Canada and Singapore are good examples of sourcing capital through FDI. Until the early 1970s, much of Canada's capital investment came from the United States, where much of its corporate control was vested. Singapore likewise encouraged FDI in hundreds of assembly plants and petrochemical facilities between the late 1960s and early 1990s.

China, with an unquenchable thirst for capital, adopted a twofold investment strategy, funded both by domestic savings and bank debt and by foreign direct investment. Through its program of special economic zones, China attracted increasingly large contributions of foreign investment, eventually reaching $60 billion in 2005. This combination of domestic debt and FDI allowed China to waste considerable capital on failing state enterprises and state banks, while still maintaining an investment rate of 39 percent and a current account surplus.

Intentional foreign debt financing is a fourth source of acquiring capital. In many developing countries, where living standards are low and capital scarce, public and private debt has been sold to foreigners. This, for example, was how the United States financed its railroads and canals—by selling bonds to affluent British savers.

Reliance on foreign debt took off after the first oil shock, in 1973–1974. At that time, huge increases in oil prices resulted in large resource flows to oil-producing countries. Much of that foreign exchange was banked, and the multinational banks loaned it to developing countries that needed to grow through the shock. Between 1974 and 1978, most countries in Latin America and sub-Saharan Africa borrowed. Mexico, for example, borrowed heavily to invest in its oil industry. Brazil, on the other hand, borrowed to finance oil imports. After the Iranian Revolution triggered a second oil shock, this pattern of petro-dollar recycling redoubled. This time, developing countries borrowed heavily both to invest and to finance government spending. However, beginning in the summer of 1982 with Mexico, and continuing through 1988, some thirty-seven countries went broke—that is, could not service their debt.

The debt crisis led to a newly expanded role for the International Monetary Fund (IMF). As the lender of last resort, the IMF kept most of these countries from defaulting. In return, the IMF imposed "conditionality," requiring reform and liberalization. After more than a decade of such efforts, however, another series of debt crises emerged with the "tequila crisis" in Mexico late in 1994, the Asian crisis of 1997–1998, the Russian default in 1998, the Brazilian crisis in 1999, and the collapse of Argentina in 2001.

A similar, fifth sort of capital accumulation could be called "unintentional foreign borrowing." Some countries, like India and Poland, had no intention of borrowing; India aimed at *swadeshi*, or "autonomy from the world," while Communist Poland planned on self-finance. But because of the oil shock (in India's case) and asymmetrical trade with the USSR (in Poland's case), both countries began borrowing in the 1970s to finance their balance of payments deficits. The result was the same—debt crisis.

As a consequence of these continuing problems, foreign debt became a less acceptable way to finance economic growth. Increasingly, countries and international institutions realized that domestic finance and foreign equity were less leveraged, sounder channels to finance economic growth. There was, in other words, no free lunch.

Efficient Usage of Resources

While it is essential to accumulate these resources, especially human skills and capital, it is nonetheless important to utilize them efficiently. Productivity is vital to economic growth. Labor must be used efficiently, resources (including technology) must be used efficiently, and capital, certainly, cannot be wasted.

Foreign competition is one channel for forcing efficiency. That is, countries that expose themselves to international competition experience one of two results: either efficient use of resources or failure. Here, Italy comes to mind. Italy has developed a host of craft industries in regional clusters. It would be difficult to imagine how these would have succeeded were it not for the constant pressure of foreign competition. Likewise in South Africa, where BMW makes vehicles for export, it has been foreign competition that pushed both firms and the country to be efficient.

Domestic competition provides another source of efficiency. While many larger countries have competitive markets, the United States no doubt sets the standard. With almost no state-owned firms and a powerful antitrust tradition dating from the 1890s, survival in domestic U.S. markets puts near-constant pressure on firms to innovate, minimize costs, reinvest, and pursue competitive advantages.

A third source of efficiency is competition for foreign direct investment. Countries that seek foreign capital compete in a world market for FDI.

Canada, for a time, was incredibly successful at attracting American investment, although largely in minerals-related sectors. More recently, the North American Free Trade Agreement sharply reduced trade barriers and encouraged significant investment in Mexico, largely from the United States.

But it is China, for certain, that has experienced the greatest success with foreign direct investment. Ever since carefully opening four special economic zones in 1978, China has enjoyed a rising surge of FDI, cumulatively amounting to nearly $500 billion by 2005. It achieved this success with low wages, tax breaks, and the promise of a huge domestic market. More recently, China has competed with huge scientific and technological incubators, called "economic and technological development zones," and venture capital for new technological enterprises.

While all these forms of competition drive firms toward greater and greater efficiency, there is a fourth channel for promoting efficiency—that is, administrative allocation. In the West—especially in the United States and the United Kingdom, the prevailing conservative ideology holds that administrative allocation is inherently inefficient. Such allocation of capital, technology, and other resources by government is deemed wasteful, insensitive to markets, and often corrupt.

In Singapore, Japan, and a few other economies, however, administrative allocation appears to have worked well—at least in the past. Government owns perhaps 25 percent of GDP in Singapore—more than a hundred firms, all real estate, and access to huge private savings. Government bureaucrats have been responsible for allocating most investment capital. The result has been high growth—about 9 percent annually—for decades. Likewise in Japan, where capital is held largely in private hands, allocation was "guided" for some time by a few key ministries staffed by intelligent, honest, and even farsighted bureaucrats.

In many, many other countries, however, capital is allocated ineptly when government is in control. Perhaps the best examples are China before 1978, India before 1985, and Russia before the collapse of the USSR. Centrally planned capital allocation, administered inefficiently or even corruptly, produced little growth of overall productivity. Economic growth occurred only thanks to pouring resources—human, capital, and natural—into the economy. Such growth, we now know, is unsustainable.

Role of Government

As is no doubt evident from the previous sections on strategy, structure, and resource growth and usage, I believe that the role of government is *crucial* to economic development. Of course, there are certainly more unsuccessful governments that have damaged growth than successful governments that have helped. Governmental power is too often misconceived or misused. Yet still, economic growth requires good government. There are a handful of things that government must do, and a larger list of things that government can do, to help economic development.

First, government must provide security—both domestic and international security—so that markets can work. Crime interferes with market transactions. Individual crime makes streets unsafe, and organized crime controls and distorts whole sectors of commerce. In Japan, for example, the *yakuza* interfered with the proper functioning of corporate governance and market adjustment of postbubble property prices. In South Africa, individual crime was so severe in some cities that it discouraged foreign investors. And in Russia, there was a breakdown of law and order throughout most of the 1990s.

Perhaps worse than crime is domestic violence caused by cultural or religious clashes. The most immediate example is in India, where Hindu and Muslim groups have occasionally engaged in large-scale, fatal violence. Revolutionary or terrorist groups can also disrupt economic growth, as in Chechnya, Kashmir, Turkey, or Saudi Arabia. Likewise, external insecurity is a persistent problem in some regions. India's conflict with Pakistan, Israel's continuing clash with Palestine, and Iraq's wars with Iran, Kuwait, and the United States simply destroy economic progress.

Second, government is responsible for creating contracts, protecting property rights, and enforcing laws. Every country needs a legal system that is trusted by people and institutions, and that works to settle commercial disputes between them. Where property rights are uncertain, for example, as in Mexico or Poland (after 1990), credit is uncertain, property markets do not function, and investment is damaged. Countries need a system of tax collection that works. Even more, they need a court system that works. Securities laws that facilitate investment, banking regulations that secure deposits, and legitimate relations between nation-states and provinces are all necessary for a country to function.

Third, government backs risk—risks of all sorts. While markets can handle ordinary risks primarily through insurance systems, government is needed to absorb extraordinary risk. Thus, incorporation in the eighteenth century and environmental regulation, health insurance, regulation of nuclear facilities, unemployment insurance, and retirement pensions in the twentieth century are a few of the sectors that only government, as the sovereign, can effectively back.[2]

Fourth, government manages the macroeconomy, using fiscal and monetary policy to do so. But even more significantly, government creates, legitimizes, and distributes money. This is a role that all governments assume. Commerce cannot occur, and markets cannot work, without a reliable medium of exchange. Where hyperinflations have destroyed the value of money, as in Brazil or Argentina, growth eventually stops. And where bank authority erodes, as in Russia after the collapse of the Soviet Union, commerce substituted barter until the legitimacy of money was reestablished.

And fifth, government implements industrial policy as an explicit or implicit result of its microeconomic choices. As previously described, most governments use tariffs to manage trade and regulate foreign investment, externalities, and competition; and they use subsidies to aid particular firms and industries. Where these measures are effective, they amount to good industrial policy. Too often, though, they produce conflicts internally, weaken productivity, and maldistribute income.

When looked at carefully and cumulatively, the range and breadth of government's influence is really amazing. Little growth or development could happen without property rights, contracts, sound financial systems, a stable money supply, security, infrastructural services, and equitable regulation of monopolies, health care, pensions, and externalities.

Competitive Advantage

In subsequent chapters, we will examine the development trajectories of some of the world's most important countries. In some, we will find a national strategy and organizational structure that fit each other, as well as the context of the region or time. In others, we'll see an ineffective strategy (Mexico) or an inept structure (India) hampering growth.

We will see big countries like China and the United States, powered in part by huge domestic markets, and smaller ones like Singapore and Italy, where exports are essential. Some countries like South Africa are rich in natural resources, while others like Japan must import virtually all inputs. Some are rich in fuel (e.g., Mexico and Saudi Arabia) but use it ineffectively. Others, including China and India, must import fuel and pay for it with their nonfuel trade surplus.

In all of the chapters, we will see the importance of sound institutions—institutions that work. They can be powerful organizations, as Japan's Ministry of International Trade and Industry once was and Singapore's Central Provident Fund still is. Or they can be less concrete, but nonetheless important, as are the United States' constitutional provisions that guarantee free speech and separation of church and state.

Throughout these chapters, we should pay special note to the time it takes to solidify sound institutions and the ways in which countries marshal resources—especially human and capital resources. And we should think about what drives efficiency in each case, as it is productivity in the long run that guarantees growth.

When strategy and structure complement each other, expand key resources and use them efficiently, and fit the domestic and international context, we will see successful, sometimes spectacular, economic growth.

PART I

Pathways to

Asian High Growth

———*m*———

Japan's Economic Miracle

AS THE AMERICAN OCCUPATION of Japan ended in the early 1950s, few were optimistic about Japan's likely economic future. Edwin O. Reischauer, perhaps the foremost *gaijin* authority on Japan, offered the following assessment:

> First of all, there is the problem of whether or not Japan, regardless of the political and economic system she eventually chooses, can maintain any satisfactory standard of living in the future. She cannot grow enough food to feed her people. She cannot produce the greater part of the fibers from which she must spin clothes for her millions. She has very little oil or iron and is lacking in adequate quantities of most of the other minerals and raw materials needed to maintain a modern industrial economy. Nylon and other synthetic fibers have destroyed most of the demand for silk, the other major export item she produced entirely within her boundaries. All she has to offer on the world market is her own energy—manpower and the energy of coal and water. With these she can transform imported raw materials into goods for re-export. The slim margin of profit from this re-export trade must be sufficient to pay for all the imports Japan must have to support her own people. To do this, Japan's export trade must be huge. But where is she to find her markets in a divided world, and in a Far East disrupted by revolutions and bitterly determined not to trade with her? Japan's situation is basically similar to England's but infinitely worse.[1]

And yet, between 1954 and 1971, Japan's real economy grew at an annual average rate of 10.1 percent per year—unprecedented in world history. Were this to continue, Japan would shortly catch the United States—which it did, in GDP per capita, by 1989. So, what happened? Why were Professor Reischauer and other economic pundits so wrong?

23

Historical Context

Imperial Japan, which gained cultural independence from China after the seventh century, eventually descended into feudalism for nearly a millennium. The feudal state, with an emperor and strong outside lords, solidified after 1281 when a great typhoon called Kamikaze ("divine wind") was credited with defeating the Mongols' one cross-ocean invasion attempt. The imperial court, rooted in Buddhism, held forth in Kyoto—a city today located between Tokyo and Osaka. In the mid-sixteenth century, Portuguese explorers arrived off the southern tip of Kyushu, looking for trading and missionary opportunities. The Japanese showed considerable interest in firearms, if not Christianity.

By the end of the sixteenth century, various feudal generals were struggling for power. After a great battle in 1600, Tokugawa Ieyasu emerged victorious and established his family's reign in Edo (today's Tokyo). Ieyasu assumed the title of *shogun*, divided up the country among about 295 *daimyo* (vassals), and created a system of roads and rice taxes to bind the country together. The shogun required that each daimyo's family live in Edo and be joined by the daimyo himself every other year. The shogun's country at this time had a population estimated at 30 million—80 percent peasants, 15 percent *ronin* (masterless samurai), 4 percent merchants, and 1 percent feudal lords.

In 1636, perhaps concerned by outside influences precipitating internal strife, the shogun issued a "closing the country" decree—virtually sealing off Japan for the next 217 years. Only in 1853 did the American government send Matthew Perry in four black ships (steamships) to Edo. There to open a coaling station and trade relations, Perry communicated U.S. demands to the shogun—Japan's ruler—before departing, with the promise to revisit Edo the following year.

When Perry did return in 1854 with nine heavily armed warships, the shogun was forced to open Japan, signing a trade treaty with the United States. This was followed, four years later, by a series of treaties with five western powers. Each got trading rights at different ports, and the shogun gave up the right to levy import duties in excess of 5 percent. These "unequal treaties" damaged the shogun's prestige in Japan, eventually pushing the outer lords to overthrow him in 1868 and return Emperor Meiji to power.

With the Meiji restoration, the lords behind the young emperor adopted a totally new strategy for Japan, characterized by the motto *fukoku-kyohei*— "rich country, strong army."[2] Now Japan opened itself to foreign education and foreign technology of all sorts, struggling to develop as quickly as possible to catch the West. Ports, railroads, telegraph, and telephone were quickly developed. Steel, shipbuilding, armaments, and eventually chemicals, vehicles, and aircraft were developed over the next few decades by the private sector in cooperation with government. Japan engaged China and then Russia in war, victoriously building a colonial empire in the East.

As early as 1907, Japan realized that the United States would soon become its strategic enemy. It chafed at the five-power pact, which limited its capital ships (battleships and heavy cruisers) to parity with the United States—well below Britain and Germany. After blowing through the Great Depression with annual growth rates of 5 percent, Japan moved to conquer Manchuria and then Southeast Asia, until the government of Franklin Roosevelt finally reacted by embargoing raw materials exports. Several months later, on December 7, 1941, the Japanese took the fateful step of attacking the United States at Pearl Harbor—precipitating a disastrous war that eventually led to nuclear bombing and unconditional defeat.

Only in 1952, after nearly seven years of occupation, did Japan regain its independence. When General Douglas MacArthur withdrew the American occupation force of several thousand, Japan's economy was barely restored to its 1936 level of output. With 2.8 million people dead and nearly 7 million having returned from once-colonial posts, Japan now faced the task of rebuilding. But its heavy industry was destroyed and its great *zaibatsu* industrial firms disbanded. With a population of more than 70 million and an island-nation nearly devoid of natural resources, it was not at all clear that Japan could survive, much less prosper.

Institutional Strengths

And yet, Japan had any number of hidden strengths—most important, its culture, distinctly Japanese with some remnants of Confucianism. Japanese were humiliated by their defeat in war. Surviving Japanese men felt a deep obligation to rebuild their defeated nation—but this time, through the economy rather than through militarism. They were willing to work incredibly hard, save, and invest if they were to reconstruct a nation for their children. Decades of this hard work, high investment in infrastructure and capital assets, and huge personal savings would bear fruit well into the future.

Japan's polity was a parliamentary democracy—entirely stable after 1955 when it came to be dominated by the Liberal Democratic Party. Its economy was essentially capitalist—that is, most assets were privately owned. There was a "widespread dualism in labor use"—large firms in heavy industries, with small firms dominating more than 70 percent of the economy.[3] Labor at the large, strategic firms joined "enterprise unions," with a seniority wage system and permanent employment. Together, these three sacred miracles—*uchiwa*—were essential to Japan's subsequent success.

Japan also benefited from an exceptionally good educational system. Its primary and secondary schools were populated by respected teachers committed to educating Japanese children. Literacy was widespread, even among women. The system was rigorously meritocratic, based on competitive entrance exams that built a hierarchical pyramid with the University of Tokyo at the top. As a consequence, Japan had managerial, scientific, and particularly engineering skills capable of adapting foreign technology effectively. During the occupation, the system was reformed, expanded, and made a bit more egalitarian.[4]

Another good turn delivered by the occupation was the evisceration of several institutional foci of political power that could have hampered economic growth. Japan's new constitution left virtually no role for the emperor, the military, or the family owners of traditional zaibatsu. Thus, when MacArthur left, only business managers and government bureaucrats remained as potential centers of power.

The bureaucracy, reformulated as twelve cabinet ministries reporting to a weak prime minister, quickly came to be dominated by two ministries—the Ministry of Finance (MOF) and the Ministry of International Trade and Industry (MITI, previously the Ministry of Munitions). Finance controlled the central bank, fiscal and monetary policy, tax collection, and the regulation of banks, insurance, and securities. MITI determined industrial policy through its control of imports, foreign exchange, foreign direct investment, and antitrust policy.

MITI, MOF, and other ministries recruited the most talented students from Japan's best universities. They provided lifetime employment, considerable power over Japan's reconstruction, and the promise of a profitable retirement. *Amakudari*, or "descent from heaven," was the practice of senior bureaucrats retiring from government and going to work as a senior executive for one of the large firms they had previously been regulating. In that capacity, they might work for another ten to twelve years, receiving a high salary and providing crucial links to their old ministry.

This was only one of several institutional mechanisms for facilitating good business-government relations. Although MITI bureaucrats had relatively limited formal power, they exercised far greater influence through "administrative guidance." This form of "administration by inducement" was developed in the late 1950s by an especially powerful MITI vice minister (head of the bureaucracy, as the minister is an elected legislator). MITI would use its statutory authority, such as foreign exchange licensing, to extend its power to control a firm's technology choices, decisions on plant scale, formation of cartels, and even mergers—"industry structuring."[5]

An analogous institutional mechanism in banking was "window guidance." As it emerged in the 1950s, the Japanese banking system was concentrated. Japanese financial assets were held by a mere seventy banks, dominated by a handful of *keiretsu* banks. Keiretsu were the industrial groups that succeeded zaibatsu in the mid-1950s. They were held together by cross-ownership, intertwined boards, interconnected trading relations, and capital from each keiretsu's lead bank. Because of Japan's fast growth and heavy investment, all of these big banks were "overloaned"—having loaned out more than 100 percent of their capital. This gave the Ministry of Finance and the Bank of Japan considerable power, which was exercised through window guidance. If loan growth were deemed excessive, perhaps fueling inflation, the central banker might request slower growth—(credit) window guidance. Banks, depending on loans from the central bank, did not hesitate to respond positively.

More broadly, postwar Japan concocted a variety of institutions to produce effective, if not cooperative, business-government relations. Advisory councils, or *shingikai*, facilitated exchange between business leaders and between them and government bureaucrats. Advisory councils were established to deal with any important policy issue—excess capacity, trade barriers, price cutting, quality control, and so on. These councils might interact with the Keidanren, the principal business organization with more than seven hundred large-company and trade-association members, or with other *zaiki* (elite business leader) groups. Often studying a problem for months and deliberating on a solution for years, such councils would eventually issue a white paper, usually indicating that consensus had been reached and new policy adopted.[6]

Three important laws, either enacted by the occupation or pushed through by MITI just afterward, were especially important. The Foreign Exchange and Foreign Trade Control Law of 1949 gave MITI the power to control imports and allocate foreign exchange. Since foreign exchange was such a scarce commodity, the occupation did not want Japan wasting it on unnecessary imports. Japan started out with an exchange budget but eventually changed to quotas. Imports were divided into three categories, depending on how essential MITI believed the imports to be; different quotas or foreign exchange restrictions were applied to each category.[7]

A second law, the Foreign Investment Act of 1950, gave MITI control of all transactions involving foreign currency. Since most technology licenses involved foreign remittances, this legislation gave MITI considerable control. Applications were screened and *mostly* (90 percent) approved. More important than the price of technology was the composition of technology imported. Especially during the 1960s, MITI used this power to guarantee that the best technologies were made available to Japanese firms, at MITI's discretion. Thus, technology licenses were used to induce all sorts of industrial policy, including scale decisions and occasionally mergers.

The third law, initially enacted in 1947, was the Anti-Monopoly Act, modeled after the antitrust provisions of the United States' Sherman and Clayton acts. However, at MITI's behest, it was revised in 1953, allowing special conditions favoring small enterprises and sectors exposed to foreign competition. In particular, it allowed two types of cartels: depression cartels, where supply exceeded demand, and rationalization cartels, to restrict technology or standardize output.[8]

Postoccupation Context

Japan's business and bureaucratic leaders faced any number of challenges in 1952. U.S. aid, which had sustained them since 1945, was terminated. Much of Japan's capital assets had been destroyed. Mao Zedong had just succeeded to power in China, closing its borders to any sort of trade. Southeast Asia was not merely impoverished; it held Japan in deep contempt. Europe too was rebuilding, drawing on Marshall Fund aid from the United States. And the cold war, between the United States and the USSR, cast a shadow over most of the world.

On the other hand, the United States eagerly cast its defense umbrella over Japan. In effect, the America would spend more than 7 percent of GDP on national security, extending it to Japan. This allowed Japan to spend less than 1 percent on defense, thereby devoting more of its GDP to commercial investment. The Korean War, meanwhile, proved to be a significant short-term stimulus, as the United States outsourced much of the production of war materials to Japan.

Energy prices, which were crucial to energy-short Japan, had begun falling in 1949. As oil production surged in the Middle East, prices fell and continued to fall (in real terms) until the early 1970s.

And finally, the international monetary system created by the United States at Bretton Woods in 1944 promised to provide favorable trading conditions for several decades. Under the gold exchange system, the U.S. dollar was pegged to gold, at $35 per ounce, and other currencies were pegged to the dollar. In 1949, the Japanese yen was fixed at ¥360 per dollar (considerably less than ¥4 per dollar, where it was set before the war). It would remain fixed at ¥360 for twenty-two years, yielding a competitive advantage for Japan that grew along with the country's sharply rising productivity.

Development Strategy

Between 1952 and the early 1960s, Japanese politicians, bureaucrats, and business leaders moved to adopt policies for economic development. Taken together, these amounted to a national development strategy. First was reconstruction—rebuilding infrastructure and basic industries. This effort required a massive commitment of capital, to which both government and business contributed, and the mobilization of Japanese savings.

This deep investment, fueled by domestic savings, helped kick GDP growth into high speed—9.8 percent annually between 1950 and 1960. (For detail on this investment, see table 2-1.)

The heart of Japan's economic development sprang from its industrial policy, authored by MITI and implemented collectively by business and government. Recognition of Japan's import dependence was the point of departure. For a large country with no natural resources, import dependence had been recognized as early as the 1880s, and certainly during the 1930s. "The position of Japan in the world economy," wrote the government in 1955, "has been completely changed by defeat, and Japan is becoming even more dependent upon the international economy than she was before the war. The future of Japan's economy, therefore, depends largely upon the course of balance of payments."[9]

So where would Japan attain her markets, and in what industries could she excel? The answers to both questions, although difficult, were obvious. The market would be the United States—the only country with an undamaged

TABLE 2-1

Gross domestic investment and savings in Japan, 1956–1960

Gross domestic investment	100%	Gross savings	100%
Private	73.7	Personal savings	37.3
Residential	7.3	Government surplus	21.0
Producers' equipment	54.4	Corporate savings	15.7
Inventories	13.1	Depreciation	30.5
Government	26.3	Net foreign balance	−0.4
Public enterprise	8.7	Error	−4.1
Other national government	7.6		
Local government	10.0		

Note: Numbers do not add to 100 in original.

Source: William W. Lockwood, ed., *The State and Economic Enterprise in Japan* © 1965 Princeton University Press,1993 renewed PUP. Reprinted with permission of Princeton University Press.

economy, a high consumption potential, and ample foreign exchange reserves. To gain access, however, Japanese companies would need to export goods at low prices—low enough to gain market share in the United States. These prices, sometimes reaching below marginal costs, gave rise to worsening trade friction and a spate of antidumping suits in the late 1970s and early 1980s. The fixed, increasingly undervalued currency also helped. Return of equity would not be much of a consideration.

The sectors Japan chose would (eventually) be high-value-added products, precisely where comparative advantage lay with the United States. Conventional logic might have suggested labor-intensive, low-value-added goods—textiles, simple assembly, toys, and knickknacks—where Japan could use her low-wage advantage. But Japan rejected this logic for several reasons: (1) the country would soon lose its wage advantage to other south Asian countries that were poorer yet; (2) affluent Americans would eventually demand higher-value-added goods that fit their higher incomes; and (3) Japan could never grow very fast and certainly not catch the United States if its national contribution were a thin margin of value added from labor. After the war, as Yoshihisa Ojimi, vice minister of MITI explained it:

> The Ministry of International Trade and Industry decided to establish in Japan industries which require extensive employment of capital and technology, industries that in consideration of comparative cost of production should be the most inappropriate for Japan, industries such as steel, oil refining, petrochemicals, automobiles, aircraft, industrial machinery of all sorts, and electronics, including electronic computers. From a short-run, static viewpoint, encouragement of such industries would seem to conflict with economic rationalism. But, from a long-range viewpoint, these are precisely the industries where income elasticity of demand is high, technological progress is rapid, and labor productivity rises fast . . . According to Napoleon and [the Prussian general] Clausewitz, the secret of a successful strategy is the concentration of fighting power on the main battle grounds; fortunately . . . Japan has been able to concentrate its scant capital in strategic industries.[10]

Accordingly, the National Diet of Japan enacted a series of industry targeting laws during the 1950s. In addition to steel and shipbuilding, it targeted aluminum, petrochemicals, automobiles, consumer electronics, machine tools, and aircraft. The choice of automobiles was perhaps the most controversial in 1955. While MITI favored including automobile production, the ministries of finance and transport opposed. Few Japanese leaders could imagine how Japan's rudimentary wartime vehicle manufacturers could possibly hope to compete with the likes of General Motors, Chrysler, and Ford. These laws, with relatively few details, directed the bureaucracy to support the chosen industries through directed financing, tax incentives, import protection and foreign currency allocation, technology acquisition, administrative guidance cartels, and if necessary, rationalization.

While the petrochemical and aluminum thrusts were eventually muted by oil shocks, and the aircraft initiative could not match defense-rich American firms like Boeing and Lockheed, several of the others would eventually become world-class successes. But it would take decades to build these industries—decades during which stable policies of a stable government were necessary.

Most of these industries were characterized by economies of scale—that is, marginal costs fell with ever-larger production units. Thus, MITI encouraged investment in large, concentrated facilities. In steel, these included nine of the world's ten largest plants, built immediately adjacent to deepwater ports; in automobiles and electronics, huge facilities near Tokyo (Toyota City) and Osaka (Matsushita). And the Japanese were perhaps the first to discover the power of the learning curve. Costs could be reduced by as much as 20 percent each time output was doubled—through learning.[11]

MITI early on searched out the best technologies available in the world and licensed them for its Japanese clients. W. Edward Deming's writings on industrial engineering and quality, and other American ideas about "scientific management," found an excited and abiding audience among Japanese managers. And finally, in the absence of vertical integration, reorganized keiretsu groups provided the organizational glue to achieve economies of scope, as well as scale.

For a poor country like Japan, raising and allocating the capital necessary to finance these industries was also a challenge. Several options were initially available: industry could acquire capital either domestically or internationally, in the form of either equity or debt. Domestic capital, at least at first, was relatively scarce. Yet, foreign capital entailed several risks. Foreign debt could cede control to foreign lenders—particularly banks—and would be priced at market interest rates, imparting no advantage to Japan. Worse yet, foreign capital would saddle Japan with significant debt-service obligations. Foreign equity was, from a Japanese perspective, even less attractive. Foreign firms would make investment decisions, as much to sell in Japan as reexport. And again, dividend obligations would flow out, leaving Japan's current account in a fragile condition.

Even domestic equity was unappealing. Were the government to facilitate a healthy stock market, capital would flow into all sorts of industries. The government would be less able to direct Japan's limited resources to the handful of its strategic sectors. Thus, domestic equity markets were discouraged in several ways, and foreign equity was sharply restricted. Only a handful of foreign firms were approved for wholly owned investments—IBM, Texas Instruments, and several American oil companies—all of which Japanese bureaucrats felt were absolutely necessary to the country's future well-being.

But since Japanese savers were also given few equity or foreign alternatives, their substantial savings flowed almost exclusively into the banks—particularly the large keiretsu banks with nationwide branches—or to the postal savings system. And because these were the only savings receptacles, they paid (and thus charged) relatively low rates. This, in turn, held down the fixed costs of capital investment. With guidance from MITI and MOF, these larger banks would funnel capital to Japan's strategic sectors.

There were many incentives for the Japanese to save. First, there was probably a considerable lag between the adjustment of consumption to higher disposable income. Second, the absence of social security undoubtedly inspired long-living Japanese to save for old age. Third, a payroll system based on lump-sum bonuses, often as much as one-third of a year's pay, probably helped. Fourth, the government provided a series of tax exemptions on savings (up to ¥3 million), on workers' savings designated for "formation of employees' assets," and on capital gains from the sale of one's residential property. And fifth, prices of Japanese consumer goods and housing remained quite high, discouraging the sort of conspicuous consumption one sees in the West. Thus, personal savings rose from 6 percent to about 13 percent of GDP between 1954 and 1971.

Government also saved during these years—a concept perhaps foreign to westerners. From 1954 to 1971, the government's fiscal balance was consistently positive—sometimes by 9–10 percent of revenues. This money too was made available for investment—especially in the public infrastructure. And then business saved. Without significant dividends (due to the absence of significant public equity markets), sizable retained earnings (after depreciation) were committed to new plants, new equipment, and R&D.

Organizational Structure

To implement this extraordinary economic strategy, Japanese leadership had to build an institutional structure—a management organization, if you will—that worked. This network of relationships is commonly referred to as Japan, Inc. In some ways, strategy is the easiest part of economic development. But putting in place a workable institutional structure, embedded in the nation's politics, economic systems, and culture, is a challenge indeed.

I've already described several of the key institutional arrangements that made this miracle work. But if we think about Japan, Inc. as an organizational chart, one could perhaps imagine something like the diagram shown in figure 2-1.

Four sets of institutions are illustrated in bold; these represent the centers of policy and economic power. (Ten other cabinet ministries are omitted, not because they lack power, but merely to simplify the chart.) Again, the Liberal Democratic Party (LDP) dominated—and continued to dominate for three subsequent decades. Also not shown are the factions—perhaps five or six—into which the LDP was divided. These groups, headed by powerful legislators who served multiple terms as a cabinet minister or the prime minister, controlled the flows of resources from contributors (mostly business) to constituents.

Sohyo, at the upper right, was one of several national labor confederations (along with Domei and Churitsuroren) into which enterprise unions were organized. During this period, Sohyo often led the *shunto*, or "spring wage offensive," picking strong unions to negotiate precedent-setting contracts. Given the practice of permanent employment, wages rather than job security were the principal objective. Strikes, although frequent, lasted no more than a few hours, usually protesting some symbolic point.

FIGURE 2-1

The organization of Japan, Inc.

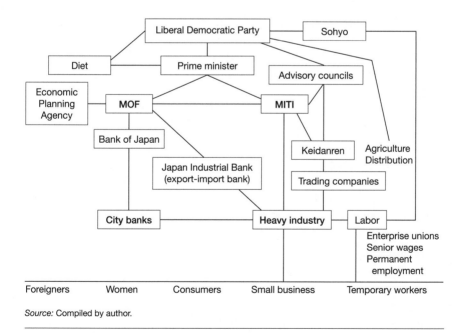

Source: Compiled by author.

A couple of other organizations deserve explanation. The Economic Planning Agency (EPA) did the macroeconomic planning (analogous to the U.S. Office of Management and Budget) to match MITI's microeconomic plans. Both MITI and MOF contributed senior bureaucrats to EPA who would serve in key positions temporarily, for two or three years.

The role of the Bank of Japan was complicated. It was not, however, an independent bank (like the European Central Bank or the U.S. Federal Reserve). Its head was appointed on the advice of MOF (and often, with the consent of MITI). Thus, it served more as a channel for financial and monetary policy passing through from MOF to the big city banks. In Japan, at least, this arrangement worked well during miracle growth—and even after, during the crises of the 1970s and the healthy period of the 1980s.

Each of the keiretsu groups had a large "trading company," which was exceedingly important in the organization of Japan's export and import businesses. These trading companies not only sourced raw materials for the manufacturing companies in their groups but also provided efficient channels for those manufacturers' export goods around the world.

Agriculture and distribution, over on the right, were (and still are) part of Japan, Inc. When Japan was first districted for voting on legislators, a much larger portion of the population lived in rural areas. Over the years, as people migrated to cities, redistricting has lagged, so that rural residents (e.g., farmers) came to exert disproportionate representation in the Diet. Since Japanese agriculture needed tariff protection and subsidies, Japanese farmers were carefully organized nationally to support the Liberal Democratic Party. They contributed to stability, and in return, the Diet maintained high prices for rice and other food commodities protected from international competition.

It was much the same with Japan's distribution system; several layers of wholesalers and retailers, overstaffed and inefficient, added to the high prices for Japanese consumer goods. All sorts of laws protected several million distribution outlets—most notoriously, mom-and-pop stores on every corner. In return, distributors were organized nationally to support the Liberal Democratic status quo.

Finally, you might be wondering about the interests and institutions below the line in figure 2-1—those who benefited from, but had no decision rights in, Japan, Inc. Small businesses, which constituted more than 70 percent of Japanese firms, were organized as subcontractors in manufacturing. They worked directly, often in long-term relationships, with larger manufacturers, providing quality inputs at increasingly low prices. Just as there was nothing small about small businesses' stake in Japan, Inc., temporary workers were not really temporary. They represented about 75 percent of the workforce (today perhaps 55 percent). They worked full time, benefiting immensely from miracle growth. But when the economy did experience a slowdown, they could be laid off.

The other groups—women, consumers, and foreigners—were important to Japan's success in many ways but had no decision rights to speak of. Although a large proportion of women worked, at least for a few years after school, the presence of women in managerial positions or top professions was rare. Consumers were relatively unorganized and consumed relatively little due to high prices. And foreigners bought things, or provided graduate education or defense.

Japan, Inc. was a much more concentrated decision structure than Americans, or even Europeans, were used to. In the 1950s and 1960s, there were probably no more than ten thousand important people running great firms and populating the ministries, almost exclusively in Tokyo. They went to school together, worked within a twenty-block area, socialized together, and commuted together. It was as if Chicago, Los Angeles, Boston, and Washington, D.C. were all wrapped up in New York. And these people worked long hours, were talented, and were very committed.

Performance

After the rebuilding of Japanese basic infrastructure and industrial capacity, the Economic Planning Agency in 1961 published a call to double Japanese national income by 1970. This would require economic growth averaging 7.2 percent annually for ten years. Yet the results were even better—10.6 percent. And much of this work was done by heavy industry (see table 2-2).

Perhaps most amazing was the composition of GDP. Consumption, which started out at 63 percent, shrank as a portion of GDP to 50 percent. In other words, as the Japanese got richer, they consumed less and less of what they produced! From a western perspective, this is peculiar, to say the least. Likewise, government spending also dropped, from 16 percent to 7 percent. It grew at 5 percent, less than half the rate of the economy. Given a steeply progressive tax structure, this rising revenue generated growing surpluses that precipitated annual tax cuts. These, in turn, stimulated economic growth—a sort of rolling supply-side economics.

The engine of this economy was clearly investment, growing from 19 percent to 37.4 percent of GDP by 1971—an annual rate of 14.5 percent. In other words, Japan, Inc. invested more than one-third of its output in new plants and equipment. This was extraordinary. No great corporation invests anywhere near this much (as a portion of its revenues). However, as we shall see, this level of investment was "typically Asian" and would be exceeded by

TABLE 2-2

Production indexes for selected Japanese manufacturing sectors, 1953–1971*

Industry	1961	1971	Growth rate (%)
Iron and steel	337.2	1,060.0	14.0
Machinery	516.0	2,489.0	19.6
Chemicals	302.7	1,200.5	14.8
Petroleum products	404.4	1,926.9	17.9
Rubber	315.8	743.2	11.8
Paper and pulp	275.6	665.0	11.1
Textiles	210.7	463.5	8.9
All manufacturing	311.7	1,056.9	14.0

*1953 = 100

Source: Edward Denison and William Chung, "Economic Growth and Its Sources," in *Asia's New Giant*, ed. Hugh Patrick and Henry Rosovsky (Washington, DC: Brookings Institution, 1976), 74. Reprinted with permission of the Brookings Institution Press.

several neighbors, including Singapore and China. All of this investment, as previously discussed, was fueled by domestic savings, which reached 34 percent of GDP in 1971.

Exports, growing at 14.7 percent, doubled in share of GDP, from 7.3 percent to 14.6 percent. Although small, these exports appeared to be the spark plug of this economic engine. Imports likewise grew rapidly but slightly slower than exports.

Less surprisingly, Japan's unemployment rates were extremely low, dropping from 2 percent to 1 percent by the mid-1960s. (These formal numbers, however, obscured significant underemployment by work in family businesses and a measurement system that weighed women and temporary workers somewhat differently than permanent employees.) Labor productivity grew at the astounding rate of 8.4 percent per year, while inflation, surprisingly, was restrained to little more than 4.1 percent annually. With productivity growing nearly twice as fast as inflation, it is little wonder that Japan's unit labor costs fell increasingly behind its major competitors, driving its international competitiveness. The results, of course, appear in the balance of payments.

Exports boomed in the second half of the 1960s as Japanese firms began to realize the results of their hard work. Imports also grew sharply, but less

FIGURE 2-2

Japan's current account, 1960–1971

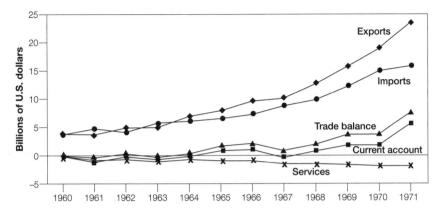

Source: Compiled by author with data from International Monetary Fund, *International Financial Statistics*, various years.

so than exports. The difference was Japan's value added. After deducting some for a negative balance in services (for technology, financial services, freight, and shipping), Japan's current account balance (trade in goods, services, and income flows) went positive by more than $5 billion by 1971 (see figure 2-2). As the capital account was still tightly closed, most of these earnings went to the Bank of Japan's foreign exchange reserves.

Japan had managed to develop and implement an economic strategy that perfectly fit its circumstances—both domestically and internationally. It built on its skilled and compliant workforce, its methods of consensual decision making, a series of institutions that stimulated savings and investment, and an effective bureaucratic planning process. Externally, it dealt with competition, targeted only the affluent market, and relied on American power and a fixed exchange rate.

And with this strategy, Japanese leaders built an effective organizational structure perfectly suited to implementing strategy. This included corporate governance, labor relations, business-government relations, and a whole host of distinctive institutions for distribution, agriculture, small business, conglomerates, unions, and so on.

Thus, the story of Japan is a perfect model of strategy, structure, and context fitting together successfully. We can use it as a comparative referent for assessing other developmental trajectories, first in Asia and then in the rest of the world.

But if anything, this miracle was too successful. U.S. foreign exchange reserves had begun to plummet, even including its hoard of gold. In the halls of Congress, lobbyists for big steel, shipbuilding, and consumer electronics were already crying about dumping. President Richard Nixon asked Commerce Secretary Pete Peterson to study the U.S. position in the international economy. But by the time Peterson had completed his gloomy assessment in April 1971, U.S. gold reserves had dropped by almost half, as French, German, and other surplus nations lost confidence in the dollar.

Early in the evening of August 15, President Nixon emerged from Camp David and went directly to the White House. At 8:03 p.m., he appeared on network TV to announce the closing of the gold window—the end of the Bretton Woods Exchange Rate System. To add insult to injury, he imposed a 10 percent import quota on Japan.

The Japanese miracle was over.

—⁄⁄⁄⁄⁄w—

Singapore, Inc.

IN HIS SWEARING-IN SPEECH in November 2004, Prime Minister Lee Hsien Loong explained to the voters of Singapore, "The trust that you have placed in Mr. Lee Kuan Yew and Mr. Goh Chok Tong who have both discharged their responsibilities admirably, is now given to me . . . I ask you to work with me to build a Singapore that will care for all our citizens, educate all our children well, and give everybody full opportunities to fulfill their aspirations."

Lee indeed had large shoes to fill. Singapore's per capita income had risen from US$427 in 1960 to US$24,793 by 2004. Income growth of 9.7 percent annually had been achieved by active government direction and control that had succeeded almost nowhere else on earth. Only the third prime minister since Singapore's founding in 1959, the young Lee faced a less stable world and an intensely competitive south Asia.

Under Lee's direction as finance minister, Singapore had recently adopted a strategy of tax cuts, both to stimulate the macroeconomy and to make the country even more attractive to foreign investors. Its Economic Development Board, meanwhile, had designed an "ecosystem" strategy to foster innovation and improved technology in five industrial clusters—petrochemicals, electronics, logistics and transport services, information communications and media, and its newest target . . . biomedical sciences.[1]

Singapore's leaders hoped that these two strategic initiatives would meet the challenges of Chinese and Indian competition and push Singapore's income into the range of developed countries. But the challenges were immense. Knowledge-based industries were deeply rooted in Japan, Europe, and the United States. Could a small city-state in Southeast Asia make the human and capital investments necessary to catch the likes of Dublin, Bangalore,

Shanghai, Taipei, and Seoul, much less London, Tokyo, Silicon Valley, and Cambridge?

Singapura: The Lion City

Singapore has been a trading center and port since the seventh century. In the fourteenth century, Chinese immigrants populated the island, before the Portuguese gained control of the region from Malay rulers in the sixteenth century. In 1819, Sir Stamford Raffles arrived in Singapore in search of a trading post for the British East India Company. After making a deal with the local Johor sultan, Raffles remarked, "It has been my good fortune to establish this station in a position combining every possible advantage, geographical and local."[2]

The island, about the size of Manhattan, was separated from Malaysia by a narrow channel. Its verdant jungle, filled with palm-roofed huts, was quaint but incredibly poor. Garbage and sewage were dumped freely in its waterways, with no concern for human health, much less the environment. Development economists describe Singapore as a staple port and as an entrepôt. Rubber and tin, both of which gained importance in the late nineteenth and early twentieth centuries, were exported from Singapore. And after 1869, when the Suez Canal was opened, Singapore became the principal port for refueling and refitting ships between east Asia and India. Only two routes could accommodate east-west trade—the Sunda Straits, between Sumatra and Java, and the far more convenient Malaccan Straits, in which Singapore was situated. Today, Singapore is the largest transshipment point for containers—with dozens of ships entering and exiting its ports daily.

By 1871, Singapore's population was estimated at sixty-five thousand. During the next thirty years, Singapore's trade expanded sixfold. Between 1910 and 1939, it grew another fourfold—to US$1.8 billion (in current dollars). The British built a major naval base there, eventually employing almost a hundred thousand people.

World War II marked a tremendous setback for the colony. The British surrendered Singapore to the Japanese in February 1942. Renamed Syonan ("Light of the South") by the Japanese, Singapore served as Japan's wartime hub for three and a half years. Singaporeans suffered terribly as some residents died of malnutrition or disease and others were executed.

After the war, the British proclaimed Singapore a Crown colony (separate from Malaya). In 1948, Britain acceded to requests from merchants to establish a legislative council. Five years later, it appointed a commission to redraft Singapore's constitution for limited self-rule. Despite electing its own legislative assembly, labor and student unrest continued. Singapore eventually sent a delegation to Britain to seek political autonomy. Lee Kuan Yew, a thirty-year-old University of Cambridge graduate who had formed the People's Action Party (PAP) in 1955, was a member of that delegation. Lee then ran for prime minister in 1959 and won.

During the next four years, the PAP worked with the Communist Party to end British colonial authority. When the British finally withdrew in 1963, Singapore joined with Malaya, Sarawak, and Sabah (North Borneo) to form the Federation of Malaysia. But this union was not to be. All sorts of problems immediately arose, over issues of revenues, common markets, and political control. Not least was the Chinese dominance of Singapore (79 percent), in contrast to Malaysia, where the majority (59.8 percent) was Malaysian. Lee Kuan Yew and the PAP government were unwilling at the time to grant any economic advantages to Malays, other than financial aid for education. Extremist leaders in Kuala Lumpur whipped up antigovernment sentiment and racial tension. In July 1964, fighting broke out between Malay and Chinese youth amid a procession celebrating Mohammed's birthday. This erupted in racial riots, in which twenty-three people were killed and hundreds injured. Two months later, Indonesian agents further provoked communal violence. Both Lee Kuan Yew and Tengku Rahman (Malaya's leader) toured the island in an effort to restore calm. Still, over the next few months, political tensions worsened, with the PAP separating entirely from the Communists and with the Malaysian government intervening in opposition to Singaporean Chinese. Lee Kuan Yew and his colleagues finally reached the point where withdrawal from Malaysia seemed the only option. On August 9, 1965, Singapore became an independent nation. Reflecting on the separation, a tearful Lee stated, "For me, it is a moment of anguish. All my life, my whole adult life, I have believed in merger and unity of the two territories."[3]

Political anguish was only part of Lee Kuan Yew's problem. He recalled, "We faced tremendous odds with an improbable chance of survival . . . Singapore was not a natural country but rather man-made, a trading post the British had developed into a nodal point in their worldwide maritime empire. We inherited the island without its hinterland, a heart without a body."[4] So Lee rationally prioritized his country's most pressing needs. First, it had to strengthen its defense and gain international recognition with a seat in the United Nations. To calm the unstable racial environment at home, the cabinet immediately formed the Ministry of Interior and Defense to build both police and army forces.

Almost as pressing was the economy. With the closure of British bases (which had contributed 20 percent of GDP), Singapore's unemployment rate of 14 percent rose sharply. To create jobs, the PAP created the Housing Development Board (HDB), which began building public housing. In eighteen months, housing for thirty thousand had been constructed, at the same time providing thousands of jobs. By 2001, more than 85 percent of the population lived in HDB-affiliated housing.

Singapore's Development Strategy

After several years of unsuccessful attempts at import substitution, Lee and his government concluded that Singapore's future lay with direct investment from American and European multinational corporations. Thus, Singapore set out on a multipronged strategy. First, it would have to leapfrog its neighbors as trading partners and attract foreign companies to manufacture in Singapore for reexport to the West. And second, Singapore sought to define itself as a first-world oasis in a third-world region. Trade and investment barriers, already low, were eliminated. The Jurong Industrial Estate, a large reclaimed area deemed by some to be a "white elephant," was prepared to host labor-intensive factories for western assembly.

The Ministry of Trade and Industry created an Economic Development Board (EDB) in 1961 to act as a one-stop shop for foreign investors. Going directly to potential customers in their home country, EDB staff tried to woo potential investors and drive investment in petrochemicals, ship refitting and repair, metal engineering, and electronics. Pioneer investors too would get special tax exemptions. In 1968, one of the EDB's early successes was National Semiconductor, which began production just two months after deciding to invest. When Texas Instruments and Hewlett-Packard relocated operations to Singapore, the rush was on.

Singapore's success, however, was dependent on many other factors besides low tariffs, cheap labor, and a nice industrial park. Singapore, Inc., conceived and implemented under the leadership of Lee Kuan Yew, was not unlike an efficient corporation. (Henry Kissinger once called Lee the "smartest man in the Western world." And the *Economist* joked that divorce from Malaysia meant that Lee's "desire to govern somewhere equal in size to his ambitions could never be fulfilled.")[5] It required a sound infrastructure, labor peace, and a noninflationary currency regime with stable exchange rates. In turn, it was necessary for the people of Singapore to save and invest—at levels never before seen. From the beginning of the PAP's rule in 1959, the government needed sufficient control to push through all the reforms necessary to make Singapore an attractive site for foreign direct investment.

Labor Policies

A productive and passive labor force was key. In postindependence Singapore, labor unrest was common. "The excesses of irresponsible trade unions," observed Singapore President Yusof bin Ishak, "are luxuries which we can no longer afford."[6] Lee wasted no time, banning antagonistic unions and arresting some labor leaders. The government established a successor union, the National Trade Union Congress (NTUC), to represent worker interests in accordance with the PAP's development philosophy. And the government created the National Wages Council to regulate wages. Union membership declined steadily, from 79 percent of the workforce to less than 25 percent by the 1990s.

The government considered labor to be in a unique partnership with business and itself. Early on, Lee created a seat in the cabinet for the secretary general of the NTUC. Thus, the unions would be aware of the reasons behind government policies and, conversely, the secretary general would represent workers' interests in the policy process. As NTUC Secretary General Lim Boon Heng told me, "The unions realize that much of what is good for business is also good for the workers. In Singapore, having a job is the most important thing. The unions must help create the necessary conditions to help encourage companies to come invest in Singapore."[7] Retrenchment policies were almost completely in the hands of management.

So successful was the EDB in attracting investors that by the late 1970s Singapore literally ran out of workers and didn't have enough of a workforce to keep up with the demand. Foreign labor eventually supplemented both skilled and unskilled labor forces. The government used the issuance of work permits as a macroeconomic tool to regulate unemployment (as well as wages and inflation). Although Singapore remained attractive to unskilled laborers, it often had difficulty retaining its skilled workforce. Emigration had become an issue by the early 2000s, so that the government had undertaken programs to encourage motherhood and keep nationals at home.

Savings

Incredibly high savings was another distinctive feature of Singapore's development strategy. The Central Provident Fund (CPF), a publicly managed, mandatory savings program, was first established in 1955—a positive legacy of the colonial era. The CPF, moreover, operated on a fully funded basis. Upon retirement, Singaporeans received tax-exempt benefits on the basis of past contributions, plus interest. The rate of interest was based on fixed-deposit and savings-deposit rates of major banks, guaranteed to pay at least 2.5 percent per annum. Mandatory pretax contributions to the CPF were made by employers and employees. Initially set at 5 percent from each, the combined contribution rates reached 50 percent in 1985, as shown in table 3-1. It is currently set at 33 percent, as the employer contribution was lowered to 13 percent in 2003 to stimulate the economy.

Virtually the entire Singaporean workforce is a member of the fund. Although originally set as a retirement plan, the fund has successfully expanded to other loan programs. Singaporeans could use their savings to buy HDB apartments. After 1981, the Residential Properties Scheme allowed for investment in private properties. College education was also a legitimate reason for borrowing. Eventually the fund provided for health care (Medisave/ Medishield) and insurance. While investment in the fund's retirement accounts was required, workers could make additional deposits for education, health, or housing. Thirty-five percent of savings could be invested in stocks on the Singapore Exchange—the earnings from which were not regulated.

The CPF's funds for the most part were invested in low-risk government bonds, used to develop Singapore's infrastructure and its government-owned businesses. As of 2001, S$89 billion (of a total of S$92 billion) was invested in government bonds. Yet it should be noted that Singaporeans actually save more than required. That is, gross domestic savings during much of the 1990s exceeded 50 percent and remained at 45 percent in 2004. This extraordinary savings, of course, helped keep interest rates low and provided the resources necessary to grow the state.

With these immense savings, Lee Kuan Yew set about investing in Singapore's infrastructure. After getting public housing started, the government built extraordinary port facilities and the Jurong Industrial Estate. More recently, Singapore has undertaken to build a new Jurong Island, filling the ocean space between seven small islands—importing the sand from Indonesia. This US$23 billion venture will allow indefinite expansion of petrochemicals and manufacturing. Over three decades, the state spent freely to clean up waterways and to build modern highways and the world's best airport (Changi), hospitals, universities, and airlines as well as a modern, fiber-optic telecommunications infrastructure. Today, the city that was once a polluted jungle village is among the cleanest, most modern cities in the world.

Perhaps the most distinctive aspect of Singapore's success is the extent to which government controlled assets directly. Besides the land and some 85 percent of the rental housing, the Singaporean government controlled about 20 percent of GDP. In addition to the utilities, the Development Bank of Singapore, and the Port of Singapore Authority, government owned Singapore Airlines, Singapore Telecom, and Singapore Technologies (munitions). In

TABLE 3-1

Rates of contribution to Singapore's Central Provident Fund, 1955–2005

	1955	1968	1970	1973	1980	1985	1986	1990	1995	1999	2001	2005
Employer (%)	5	6.5	8	15	20.5	25	10	16.5	20	10	16	13
Employee (%)	5	6.5	8	11	18	25	25	23	20	20	20	20
Total (%)	10	13	16	26	38.5	50	35	39.5	40	30	36	33

Source: Central Provident Fund of Singapore, Annual Report, 2003.

addition, government held stakes in almost all areas of the economy, including food supply, travel, and biotechnology.

Many of the government-linked companies were supervised through the government's investment arm, Temasek Holdings. Temasek, at least in 2002, owned more than forty firms, or 20 percent of Singapore's market capitalization. Ho Ching, the chairperson of Temasek (and wife of the prime minister) ran Temasek tightly and independently. Because the company was a government-owned firm, she told me, did not mean it had to answer to government; rather, it was run like a business, with independent boards.

To help assure that these investments yielded productivity growth, the Singaporean government launched a productivity movement and created the Productivity Standards Board in 1981. Because Singapore was investing so much capital, it was important to understand the productivity of that capital, as well as of labor. Those large investments in the 1970s and early 1980s caused Singapore's total factor productivity (TFP, the growth in output not attributable to labor or capital) to decline by 0.6 percent annually through 1985. However, as those investments began to pay off, Singapore's TFP accelerated to a growth rate of 3.8 percent annually in the late 1980s and 2.9 percent in the early 1990s. Demand shocks associated with the Asian financial crisis caused productivity to slip again in the late 1990s and then turn sharply negative in 2001. And it has only recently recovered.

To address this situation, the government renewed the productivity movement vigorously, renaming the board SPRING (Standards, Productivity and Innovation). A nationwide productivity rally, held September 5, 2001, was chaired by then Deputy Prime Minister Lee Hsien Loong. SPRING, with more than eight hundred employees, would now aggressively push productivity in more than two thousand organizations—business, labor, and government. Productivity training, quality circles, work redesign, improvements in standards, incentives for small and medium enterprises, retailer networks, promotion of wellness—no potential project for improving productivity was overlooked.[8] As figure 3-1 illustrates, these efforts worked initially—productivity rebounded.

When I was visiting the CEO of SPRING, I ran into Lim Boon Heng, secretary of the National Trade Union Congress, walking down the hall of SPRING's offices. When I told the CEO of this surprise meeting, he responded, nonplussed: "Of course, Lim Boon Heng is also chairman of SPRING." "We believe in promoting productivity," said Lim, "because if we increase this, we can negotiate sustainable increases in wages. Instead of just concentrating on sharing the cake, we concentrate on making a bigger cake."[9] I was in awe. And as SPRING's CEO added, "We need to move from being an efficiency city to being an innovation nation."[10]

FIGURE 3-1

GDP, labor productivity, and TFP growth

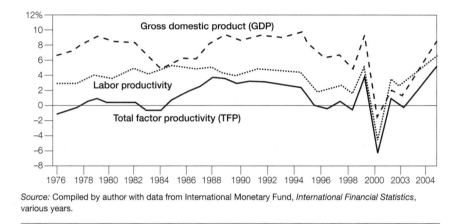

Source: Compiled by author with data from International Monetary Fund, *International Financial Statistics*, various years.

It is government officials who think like this that have made Singapore such a success. Repeatedly I spoke with civil servants who talked about "business as the customer." One actually commented on his department's objective of "delighting the customer." It was the same in A*STAR (which we'll look at later in this chapter), the EDB, and the Jurong Town Corporation. Even in Japan, I've never heard bureaucrats speak that way!

Political System

Judging from its civil service, Singapore has been run much like a corporation. While cabinet officers are politicians, they tend to be particularly talented individuals—often educated abroad in business or economics. And the civil service itself is extraordinarily well educated, motivated, talented, and well compensated.

Singapore is governed by a parliamentary system consisting of eighty-four elected members (nine elected directly, and seventy-five elected in teams of four to six to represent the fourteen group constituencies and ensure at least one racial minority member per team). Members of Parliament are elected every five years. Voting is compulsory for all elections. A president, elected directly, appoints the prime minister with the Parliament's support. The cabinet consists of fourteen to sixteen ministers, and each meritocratic ministry is headed by a permanent secretary.

Compensation for senior ministers is exceedingly generous. The prime minister's salary in 2000 was a bit more than US$1.1 million; even his most junior minister received US$550,000—more than the president of the United States! The government argued that high salaries were necessary to retain talent. Lee Kuan Yew, Lee's father and the first prime minister, defended the practice, stating, "See it in proportion to what is at stake." Goh Chok Tong further reasoned, "The damage we had prevented to the economy from the Asian financial crisis is more than enough to pay the ministers and the other political office holders for the rest of their political lives and in fact over many lifetimes."[11]

Government pay scales were guided by a careful formula. Entry-level ministers or permanent senior secretaries earned 60 percent of the median salary of the eight top earners in six professions, ranging from bankers to multinational CEOs. And like large corporations, senior officials' bonuses and many departmental budgets were tied to the country's GDP performance. "We are 100 percent government, but in terms of operational discipline, we are run like the private sector," explained a senior director at the EDB.[12] Thus, in 2002, with an economic downturn, senior ministers suffered appropriately.

Still another practice that emulated some corporations was frequent lateral job switching. That is, senior bureaucrats often switched jobs every few years, from the Central Provident Fund, to defense, to trade, to labor. While this sometimes resulted in less experienced professionals heading a particular ministry, the benefits were significant. Everyone knew everyone else and had a pretty good sense of broad issues and strategy. As the minister of information technology and the arts observed, "The initial start is a challenge, but it keeps our perspective fresh and the government flexible."[13]

Perhaps most importantly, there was no corruption among Singaporean bureaucrats. In fact, there was relatively little corruption of any kind in Singapore. The authoritarian government was renowned for its honesty and transparency. It consistently ranked high in Transparency International's Corruption Perceptions Index. In 2004, for example, Singapore ranked fifth best, of 145 countries—the only Asian country in the top fifteen.[14] As early as 1952, the government had established the Corrupt Practices Investigation Board—an independent group that enforced anticorruption laws. Any person found guilty of corruption could be imprisoned for five years or fined S$100,000—or both.

From anti-spitting campaigns to a ban on chewing gum, Singapore has been called the "nanny state" by cynics. But Lee Kuan Yew believed that it was necessary to maintain a tight control over the social and physical environment of so small an island. Thus, for example, Singapore had instituted a "clean and green" movement to beautify its surroundings. Millions of trees were planted, by everyone including cabinet ministers and the prime minister, every National Tree Planting Day. The Singapore River, once an open sewer, was cleaned enough to become fishable and swimmable. Stagnant water was drained, so that the insect population was reduced and public health, enhanced.

Automobile pricing and taxation exemplifies control of the government for social purposes. Taxes kept imported automobiles exceedingly expensive, to limit the number of automobiles. On top of that, Singaporeans had to bid at auction for a restricted number of certificates of entitlement. Thus, for a car that cost US$50,000, taxes might be US$20,000 and the registration fee, an additional US$30,000. And to control downtown traffic, a system of electronic cordons charged higher rates at peak hours to control congestion. Obviously, for most Singaporeans, mass transit was popular.

Perhaps the best-known example of the "nanny state" is the case of Michael Fay, an eighteen-year-old American resident found guilty of vandalism (spray-painting automobiles) in 1994. Singaporean authorities sentenced him to six strokes of the cane. When President Clinton pleaded for leniency, Singaporean authorities grudgingly reduced the sentence to four strokes. "Singaporeans," surmised a columnist for the *Straits Times*, "appear willing to overlook the sacrifice of civil liberties for the practical benefits of an orderly and comfortable society."[15]

Singaporeans speak any of four languages—English, Mandarin Chinese, Malay, or Hindi. In 1979, interestingly, Lee Kuan Yew decided that Singaporean youth were becoming too westernized in their tastes for games, music, and movies. He actually called the English-educated a deracinated, devitalized lot. So he switched the required language in Singaporean schools to Mandarin, to the disgust of Malays and Indians. Lee hoped that individualism would be deemphasized, while the Confucian focus on the national group would become dominant. Today, Singaporean children choose schools where the curriculum is dominated by Mandarin, Malay, Hindi, or English, but English is always at least the second language.

Fiscal and Monetary Policy

This strategy would not be complete without effective macroeconomic management. Singapore's fiscal and monetary policies were exemplary. Ever since 1970, the central government had generally run a balanced budget—falling into deficit only occasionally, when stimulus was absolutely necessary. Although the tax rate was low, noncapital expenditures were also minimized. Investment spending by the government was financed largely by bonds purchased by the Central Provident Fund. In the 1990s, for example, the government generally maintained surpluses of 20 percent of revenues

(25 percent of expenditures). Only in 2001, in deep recession, did the government cut taxes and run a deficit of S$2.7 billion (about 9 percent of expenditures, or 1.7 percent of GDP).

Monetary policy, meanwhile, was controlled by the Monetary Authority of Singapore (MAS), the powerful central bank that also controlled bank regulation, securities, insurance, and exchange rates. Through an exchange-rate-centered policy, MAS maintained a low inflation rate and kept interest rates on a par with foreign rates. MAS tied the exchange rate to a trade-weighted basket of currencies. From the early 1970s, it gradually appreciated against the U.S. dollar, rising from 3.06 to 1.41 in 1996, before it gradually depreciated again (currently at S$1.63 per U.S. dollar). After the second oil shock (1979–1980), the inflation rate was held below 3.4 percent and generally in the range of 1.5–2 percent. The prime lending rate was usually less than 7 percent after 1990—and recently as low as 4 percent.

Industrial Policy

Singapore's industrial policy was to attract foreign investors from Europe and the United States (and eventually Japan) to build petrochemical, shipping, and assembly facilities in their "first-world oasis." This worked well until the early 1980s after the second oil shock, when other, lower-wage Asian countries (Malaysia, Thailand, and China) began to emerge as competitors. Rather than try to hold down wages, Lee's government decided to push wages higher, hoping that such a policy would force foreign investors to increase the value added of their operations, deploying even more technology and capital in their Singaporean plants. "Our strategy," said Goh Chok Tong, at the time minister of trade and industry, was "to induce entrepreneurs and managers of capital to increase efficiency of production by restructuring, automation and rationalization. We also encourage[d] them to upgrade into higher-technology industries that can generate more value-added products."[16]

While this policy worked for several years, the economy nonetheless slipped into a deep recession in 1985. Unemployment jumped, and manufacturing investment dropped sharply. A task force was appointed, headed by Lee's son, Lee Hsien Loong (who became prime minister in 2004). This committee found that the wage policy was overambitious, as labor productivity had not kept pace. It also found excessive government intervention. The committee recommended less government, more flexible wage setting, and a reduction of forced savings. These actions, taken immediately, helped stimulate recovery in 1986 and growth of 7.8 percent annually for the succeeding five years.

Two things are interesting about this episode. First, Singapore's technocrats were able to study a problem, take action, and recover. Few other states could implement a remedy so effectively or quickly. The second lesson was the challenge of low wages. With China opening up, this would last indefinitely. Thus, Singapore would have to change its strategy, finding ways to continually increase the value added of its economy, and itself become a foreign investor in lower-wage countries.

Singapore increasingly became a trading powerhouse. By the early 1990s, its trade volume had grown to two or three times its GDP—the highest ratio in the world. Its Trade Development Board, later renamed International Enterprise Singapore, had established Singapore as a trading hub. And in 1989, Singapore had launched TradeNet—the first e-trade processing system, which dramatically improved efficiency and turnaround time for investing businesses. By 2001, Singapore's total trade was 277 percent of GDP. Although the country had long-run deficits, the current account had turned positive in 1988 as Singapore's trade in services exceeded its deficit in goods. But even the goods balance turned positive in 1994, and since then, Singapore has not looked back. By 2004, Singapore's trade balance in goods was a surplus of US\$32 billion, in services it was US\$8.5 billion, and in income it was S\$8.9 billion. Together, these produced a current account surplus of US\$28.8 billion. This was 30 percent of GDP . . . the highest in the world!

The flow of net income is perhaps the most telling number in Singapore's balance of payments. Net income represents the interest and dividends Singapore pays on all the foreign investment in Singapore, minus what it earns on its investments abroad. As shown in table 3-2, this number, long negative, went positive in 1985 and remained so until 2002. This figure represents Singaporean savings and growing investment abroad. That is, increasingly Singaporeans saved more than they invested at home, using the difference to invest abroad. Another way to put it, they invested a large portion of the current account surplus abroad (while keeping some of it as reserve assets).

We can see this on the capital account. Direct investment increased of late, to US\$6.4 billion, while portfolio investment and other investments (e.g., government bonds) are hugely negative. Again, this indicates that Singaporeans are saving more than they need and purchasing more and more, primarily foreign financial assets.

Moving Up Again

Faced with repeated slowdowns in economic growth, low-wage competition from China, and bouts of negative productivity, the government of Singapore began consciously to change strategies again. These efforts, which

TABLE 3-2

Singapore's balance of payments, 1975–2005 (billions of U.S. dollars)

	1975	1980	1985	1988	1991	1994	1997	2000	2001	2002	2003	2004	2005
Trade balance	-2.4	-4.2	-2.8	-2.3	-4.1	1.4	1.1	11.6	12.9	22.2	31.9	32.3	33.4
Exports	5.1	18.2	21.5	37.9	56.8	97.9	126	139	122	154	172	204.1	233.1
Imports	-7.5	-22.4	-23.4	-40.3	-60.9	-96.6	96	127	110	131	140	171.8	195.0
Net services	1.8	3.1	2.4	3.1	6.9	9.1	11.5	5	5.7	0.4	2	0.5	2.9
Net income	0.04	-0.4	0.6	0.3	1.9	1.6	6.5	0.6	0.7	-0.2	-1.9	-2.8	-0.6
Current account	**-0.6**	**-1.6**	**-0.04**	**0.9**	**4.2**	**11.4**	**17.9**	**15.9**	**17.9**	**21.1**	**30.7**	**28.8**	**33.4**
Direct investment	0.3	1.1	0.8	0.9	2.9	4	3.3	0.5	-1.6	2.2	6.4	5.8	14.6
Portfolio net	-0.02	0.01	0.2	-0.3	0.2	-7.7	-0.1	0.5	-1.2	-12.5	-11.9	-11.7	-13.7
Other	0.04	0.02	0.03	-0.2	-0.01	-5	-1.5	-1.4	-12.6	-4.9	-21.9	-7.2	-21.0

Source: Compiled by author with data from International Monetary Fund, *International Financial Statistics Yearbook*, 2005.

would unfold over several years, entailed microeconomic changes, institutional changes, and a new macroeconomic thrust.

At the microeconomic level, the Economic Development Board took the lead. The EDB stated, "[The board] will endeavor to do even better to entrench Singapore as a compelling hub for business and investment. The linchpin of our new approach rests on building a vibrant enterprise ecosystem—a total environment bringing together companies big and small, foreign and local, thriving in synergy and symbiosis."[17] This strategy would entail a dual approach: (1) continue to focus on the already strong "clusters" of chemicals, electronics and precision engineering, logistics and transport services, and information communications and (2) encourage innovation and entrepreneurship in these sectors. "We want to encourage innovation and entrepreneurship throughout the economy," said Chua Taik Him, assistant managing director of the EDB. "We'll do this by investing in our human capital, technology, and infrastructure. This will be done by Singapore, not just [the] EDB. We have a *national* mind-set."[18]

Perhaps the best example of Singapore's single-minded focus on industrial clusters was the next "big thing"—biomedical sciences. This cluster encompassed the pharmaceutical, medical technology, biotechnology, and health-care industries. As the chairman of the EDB noted, "[B]iomedical sciences is an industry that amply suits Singapore. It is not labor and land intensive; it requires a well-trusted system of operation; it is intellectually capital intensive, and intellectual property is well-protected. We don't have much in the way of resources to offer, but what we do have is brains!"[19]

To build on Singapore's competitive advantage of its infrastructure, intellectual property laws, and first-rate health-care system, the government took a number of initiatives to transform Singapore into the biomedical hub of Asia, called Biopolis. It aggressively sought to entice established biomedical and pharmaceutical firms to locate manufacturing (and hopefully research and development) in Singapore. The EDB strove to provide a one-stop service for potential investors. Its Biomedical Services Group was organized to assist companies in the planning, investment, and marketing aspects of biomedicine.

As it had done earlier with petrochemicals, Singapore invested in infrastructure. One-north, a visionary industrial park for both start-up and established biomedical firms, encompasses a nineteen-acre complex of new high-rise buildings devoted exclusively to biomedicine. Located near the National University of Singapore (which itself contributed by investing in strengthened biomedical degree offerings), Biopolis expected to meet both the residential and research needs of two thousand scientists and professionals. The government built the first seven buildings to attract further investment by the private sector. Not far away, a four hundred-acre plot was set aside for the manufacturing needs of pharmaceutical companies. A goal of attracting fifteen global life-science manufacturers had already been surpassed by 2004.

Financial capital, meanwhile, was earmarked for the Biomedical Sciences Investment Fund to assist new ventures. "The government now serves as a facilitator and catalyst to the private sector," said Chua.

Intellectual capital would also be necessary if Singapore's ecosystem strategy were to succeed. The education system would need to support it. Since many believed that traditional rote learning stifled creativity and entrepreneurship, the government was making investments to promote new ways to teach and encourage innovation. The EDB planned to have at least ten world-class institutions in Singapore by 2008; already, INSEAD, John Hopkins, Wharton, and MIT had set up satellite campuses or educational joint ventures there.

Perhaps the centerpiece of the biomedical thrust was the Agency for Science, Technology and Research (A*STAR). Originally organized under another name in 1991, A*STAR was building Singapore's scientific knowledge base through a series of five-year plans. Headed by Philip Yeo since 2001, A*STAR's third plan (2001–2005) was budgeted at S$7 billion. This organization had four divisions: the Biomedical Research Council, the Science and Engineering Research Council, the Exploit Technology Pte Ltd., and the Corporate Planning and Administration Division. The research councils oversaw R&D efforts in the Singaporean public sector.

Each of the four divisions worked to fund and promote scientific research and education with a goal of creating the "Boston of the East." In addition to helping start the Genome Institute of Singapore, the Institute of Molecular and Cell Biology, and the Institute of Bioengineering, A*STAR awarded research and educational grants to promising students. When I met with Philip Yeo in Boston, he proudly described the science scholars he was supporting at Harvard and MIT, not to mention Stanford, Columbia, and five or six other great schools throughout Europe.

In 2001, Prime Minister Goh convened the Economic Review Committee (ERC) to review Singapore's macroeconomic policy, further diversify Singapore's economy, and develop the entrepreneurial, innovative, and science-focused environment necessary to facilitate the move to a knowledge-based economy. Lee Hsien Loong, then deputy prime minister, was chosen as chair.

In mid-2002, the ERC recommended that government cut its corporate tax rate from 24.5 percent to 22 percent, and personal income taxes from 26 percent to 22 percent. Both would be lowered to 20 percent by 2005. This would encourage foreign direct investment into knowledge-based industries. And the budget would offer additional tax breaks for research and development. MAS believed that these tax cuts would push Singapore's real GDP growth up by 1.2 percent and investment by as much as 10 percent.

Although this would likely produce budgetary deficits, it would be partially offset by a hike in the goods and services tax (GST) from 3 percent to 5 percent. "GST preserves the incentive to work and encourages enterprise," concluded the ERC. "As people's income increases, income tax will push them into higher tax brackets, which take larger proportions of their incomes; GST will not."[20] The higher GST was expected to raise most of the revenue lost to income tax cuts.

The ERC also recommended increasing competition to help stimulate entrepreneurship. Government was urged to divest itself from nonstrategic sectors gradually. As Lee Hsien Loong observed, "You can change taxes, you can change policies quickly, but if you want to change mind-sets, promote entrepreneurship or innovation . . . those are not changes you can cause overnight."[21]

Singapore, Inc.

Singapore has become a rich country—equal to the Organisation for Economic Co-operation and Development (OECD) average and better off than Spain, Portugal, Greece, and Italy. It has remained secure in Southeast Asia, amid countries far larger, and somewhat less stable, than itself. These achievements are indeed considerable.

Singapore has done this through a combination of great leadership, effective developmental strategy, and strong governmental institutions. Lee Kuan Yew, who led Singapore's development from 1959 to 1990, was indeed unusual—an intelligent, ambitious, and honest leader who served for an entire generation. The strategy he adopted, of export-led growth based on foreign direct investment, was prescient—the right strategy at the right time, for a country without resources in a globalizing world.

But I believe that Singapore's success derives most from its extraordinary institutions—the institutions created by the PAP government. These institutions—organizations implementing policies under law—have made Singapore work as well as it has. These include the Housing Development Board, the Jurong Industrial Estate, the Economic Development Board, the Central Provident Fund, the Monetary Authority of Singapore, SPRING, and A*STAR. Together, these institutions formed a web of organizational structure that fit Singapore's strategy almost perfectly. It is difficult to think of another country with a similar set of governmental institutions that work so well.

In fact, Singapore is almost certainly the best example of government that works—more than a quarter of Singapore's GDP and virtually all of its policy endowment is government controlled. Effective macroeconomic management is a significant part of this. Nowhere else do we find such high levels of savings and investment directed so effectively at building the infrastructure, skills, and institutions necessary for economic performance.

Yet Singapore's future remains uncertain. While it continues to grow quickly and develop its biomedical resources, the challenges of becoming a knowledge-based economy in competition with the older and richer nations of Japan, Europe, and the United States are immense. But Singapore has made its bet—that a government-led country can work as well as market-dominated capitalist states. Either way, Singapore has done it in the past and thus serves as an admirable model of what is possible. It remains to be seen if the country can continue in the future.

—⟋⟋⟋⟋—

China

THE PRAGMATIC STATE

IN 1992, as the economic slowdown and political stillness following
Tiananmen Square gradually subsided, Deng Xiaoping once again took the
initiative. Getting his second wind after fourteen years in power, the octoge-
narian flew to Shenzhen and planted a tree, repeating his old slogan, "to get
rich is glorious." Then he traveled up the coast, visiting factories, until he
reached Shanghai's huge industrial park. All the while, he encouraged managers and pushed his reform agenda.

The gross domestic product at the time stood at $484 billion, or $413 per
capita. China had already come a long way, growing 8.9 percent annually
since 1978, but with nearly a third of the world's poor, it still had a considerable way to go.

Later in the same year of Deng's southern tour, Tim Clissold, a young
British investment banker, set off across China to find potential investments.
He eventually described his visits grimly:

> *Most of the factories that we saw were vast, more like towns than manufac-*
> *turing plants, with populations of many thousands hidden behind high walls*
> *and gateways with their own hospitals, kindergartens, cinemas and shops . . .*
> *We hadn't found a single factory that made the remotest sense for investment.*
> *We had been presented with scenes of complete anarchy at most of them: huge*
> *workshops with vats of boiling metal and men wearing cloth shoes pouring it*
> *into moulds on the floor; groups of women squatting down on their hunkers,*
> *with rusty old files gnawing away on vast heaps of aluminum castings; ac-*
> *countants' offices piled high with shoeboxes stuffed full of wafer-thin paper*
> *covered in indecipherable characters.*[1]

Twelve years later still, in 2004, I visited Shanghai for several days. The reception area of my hotel was on the forty-fourth floor of the world's second-tallest building. The city was stunning. When I last had seen Pu Dong, it was a filthy industrial swamp. Now it was nothing but skyscrapers and apartment buildings stretching as far as one could see. On this visit to Pu Dong's industrial park in 2004, I drove by more than a thousand plants—a biotech area, a high-tech research park, electronics assembly, and virtually every recognizable brand name in the West. I visited GE's newest research facility, staffed with more than six hundred scientists. And I was stunned to learn that Pu Dong officials were planning an expansion of two thousand acres.

China's GDP had reached $1.587 trillion, or about $1,588 per capita. Adjusted for purchasing power parity, this amounted to more than $5,000 per capita, with fewer than 4 percent of the population in poverty. On January 5, 2005, the government announced the birth of the 1.3 billionth Chinese.

How had China done this? How could a country with so huge a population and so awful a government have grown its income more than 9 percent annually for twenty-six years? While *glasnost* (political liberalization) had made little progress, *perestroika* (economic liberalization) had gone wild! What had the government done to unleash the productive capabilities of its people while maintaining peace and preserving power? China was not quite capitalist yet, but its social market economy was still growing more than 8 percent annually in 2005.

China's Long History and Broad Geography

It is nearly a cliché to speak of China's long history. Its civilization arose more than four thousand years ago, in the rich, moist soil of the Yellow River Valley. The development of rice farming, with the use of water buffalo for power, led to significant yields and the rapid growth of population. Farmers evolved into family clans, clustered around villages and eventually central towns. By 1120 BC, the Zhou family of warrior priests managed to subjugate adjacent villages and establish control over the Yellow River Valley. The Zhou dynasty ruled for nearly six hundred years, collecting taxes and raising armies that supported the emperor and his bureaucrats. Art and scholarship flourished, producing the great philosophers Confucius and Lao-tzu.

After 480 BC, however, China split into warring states. Political anarchy ruled until 221 BC, when the Qin family consolidated power brutally. For eleven years, the emperor killed thousands of Confucian scholars, used forced labor to build roads and repair the Great Wall, and standardized coinage and the Chinese writing system. The body of political and moral philosophy that emerged under Confucianism was officially adopted by the Han dynasty, which ruled from 206 BC until AD 220.[2]

The Chinese imperial system rested on three pillars. First was the emperor, who enjoyed a "Mandate of Heaven." The mandate gave the emperor a divine right to rule, but that right depended on certain standards of good conduct. There are many instances of peasant uprisings when this right was deemed forfeit. The second pillar was the imperial bureaucracy. This bureaucracy, which ran the empire, was guided by sophisticated procedures, exams, and rewards. The third pillar was Confucianism, defining bonds between subject and ruler, son and father, husband and wife. These intrinsic rules, or relationships, were key to the political institutions that governed China.[3] Chinese considered their land the Middle Kingdom, a civilization surrounded by the "four barbarians"—Annam, Mongolia, Korea, and Japan.

In addition to stable government and an effective administrative bureaucracy, the Chinese enjoyed an active and inventive intellectual climate. They invented paper, the printing press, the compass, mechanical clocks, and gunpowder centuries before those innovations were discovered in the West.

Non-Chinese people, however, were generally deemed inferior. Chinese emperors remained pointedly uninterested in the outside world. "We possess all things," observed one emperor in 1792, "and have no need for the strange or ingenious manufactures of foreign barbarians."[4] Or as historian R. H. Tawney observed, Chinese peasants "ploughed with iron when Europe used wood, and continued to plough with it when Europe used steel."[5]

Portuguese sailors arrived in 1514, followed shortly by the Dutch, British, and Russians. To balance their trade with China, British merchants smuggled opium into China, causing widespread addiction and resulting in a series of military defeats known as the Opium Wars. These conflicts, finally settled by the series of Unequal Treaties, allowed western powers to carve up China through access to coastal cities. The combination of colonial depredation, rapid population growth (from 143 million in the mid-eighteenth century to 423 million by the mid-nineteenth century), food shortages, declining control of the bureaucracy, and increasing corruption gave rise to internal struggles and revolution. The Qing dynasty (1644–1911) finally collapsed, giving way to an even less stable Republic of China, under Sun Yat-sen.

Although many of the provinces declared their loyalty to Sun and his nationalist Kuomintang (KMT) party, his central government in Nanjing had little power over rapacious warlords. After Sun's death in 1925, two competing centers of political power emerged. General Chiang Kai-shek took control of the KMT and began unifying the country. And leftist students and urban intellectuals formed the Chinese Communist Party (CCP). In 1927, after Chiang Kai-shek attacked and killed hundreds of Communists in the Shanghai Massacre, the CCP fled to the countryside under the leadership of Mao Zedong. Mao and his Communist followers were eventually forced to move north in the fantastic Long March from Jiangxi to Shaanxi. Although many died during the trek, Mao's power was consolidated and legitimized.

The Japanese invasion in 1931 forced the two sides to cooperate. The KMT moved west, operating out of Chongqing, while Mao's Communists went underground and employed guerrilla tactics. After the war, Chiang launched another attack on the CCP but was routed and eventually fled to Taiwan. On October 1, 1949, Mao stood atop the Tiananmen Gate of Heavenly Peace and proclaimed the establishment of the People's Republic of China.

The country Mao inherited was vast, stretching from Heilongjiang in the northern reaches of Mongolia to Hainan Island in the subtropical south. More than twenty-five hundred miles separated Shanghai on the eastern coast from the border of Tajikistan far to the west. Modern China borders fourteen countries—from North Korea; through Russia, Mongolia, and several ex-Soviet states; around past India; to Myanmar, Laos, and Vietnam.

Although about the size of the continental United States, China has perhaps one-fifth of America's arable land, with four times the population. Urbanization and desertification have combined to reduce this amount by hundreds of thousands of hectares annually. Farmers in southern China grow two or three crops annually—this is the rice bowl. In the north, one crop is grown each year, usually maize, soybeans, or wheat. Rain and water availability are crucial to China's agriculture. Several huge river systems—particularly the Yellow and the Yangtze—irrigate, but also flood, China's breadbasket. (See figure 4-1 for a map of China.)

Today, China's population of 1.3 billion is increasingly urban (40 percent). China has a hundred cities with populations greater than 1 million. Chongqing, perhaps the world's largest, is home to 30 million. Shanghai has more than 16 million, with Beijing not far behind.

Communist Revolution

Mao sought to transform China by achieving rapid economic development through a peasant-led Socialist revolution. Unlike his successor, Deng Xiaoping, Mao was driven by ideology—and a somewhat muddled, inconsistent ideology at that. He started by deploying the People's Liberation Army to gain control of the provinces. He established two parallel political structures. There was the Communist Party structure, which reached from Beijing down through provincial government, local authorities, and finally to *danwei*, or "village units." These local units were responsible for schooling,

FIGURE 4-1

Provinces of China

provision of housing, administration of birth control, resolution of personal disputes, and providing pensions. Workers were tied to the danwei through their *hukou*, or "residence registration." The general secretary of the Communist Party, and head of the politburo, was generally the ruler of China. But there was also an administrative government structure with ministries and a federal bureaucracy. The National People's Congress, with some three thousand members, enacted laws and elected a premier. (Deng held both positions.) A third source of power is Chairman of the Central Military Commission—a title that Jiang Zemin gave up grudgingly to Hu Jintao, secretary of the Communist Party, in 2004.

Early on, Mao targeted potential opponents with mass political campaigns. He suppressed landowners and rich peasants, counterrevolutionaries (former KMT officials), intellectuals, and other rightists. Violence, "struggle meetings" (attesting loyalty to the government), and forced public confessions were all part of this. Adopting a Soviet development model, he issued a first five-year plan (1953–1957), with central planning and investment in heavy industry. Like the USSR, this approach produced rapid economic growth (9 percent annually).

The second phase of the Maoist era, and certainly the most egregious, was the Great Leap Forward. Mao became disenchanted with Soviet economics after Khrushchev's attack on Stalin's legacy in 1956. He longed for some other approach, where mass action by peasants could lead development. In 1958, he introduced the Great Leap Forward. Land was redistributed into rural communes, where peasants would be mobilized to increase production and build an industrial base in the countryside. Ambitious targets were set for backyard furnaces to produce iron. Farmers actually melted down agricultural implements to meet their targets for low-quality iron that was fairly useless. Local officials falsified figures, fearfully living in a world where quotas could increase without warning. Economic growth halted, with GDP dropping by one-third. Perhaps 20 million to 30 million people— mostly elderly—starved to death.

In 1960, when this tragedy became evident, Mao quietly shifted strategies. He withdrew from day-to-day decision making and called in Deng Xiaoping to make things work. Under the control of Deng and his pragmatic bureaucrats, agriculture and industrial production returned to stable growth. By 1965, the economy was growing at about 11 percent, with declining unemployment. But no sooner was rapid growth attained than Mao again worried for his Socialist revolution.

To "put China back on track," he announced a Cultural Revolution in 1966, led by his third wife, Jiang Qing, and guided by so-called Mao Zedong Thought (based on his small red book). Under orders to destroy the Four Olds (old thoughts, culture, customs, and habits), gangs of teenage Red Guards roamed the countryside, burning books, destroying centers of science and learning, beating and killing intellectuals and the wealthy. Deng Xiaoping was among those "sent down" (exiled) to the countryside. His son was permanently crippled when thrown out a window by the Red Guard.

By the early 1970s, China had descended into anarchy, with factions of Red Guards fighting one another. Mao finally called on the army to restore order and disband the guards. In 1973, he recalled Deng to Beijing to begin rebuilding once again. Three years later, Mao was dead. With no succession process in place, a power struggle ensued between leaders of the Communist Party. Only in 1978 did Deng Xiaoping emerge victorious.

The Pragmatic Reforms of Deng Xiaoping

Deng, unlike Mao, was a pragmatic individual who wanted stable government and economic growth. How he attained these would depend on what worked. "Who cares if a cat is black or white," he famously said, "as long as it catches the mice." Deng would seek to depoliticize the economy, creating a sphere of private activity increasingly beyond government.

Deng immediately turned his attention to population control. China's population, at 950 million in 1978, was too large and growing too fast (1.6 percent annually). Mao had encouraged a large population, as "every person added two more hands to work." After 1971, Premier Zhou Enlai had begun discouraging population growth, with a slogan of "late, sparse, and few." While the birthrate had fallen some, it was still too high for Deng. In 1978, he adopted a one-child policy. Without special permission otherwise, women were allowed to have one child only. Financial incentives (i.e., tax penalties), social sanctions, sterilization, and occasionally, forced abortion were deployed—especially in the countryside. According to the *China Statistical Yearbook*, the population growth rate had fallen to 0.9 percent by the end of the century.[6]

In 2000, these rules were modified to allow a second child for families whose first was a daughter. As it was, China had many more male births than female ones, gradually leading to a disturbing imbalance. Even at this lower rate, however, China's population recently surpassed 1.3 billion and will likely reach 1.5 billion by 2020 or so. These numbers have huge implications for food, energy, jobs, and pensions, to which we'll return later in this chapter.

After population, agriculture was in desperate need of reform. Mao's communalization of agriculture was a disaster. Farm output had dropped to the point where food needed to be imported. Communal farmers had few incentives to produce and thousands of ancillary people to support. In some local districts, officials had begun to allow peasants to retain part of their production above their contracted contribution to the commune. This they could sell on the black market. A related innovation was the Household Responsibility System, in which officials leased plots to individual households. Here again, after contracted sales, surplus could be sold freely. Deng immediately raised contract prices and ordered that farmers be allowed to sell extra produce at market-determined prices—a dual-price system. This system spread quickly after 1979, eventually applying to 99 percent of farming households.

These reforms had an immediate impact. Agricultural output experienced rapid gains during the next six years, with grain yields growing at nearly 6 percent annually; meat output nearly doubled.

Success on the farms led to further reforms. With their significant new savings, farmers began to demand consumer goods—in short supply. Towns, villages, and other rural organizations began to create firms, called "township and village enterprises" (TVEs), to use surplus resources and create consumer goods. These TVEs might also make agricultural implements, steel, machinery, textiles, or simple electronics. Over the next two decades, the output of TVEs grew at 30 percent annually. Increasingly, TVEs produced Christmas ornaments, footwear, and other labor value-added goods for export. By 1995, some 22 million TVEs employed 129 million people and produced about 38 percent of all manufactured output.[7]

Another step, taken by the Central Committee in 1978, was to acknowledge the need for greater openness. Although trade was opening through the expansion of foreign trade corporations, there had been no foreign direct investment (FDI). Hard-liners, in fact, worried that FDI would jeopardize Chinese assets and threaten the Socialist character of the economy. Thus, as an experiment, the government in 1979 created four special economic zones (SEZs) along the coast—three in Guangdong province next to Hong Kong and one in Fujian province, across the straits from Taiwan. These zones—with tax incentives, easy approval procedures, plant sites, guaranteed power, and available labor—were designed to attract foreign capital. And with the capital would come technology, management skills, and access to distribution channels in the world economy.

In 1984, SEZs were expanded to Shenzhen, Zhuhai, Shantou, Xiamen, and Hainan. In 1988, zones were extended to coastal areas along the Yangtze River, the Pearl River, the Shandong Peninsula, and the Liaodong Peninsula. And in 1992, the definition of a *zone* was broadened to embrace any special economic area, in various inland cities and autonomous regions. Moreover, fifteen new free-trade zones, thirty-two state-level economic and technological development zones, and fifty-three new high-tech parks were authorized in large and medium-sized cities. All of these SEZs served as catalysts for developing the foreign-oriented economy and generating commerce through trade.

SEZs started up slowly, with but $1.9 billion during the first four years. Most of this came from offshore Chinese in Hong Kong and Macao. These people had relatives and friends in China and understood business practices there—how to attract and manage labor, how to organize suppliers, how to ensure timely delivery, and how to manage foreign exchange and taxes. Before long, Taiwanese investors joined in—taking some risks but eager to be involved in China's development boom. Then Europeans and Americans began investing in the late 1980s, and the Japanese in the mid-1990s. As shown in figure 4-2, after a post-Tiananmen lull, direct investment took off, reaching $60 billion in the aftermath of China joining the World Trade Organization in 2001.

Nearly every multinational felt obligated to be in China. The domestic market appeared limitless, and for reexports, the labor costs were minimal.

Still, the majority of the investment came from expatriot Chinese. Their ability to manage a business in China generally exceeded that of foreigners.

This massive inward flow of investment, at 2–4 percent of China's GDP, had several implications. Foremost, it created jobs and generated wealth along China's coast. It also brought technology and management know-how, both of which were quickly absorbed. And it generated an immense volume of trade. China's exports grew from $10 billion in 1978 to $570 billion by 2004; imports grew from $11 billion to $540 billion. As much as 60 percent of this volume was thought to pass through foreign-invested plants. These products, the incomes generated, and the brands that proliferated were changing China fundamentally. It was being westernized rapidly, just as hard-liners had feared.

Another step by Deng was an attempt to fix the state-owned enterprises (SOEs). In 1978, China's entire economic infrastructure was government owned—either owned by the national government in Beijing, by provincial governments, or by TVEs. Thousands of such companies, both big and small, produced goods inefficiently, with excessive staff and outdated equipment. There was no quality control, no R&D to improve product performance, no channel management, no marketing. As in Russia, production targets and inputs were allocated according to a central plan. Price was administered, usually for policy reasons. The World Bank estimated that SOE productivity was –1.2 percent annually. There was no market.

In the early 1980s, some local officials encouraged the Management Responsibility System, modeled on the Household Responsibility System in

FIGURE 4-2

Foreign direct investment into China, 1979–2005

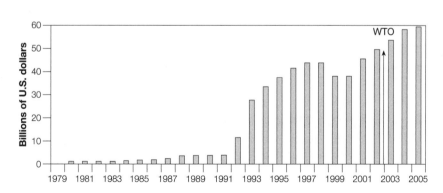

Source: Compiled by author with data from International Monetary Fund, *International Financial Statistics,* various years.

agriculture. Firms were allowed increased autonomy over production and investment decisions. Once they fulfilled their contractual obligations for the state, they could sell their surplus output at market prices. Dual-track pricing was generally allowed after 1985.

These initiatives had limited success for a number of reasons. First, SOEs were not allowed to lay off surplus workers. Thus, cutting costs was difficult. Second, many of the SOEs operated in monopoly markets where the incentive to fix things was limited. Third, it was difficult to import modern equipment even when investment funds were available. And finally, when these firms lost money, they could merely turn to the state bank for loans. By the early 1990s, two-thirds of China's SOEs were losing money.[8] Meanwhile their share of national output shrank, as TVEs and foreign-invested firms boomed.

A fifth piece of China's development strategy was price decontrol—gradually. In the late 1970s, all prices were set by the state. Food, public transportation, housing, power (and coal), communications, and many manufactured goods were sold below cost. Deng Xiaoping realized that prices had to reflect costs eventually. So the government began raising prices toward a market-clearing level. Rice, power, and housing, however, were still not fully decontrolled by the twenty-first century.

Shortly after Deng's southern tour in 1992, Beijing turned to two of its most difficult structural problems—fiscal policy and exchange rate policy. The central government generally ran deficits, primarily due to inadequate revenues. The tax system in China was decentralized. Local and provincial governments collected property taxes and excise taxes. Under the "tax contract" system, the provinces had a tax quota to the central government, yet the latter's revenue, even with revenue from SOEs, was generally less than 30 percent of all government revenue. The larger, faster-growing provinces, like Shanghai and Guangdong, were getting rich and reinvesting their own tax revenues in infrastructure. By 1993, the central government's revenues had fallen to 20 percent of all government revenues, and its fiscal deficits were growing.

On January 1, 1994, the government implemented a new tax system. It reduced the number of taxes from thirty-two to eighteen and introduced a value-added tax (VAT), an enterprise income tax, and a personal income tax. Revenue sharing changed abruptly. Three-quarters of the VAT were reserved for the central government, along with excise taxes, trade-related taxes, and enterprise income taxes from centrally owned SOEs. The new State Tax Administration was made responsible for the collection of central taxes. Suddenly, the central government's revenues jumped to more than 50 percent of the total, and tax revenues generally rose from 12 percent to 18 percent of GDP.[9]

Exchange rates posed another difficult problem. Before 1986, the yuan was largely inconvertible. Its price, in dollars, was 1.68 in 1978, but was steadily devalued over the next sixteen years, to 5.75 in 1993. In 1986, however, China had adopted a system of dual exchange rates—the yuan or renminbi (RMB) for domestic transactions and Foreign Exchange Certificates for foreign investors. The latter was traded on a swap market, at about 10 yuan per dollar, reflecting market prices on the coast. Domestic exporters had to turn over most foreign exchange earnings to the central bank at the fixed rate but could trade a portion of earnings on the swap market. Conversely, foreigners bought currency on the swap market to do business in China.

This complicated system engendered a huge amount of corruption, as businesspeople of all sorts tried to hedge the exchange rate gap. In 1994, the government abandoned the system, unifying the currency and devaluing it by 50 percent, where it stabilized late in the year at 8.3 yuan per dollar. This sharp devaluation, of course, gave China a huge advantage in trade over its south Asian competitors. While China's exports boomed and imports were constrained, Korea, Indonesia, Malaysia, Singapore, Thailand, and the Philippines lunged toward the Asian crisis of 1997–1998.

Inflation, fueled by years of hypergrowth, was nearly out of control in February 1994. At that time, Deng appointed Zhu Rongji—the number-three man in the politburo—to take responsibility for the economy and curb inflation. The problem was the banks. The People's Bank of China and three other large state banks had been lending wildly for years—to failing SOEs, growing TVEs, and aspiring private firms. Credit growth, often more than 30 percent annually, had reached 42 percent in 1993. This amount of monetary injection had fueled inflation, reaching 24 percent in the early months of 1994.

Zhu tried to get a hold of things by ordering the banks to slow formation of credit. But borrowing by SOEs continued, and local branches were unwilling to bankrupt local firms. In the late summer, Zhu raised interest rates and arrested some bankers for making illegal loans; one was executed. Thereafter, inflation fell sharply, reaching 1.2 percent by 1999. But Zhu had not made much progress with outstanding loans. It was estimated that nonperforming loans of the state banks amounted to 25 percent of GDP. In other words, the banking system was broke!

Also in 1994, the government adopted a new strategy for dealing with SOEs, summarized by the slogan zhuada fangxiao—"grasping the big ones and letting go of the small ones." First, the government would attempt reform of the larger SOEs, those involved in heavy industry. Second, the provinces were allowed to begin privatizing smaller SOEs. And third, the government would allow some of the worst to merge or go bankrupt. Three years later, the Fifteenth Party Congress endorsed this approach.

Deng's implicit economic development strategy included two final pieces. First was China's industrial policy. Intent on improving productivity and increasing R&D expenditures, the ninth five-year plan (1996–2000) adopted a clear industrial policy. Five pillar industries were targeted for special protection and increased investment: machinery, electronics, petrochemicals, automobiles, and construction. And the second part of strategy was trade liberalization. For years China had been negotiating for "most favored nation" status and entry into the GATT. After 1995, Deng's government began again to negotiate entry into the World Trade Organization (WTO). Political tensions and conflicts over human rights hampered these efforts until after Deng was dead.

Successful Growth and Institutional Problems

When Deng died in the spring of 1997, China had become a different place. The country's economy had tripled in size. Private consumption was but 48 percent of GDP, while capital investment had risen to 39 percent. Trade had quintupled, and government spending was still only 12 percent. Inflation was dissipating fast and soon to go negative (deflation). And the balance of payments was spectacular! One can see in table 4-1 the effect of China's devaluation and the accumulation of reserves that had already begun. At the time, the Bank of China reported $107 billion in foreign exchange reserves, soon to exceed $500 billion.

But as Jiang Zemin took power, he faced a range of difficult structural and institutional problems that needed solutions if the miracle were to continue. Among these problems were the SOEs, the banks, corruption, unemployment, provincial-central relations, energy and the environment, various aspects of foreign policy, negotiated entry into the WTO, and the yuan's exchange rate.

To stem government budgetary losses and to force improvement of state-owned enterprises, the government began privatizing after 1997. By 2000, many of the town and village enterprises had been sold (most often to their managers), and according to the Ministry of Commerce, 81 percent of the 63,490 small SOEs owned by the federal government had been privatized. This followed part of the government's dictum to "let go of the small ones," but by 2002, there still appeared to be some 159,000 government-owned enterprises, with assets of 18 trillion yuan. Of these, some 9,400 were large firms.

To "grasp the big ones," the government in 2002 created the State Asset Supervision and Administration Commission (SASAC). Early in 2003,

SASAC assumed control over 196 large enterprise groups, with 7.1 trillion yuan in assets (about half of all central government business assets).[10] Among these were China's three major oil companies (PetroChina, Sinopec, and CNOOC), several major power companies, the four big steel companies, an aluminum company (Chalco), two big auto manufacturers, airlines, telecommunications, coal-mining companies, the Three Gorges (power authority), and eleven military equipment companies. The SASAC's task was to rationalize government's management and improve performance of these key firms.

To privatize the rest of the government's assets, several problems needed to be solved: what to do with laid-off employees, what to do with the SOEs' debt to the banks, and how to make transactions more transparent. The central government had begun transferring funds to local governments to pay minimal unemployment and pension benefits. As to the debt, the government tried to pay as much as possible from the sale and then had the banks assume the rest. Transparency had suffered, resulting in too many nonpublicly negotiated privatizations, which were extremely vulnerable to corruption.

The banks were a bigger problem, obviously made worse by the privatization process. China's state banking system consisted of four big banks, which owned 60 percent of all banking assets, plus several state policy

TABLE 4-1

China's balance of payments, 1980–1996 (billions of U.S. dollars)

	1980	1988	1993	1996
Merchandise exports	18,188	41,045	75,659	151,077
Merchandise imports	−18,294	−46,369	−86,313	−131,542
Trade balance	**−106**	**−5,315**	**−10,654**	**19,535**
Net services	241	1,220	−868	−1,984
Net factor payments	195	−126	−1,259	−12,437
Net transfers	570	419	1,172	2,130
Current account	**900**	**−3,802**	**−11,609**	**7,243**
Net FDI	57	2,344	23,115	38,066
Net portfolio	na	876	3,049	1,744
Net other	−290	3,913	−2,690	156
Errors and omissions	na	−957	−10,096	−15,504
Overall balance	**561**	**2,374**	**1,769**	**31,705**

Source: Compiled by author with data from National Bureau of Statistics of China, *China Statistical Yearbooks*, various years.

banks, thirty-nine thousand credit cooperatives, eleven shareholder banks, and a few finance companies and investment trusts. By lending so long and so freely to SOEs, all of these institutions carried a huge amount of bad debt (i.e., nonperforming loans).

In 1999, the government created four asset management companies—one for each of the big banks—to begin buying the nonperforming assets and then selling them at deep discount. The government capitalized these asset management companies with injections of billions of dollars in foreign exchange. Finally, the government allowed the big banks to list on China's stock markets.

Meanwhile, with the economy growing so fast, the banks moved to increase their asset base relative to nonperforming loans. During the next three years, there was an immense amount of investment in the Chinese economy—indeed overinvestment—as these banks built their loan assets instead of reducing nonperforming loans. By 2003, the ratio of loans to GDP had reached 135 percent—the highest such ratio in the world. China's banking system was out of control.

In another policy reversal, the government created a new bank regulator—the China Banking Regulatory Commission (CBRC)—and in 2004 issued its Regulation Governing Capital Adequacy of Commercial Banks. The CBRC explained that its new aim was to build capital adequacy—making capital, rather than deposit-based funding, the key constraint. In a financial revolution, the CBRC was moving to bring Chinese bank regulation into compliance with global (e.g., Bank for International Settlements) standards.

Banks would have to maintain capital adequacy (capital to risk-weighted assets) at 8 percent, with core capital (equity, reserves, and retained earnings) at 4 percent. To improve transparency, the CBRC would require all banks to publicly disclose their ratios and report quarterly to the CBRC. The commission would conduct quarterly reviews, and bank boards would be held responsible for capital-adequacy management. The CBRC could choose from a range of draconian sanctions.[11]

Corruption was deeply embedded in these structural relationships. China had no Anglo-Saxon tradition of the rule of law. Its concept of property rights was rooted in a long history of imperial Confucianism. *Quanxi*, the cultivation of relationships, seemed to govern most individual and business economic interactions. Quanxi was crucial to any sort of economic transaction, from getting phone service installed to entering a billion-dollar real estate deal. In the absence of property rights and common law, quanxi worked well to facilitate the transactional side of development in China.

There was a fine line between quanxi and corruption. Relationships between officials and managers of publicly owned assets could easily go beyond mere reciprocal obligations. When a large, poorly paid bureaucracy interacted with a rapidly growing capitalist community, it is little wonder that corruption deepened quickly. By 1993, Transparency International—a European nongovernmental organization (NGO) that evaluated corruption—found China to be among the most corrupt nations. Early on, American firms in particular found it difficult to enter joint-venture agreements in China without breaching the Corrupt Practices Act.

Jiang Zemin was particularly aware of this issue and the risks it posed for successful foreign direct investment. Thus, as early as 1996, he launched a series of "strike hard" campaigns against not only corruption but other petty economic crimes as well. These campaigns resulted in a thousand executions in 1996 and more than three thousand annually by 2004. These were accompanied by the enactment of important laws to protect and enhance market transactions.[12]

By 2004, China had made progress with corruption. Most large companies reported that business was possible without pressure to give gifts. Still, in its Corruption Perceptions Index, Transparency International ranked China 71 in its index of 146 countries. (This index, ranging from 10 [perfectly noncorrupt] to 0 [perfectly corrupt], was based on surveys of businesspeople by NGOs and chambers of commerce.) At 3.4, China was tied with Saudi Arabia—well ahead of India and Russia (ninetieth), a bit behind Mexico (sixty-fourth), but far, far from developed countries like the United States (seventeenth) and Singapore (fifth).[13]

Unemployment was perhaps the largest problem associated with restructuring. By the turn of the century, China's unemployment sprang from two sources—privatization and restructuring of SOEs, and rationalization of agriculture.

Reliable unemployment figures are difficult to come by. However, SOE restructuring is thought to have made some 41 million workers redundant. Restructured TVEs shed another 21 million. Some of these people (estimated at 13 million) have found jobs in the emerging private sector or service jobs in the underground economy. But because these are middle-aged or older workers, with no significant safety net, they have posed a huge problem for China.[14] If Goldman Sachs's estimates are correct, about 81 million are currently unemployed. (See figure 4-3 for details on China's unemployment rates since 1985.)

Rural peasants, migrating east to find more attractive jobs in the cities, constituted another floating pool of poorly educated, underemployed workers, ranging in number from 90 million to 150 million. As agriculture has been rationalized, these people have been driven off the farms or out of rural towns, but they lack an urban *hukou*—the household registration necessary

FIGURE 4-3

Unemployment in China, 1985–2002

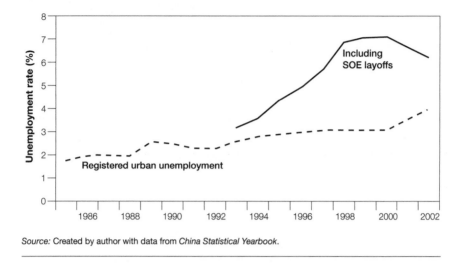

Source: Created by author with data from *China Statistical Yearbook*.

to formally live and work in a city. A hukou is necessary not only for a job but also for access to any city services, such as education, health care, and social security. While the government initiated reforms to the hukou system in 2001 and 2003, there remain a number of barriers that continue to marginalize this floating population.[15]

Given China's demographic profile, something between 80 million and 100 million net new jobs need to be created in the next decade for the workforce coming of age. This is one reason why government has been running significant deficits and why banks have been lending so freely. To create 8 million to 9 million jobs annually the real economy needs to grow at 8 percent or more—a tall order, indeed.

Still another set of structural problems pertains to China's energy consumption and the impact of economic development on its environment. The two issues are obviously related.

From a very low (per capita) base, China's use of power has grown quickly since the onset of its economic miracle (see figure 4-4). With 11 percent of the world's coal, and relatively little oil or gas, China's electricity has been either coal-fired (84 percent) or hydroelectric (14 percent). Added to this, some 300 million tons of coal per year were used for cooking, mostly in open stoves. With 1 percent sulfur and relatively high ash, this coal generated a lot of air pollution. During the past decade, rapid development of

FIGURE 4-4

China's production and consumption of selected power sources, 1968–2003

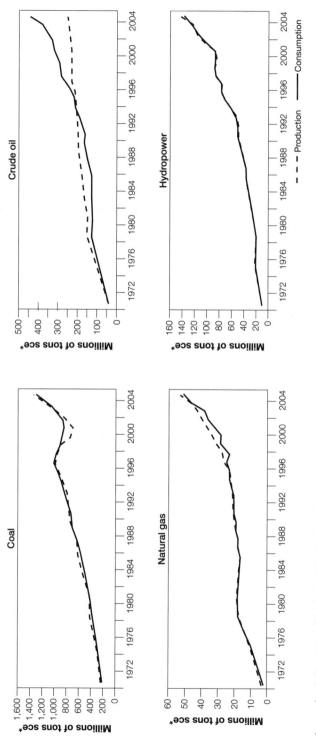

Source: Created by author with data from *China Statistical Yearbook.*

*From the *China Statistical Yearbook 2005*: "The coefficient for conversion of electric power into SCE (standard coal equivalent) is calculated on the basis of the data on the average coal consumption in generating electric power in the same year."

natural gas has displaced much of this urban coal use. At the same time, however, the development of a highway system has stimulated massive demand for petroleum—demand that exceeded China's supply after 1993.

From the charts in figure 4-4, one can see that China reported a sharp drop in coal consumption between 1997 and 2000, as some thirty thousand small, inefficient mines were forced to close (or at least consolidate). These dubious figures, however, were followed by a burst of increased output, taking China's coal production to 1.4 billion tons by 2003. One also sees gas consumption surpassing production in 2003, as China began importing liquefied natural gas. But most significantly, one sees oil imports rising sharply, reaching 30 percent or more of consumption. In 2003, China's increased need for fossil energy amounted to 52 percent of the world's increased demand. This trend continued in 2004, pushing up coal, oil, and gas prices to record highs.

There is no reason to think that this will moderate in the next few years, as long as the economy continues to boom. For the past three years, since the fourth-generation leadership took over, China's three oil companies have been traveling the world searching for oil and gas supplies. Several huge pipelines from Russia and Kazakhstan were being negotiated, as well as joint-venture developments in Iran, Saudi Arabia, and Indonesia. Over the next twenty years, China's energy import bill will rise above $100 billion annually (at current prices), which must be paid for by revenues from net goods exports. And the same is true for iron ore, copper, and grain imports. China's consumption is simply bursting at the seams.

The related consequence, of course, is environmental pollution. Two and a half decades of rapid development, for a population as large as China's, has resulted in awesome environmental problems of all kinds—air, water, toxic waste, land, and carbon dioxide. For any western visitor to China, air pollution is most evident. According to the World Health Organization, seven of the world's ten most polluted cities are in China. When visiting Shanghai or Beijing, one often does not see the sun for days at a time. The World Bank estimates that 20 percent of all deaths in China are attributable to air pollution.

Water is no better. Of China's seven large rivers, nearly 80 percent of the mileage is thoroughly polluted and unable to support fish. Human and industrial wastes make most of these rivers unfit for human consumption or for irrigation. Toxic wastes are carelessly disposed of in many parts of China, laying the groundwork for long-term ill effects on health. Ocean pollution is no better. In the East China Sea, waste and fertilizer runoff cause frequent red tides, and overfishing is rife. In China's north, wasteful irrigation and excessive draws on underground aquifers are causing subsidence and water shortages in five hundred of China's seven hundred cities.

In the west, erosion (for lack of control) and deforestation have reduced China's arable land by one-fifth since 1949. Given that China's arable land is but one-tenth of its total and its livestock herds are four times those of the United States, China faces an almost insolvable challenge feeding itself.[16]

The Chinese government is well aware of these problems. In recent years, it has enacted much tougher environmental laws and has upgraded the status of the State Environmental Protection Administration, although this organization still has subcabinet rank. The problems are twofold. The government does not have the resources to adequately finance cleanup, and enforcement of the law is weak and local. If a choice must be made between a growth-oriented investment and pollution control, the former generally wins unless the problem is so severe that both public criticism and NGOs successfully intervene.

Perhaps the most severe problem on the horizon is climate change. China emits about 13 percent of the total global carbon dioxide. While not as bad as the United States (at 25 percent), China's huge growth rate is likely to put it in the lead by 2020. Without U.S. leadership, China has thus far been unwilling to take any action. Yet continuous high emissions will only make the problem worse. China, especially its coastal lowlands, will eventually suffer irreparable harm.

World Trade Organization

After years of halting negotiations with half a dozen major trading nations, and especially the United States, China finally reached an agreement with the Clinton administration late in 1999. China had wanted admission to the WTO for any number of reasons: to protect its "most favored nation" status; to ensure it received national treatment from other member countries (i.e., its goods and investments would be treated equally with domestic goods and investments); to give China access to multilateral dispute resolution; and to separate China's trade from near constant human-rights criticisms from the United States. But perhaps most importantly, entry into the WTO would force China's huge domestic economy—especially its protected sectors—to adjust to the realities of global competition.

On December 11, 2001, China formally entered the WTO. China had preferred to gain "developing country" status, which would have provided "special and different treatment," with regard to length of implementation periods, continuing rights to subsidize 10 percent of agricultural output, and relaxed liberalization requirements. The United States, however, refused to concede to "developing country" status. Thus, a compromise was reached, in which China could maintain 8.5 percent subsidies in domestic agriculture (but not exports) and would eliminate subsidies on all industrial products.

For China, accession to the WTO encompassed three broad market-opening principles:

1. Commitments by China to abolish nontariff barriers, reduce tariffs, and open service sectors

2. Commitments by importing countries to abolish the quotas on textiles and clothing, originally imposed under the multifiber arrangement (long-standing textile quotas allocated by developed countries)

3. Agreement from the United States and other countries to impose "most favored nation" status on China

China agreed to lower tariffs from 12 percent to 6.8 percent; to open closed sectors, such as banking, insurance, and telecommunications to foreign direct investment; to open retail and wholesale distribution to foreign competition; to remove asymmetrical regulations on trading for foreign, as opposed to domestic, firms; and to protect intellectual property according to generally accepted international standards.[17] At the same time, China acceded to a couple of American protective demands, including the United States' dumping laws and special protection for textiles. Moreover, even after full implementation of the WTO provisions, some tariffs (on sugar, feed grains, cotton, apparel, and automobiles) would remain well above 10 percent. Since China's accession took place, its trade—both exports and imports—have grown stupendously. As of mid-2004, exports had grown 22 percent in 2002, 34.6 percent in 2003, and 39.7 percent in the first quarter of 2004. Imports in those years had expanded by 21 percent, 39.9 percent, and 42.6 percent, respectively. China's top exports are still garments, followed by computers, textiles, computer components, shoes, and mobile phones. Its principal imports include integrated circuits, crude oil, rolled steel, primary plastics, and iron ore. In the first quarter of 2005 (after the Multifiber Agreement had lapsed), China's exports of garments to the United States increased by 1,000 percent.

China's compliance with its WTO commitments appeared mixed. On tariff reductions, China was performing on schedule, although customs procedures were problematic. On trading and distribution rights, China had put the new Foreign Trade Law in place, but multinationals were grumbling about implementation of its regulations and a lack of transparency in the proceedings. Expanded access to markets was also mixed, with banking being opened more slowly than scheduled. Transparency remained a key complaint of foreign firms, along with standards-setting procedures. And protection of intellectual property was far behind schedule.[18]

Fourth-Generation Leadership and Issues

After three generations (Mao Zedong, Deng Xiaoping, and Jiang Zemin) had presided over China's rapid growth, a so-called fourth generation emerged in 2002, when Hu Jintao replaced Jiang Zemin as general secretary of the Communist Party. Of the politburo's standing committee, only Hu remained. One year later, he was joined by Wen Jiabao, replacing Zhu Rongji as premier, and Wu Bangguo, replacing Li Peng as head of the National People's Congress. The final step occurred in September 2004, when Hu assumed the chair of the Central Military Commission.

Jiang's influence, however, was not entirely lost. The constitution was amended to enshrine Jiang's Theory of Three Represents, alongside Marxism-Leninism, Mao Zedong Thought, and Deng Xiaoping Theory. The Communist Party, according to this theory, represents the foremost productive force, the most advanced culture, and the fundamental interests of the people.[19]

Although they took over a rapidly growing, newly prosperous economy, Hu and Wen faced a great many issues. On the political front, they needed to consolidate their power within China, to control Hong Kong without appearing too hard-line, to discipline North Korea, to straighten out relations with the United States, and to foster a sustainable relationship with Taiwan.

Of these issues, Taiwan was by far the most serious. China has always claimed sovereignty over the island, refusing to recognize any sort of independent relationship. Since 1979, however, when the U.S. Congress passed the Taiwan Relations Act, the United States has gone on record defending Taiwanese independence. In 2003, Paul Wolfowitz of the U.S. Department of Defense said the United States would do "whatever it takes" to defend Taiwan. The current Taiwanese president, Chen Shui-bian, continues to stir pro-independence sentiment on the island, enraging the mainland China government. With his own hands fairly full with foreign policy, President George W. Bush has opposed any unilateral decision, by either China or Taiwan, to change the status quo.

Meanwhile, the determination of the People's Liberation Army (PLA) to "focus on preparing for conflict in the Taiwan Strait—including deployments of short-range ballistic missiles opposite Taiwan—[cast] a cloud over Beijing's declared policy seeking 'peaceful reunification.'" In 2004, China granted the PLA a significantly enlarged budget to foster modernization. Officially, the budget is $22 billion, but careful observers believe it to be as much as $70 billion. After the Gulf War, China realized that its military was grossly outdated. Since then, it has shrunk the PLA and is working to make the army mobile, with high-tech weaponry. China, meanwhile, maintains a small force of twenty nuclear-armed intercontinental ballistic missiles.[20]

Social issues were also pressing. No sooner had Hu assumed power than China was struck by the Sudden Acute Respiratory Syndrome (SARS) crisis. After initial problems of bureaucratic denial, Hu mobilized government to gain control of SARS effectively. Other problems, however, were not as malleable. The Falun Gong, a quasi-religious sect that had demonstrated in Beijing back in 1999, still had upwards of five thousand members residing in Chinese prisons.

Income distribution—especially between rural and urban, and east and west—was worsening. At the turn of the twenty-first century, rural income was about one-third of urban income but, because of rural out-migration, was getting no worse. Within the urban sector, however, income distribution was worsening. The richest 5 percent had ten times the income of the poorest. In both sectors, the Gini index had risen steadily, with the national index approaching 0.40. (The Gini index is a measure of income inequality. At 0, everyone has an equal share of net income; at 1, a single person has it all.) The central government, concerned that income inequality might destabilize politics, was working to mitigate these trends by focusing infrastructural investment on rural regions and attracting FDI to the west.

Unemployment, continuing structural adjustment to the WTO, the yuan's exchange rate, and China's bilateral trade surplus with the United States were probably the most pressing economic issues facing the fourth generation.

Since Deng Xiaoping's era, China had continued to grow fast and perform extraordinarily well in global competition. With foreign direct investment continuing to pour in at the rate of $60 billion annually, with eager workers still seeking jobs for wages of $0.64 an hour, and with its exchange rate pegged at 8.3 yuan per dollar, China continued to run trade and current account surpluses—and an extraordinary trade surplus with the United States. Figure 4-5 shows this data for the post-Deng period. These substantial current account surpluses have resulted in the buildup of approximately $590 billion in foreign exchange reserves. Moreover, the trade balance, since China runs deficits with many east Asian countries, obscures the huge bilateral surplus with the United States—approaching $200 billion by 2006.

It is this bilateral imbalance that has threatened good economic relations between the two superpowers and has shone the spotlight on the yuan's exchange rate. Most western economists presume that China's currency is undervalued in terms of the U.S. dollar, to which it has been pegged since 1994. China's productivity has been growing at 5–6 percent annually—about 3 percent faster than U.S. productivity growth. And it has been running a trade and current account surplus for the past ten years. This suggests that the currency might be undervalued by 35 percent or more and severely in need of revaluation.

Early in 2004, John Snow, the U.S. treasury secretary, visited China, urging revaluation. The Chinese demurred. Although its government has made noises about adjusting rates, nothing had happened as of April 2005. Out of frustration, the U.S. Senate passed a procedural motion (on April 6), by a significant majority, to impose a 27 percent tariff on all Chinese imports if Beijing did not revalue.

To keep its currency undervalued, China's central bank has had to use significant reserves to buy U.S. debt. In both 2003 and 2004, China was a leading purchaser of U.S. bonds, helping maintain low interest rates and keep the world economy growing. But as the government's dollar-denominated holdings increase, China's money supply continues to expand rapidly, and the government runs increasing risks of inflation and of seeing its reserves depreciate. Even the 2 percent appreciation of the yuan in mid-2005 did little to change China's trading advantage or sap the growing criticism in the United States.

China had certainly confounded the pundits. Without democracy, or virtually any political freedom, the Communist government had overseen a widespread economic liberalization—gradually and peacefully. As much as 50 percent of enterprise was now in private hands. Incomes had quadrupled. Debt was low, the current account in surplus, and the central bank comfortable with a huge stock of foreign exchange. When compared to India or Russia, China could surely be proud.

FIGURE 4-5

China's trade, 1997–2005

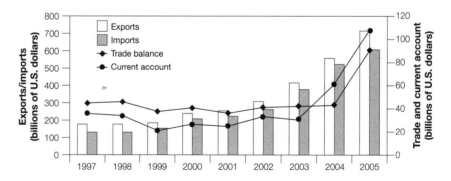

Source: Compiled by author with data from International Monetary Fund, *International Financial Statistics*, various years.

China had used its strong, centralized government to implement this strategy of gradual liberalization. Even though its institutions were inept and often corrupt, government power with informed leadership sufficed. Instead of institutions to encourage savings, China could rely on a culture of thrift. With capital controls tightly in place, Chinese banks could pour money into investment by state enterprises, even though they used it ineffectively. The currency reform in 1994 underwrote China's cheap labor and strong FDI to generate massive current account deficits by 2005. Surprisingly, the Chinese Communist government was able to match its pragmatic strategy with a forceful Communist structure.

Yet Hu and Wen have their work cut out for them. Without increasing the government's deficit much more, they need continued growth of at least 8 percent annually to create 8 million to 9 million new jobs each year. They need to fix or privatize the large state enterprises, and they need to fix the banks—all the while, adjusting to the World Trade Organization. They need to maintain a positive trade balance in manufactured goods to pay for the growing imports of petroleum, natural gas, and food products necessary to fuel their country.

Doing all this, while preserving the center's autocratic power, will be a difficult task indeed. Under Deng Xiaoping, China implemented a pragmatic development strategy, liberalizing the economy while holding political power at the center. Given the incredibly low base from which it started and the Chinese dedication to savings and work, this strategy worked stupendously. Yet despite continuing great performance since 1998, the country has been experiencing the intensifying pressures between decentralized capitalism and centralized communism—with more than forty thousand demonstrations in 2005 alone!

But more of the same won't work indefinitely. There is a limit to how much the United States can import and consume. If the yuan does not appreciate significantly, the United States will eventually retaliate. Moreover, the schism between central power and market liberalization cannot last indefinitely. Political reform is increasingly overdue. In the conclusion, we'll consider future scenarios to think about what this may mean for business.

——⟋⟋⟍⟍⟋——

FIVE

India on the Move

IN MAY 2004, after a year of extraordinary economic growth, the Indian people nonetheless voted out the ruling Bharatiya Janata Party. In a surprising upset, they chose the Congress Party and its allies (United Progressive Alliance) who had appealed more effectively to rural Indians—still two-thirds of the population. As prime minister the alliance chose Manmohan Singh, the former finance minister who had led the recovery from financial crisis in 1991, away from *swadeshi* (self-sufficiency) toward more open, global competitiveness.

Singh's challenge was considerable. He needed to fulfill campaign promises to redirect resources to rural India. And he needed to grow the economy fast enough to create the millions of jobs necessary to stabilize or reduce India's unemployment. At the same time, he knew that India's fiscal deficits were unsustainable and must be cut if investor confidence in India were to be restored. But his political alliance, which included the Communist Party, rejected privatization out of hand and was unwilling to curtail needed domestic spending programs. Singh also inherited India's troubled relationship with Pakistan. Here too he needed to reestablish investor confidence by deepening the peace process toward normalized relations.

India's Long History

Populated for at least eight thousand years, India has deep cultural roots. Archeologists have discovered evidence of an extensive, multicity Indus Valley Civilization, dating back five thousand years in northern India. Carefully planned cities with broad streets organized in grids had clearly identifiable residential and commercial districts. Bronze tools, pottery, and household goods, together with an elaborate sewage system, attest to a sophisticated civilization, compatible with those of Egypt, Mesopotamia, and China.

As agriculture, crafts, and trade developed, India evolved into a series of kingdoms and tribal republics spreading south through central India. Although Buddhist literature was evident in the north from about 500 BC, the region's primary religion was Hindu—an indigenous set of beliefs and cultural norms that spread and evolved organically. For the next two millennia, India was invaded and conquered repeatedly by visitors from the north and west. First came the Persians and then the Greeks under Alexander the Great. Indian empires—the Mauryan and the Gupta—were interspersed with Hun and Afghan invaders until the Portuguese arrived in 1497. Babur and Akbar from Pakistan displaced the Portuguese, creating an empire whose signature monument is the Taj Mahal. But finally, in 1640, the British East India Company arrived, building a fort in Madras, in the south.

To expand its lucrative India trade, the East India Company built roads, bridges, ports, and eventually a railway, in 1853. The company, however, exploited resources and extorted heavy taxes. In 1857, the Indian-manned army rebelled in a bloody uprising. After the British army quelled the mutiny, Britain reclaimed the territory held by the company, establishing it as a Crown colony in 1858.

British rule in India was scarcely a model of Anglo-Saxon egalitarianism. The British set out to build a modern colony—railroads, roads, universities, banks, trading houses, and so on—creating an Indian bureaucracy (the Raj) to administer the colonial economy. The Indian civil service was staffed by Indians educated in England. But they were "Indians," deemed inferior by British—"oriental others" who were ill-suited to rule by law and system. Indeed, during the entire eighty-nine years of British rule, the distaste for "orientalism" never subsided.[1]

Tightening control by the British empire inspired British-educated Indians to create the Indian National Congress in 1885—an organization intended to give Indians a greater role in their own destiny. It was most certainly the role model for the African National Congress, created in 1912 in South Africa for the same purpose. In fact, Mohandas Gandhi, an Indian lawyer, had been living in South Africa and actively opposing apartheid. In 1915, he returned to India, where he soon got involved in his own country's freedom struggle.

Gandhi, now called Mahatma ("the great soul"), strove to build a self-sufficient economy that would restore unity and balance to village life, stolen by colonial exploitation. But an ardent believer in nonviolence, he strove to oust the British through peaceful resistance. He fasted, protested, and parlayed with British officials, despite thousands of casualties of peaceful resistance. Although Indians fought beside Britain to resist Nazism during the

Second World War, peace brought an immediate renewal of the freedom movement.

The Muslim League, headed by Muhammad Ali Jinnah, exacerbated the unrest by demanding a separate Muslim state. To retain control, the British tried to exploit these frictions, eventually deciding to partition India into two countries on the basis of religious majority: a democratic India, and an Islamic East and West Pakistan. Believing in a unified, secular country, Gandhi declared, "Even if the whole of India, ranged on one side, were to declare that Hindu-Muslim unity is impossible, I will declare that it is perfectly possible."[2] Gandhi's protests, however, fell on deaf ears. Ten to fifteen million Hindu and Muslim refugees moved either to or from Pakistan amid violence that eventually claimed more than six hundred thousand lives. On August 15, 1947, Lord Mountbatten (the British viceroy) handed over the reins of government to an independent India. A year later, while still working for peace, Gandhi was assassinated by a Hindu extremist.

Diversity

India is incredibly diverse—climactically and topographically, linguistically, religiously, and culturally. At 3.3 million square kilometers, modern India is just over a third the area of the United States. Today it is bordered by Pakistan, China, Nepal, Bhutan, Myanmar, and Bangladesh. (See figure 5-1 for a map of present-day India.) The subcontinent is incredibly fertile and reasonably mineral-rich. In addition to iron ore, precious metals, and bauxite, it holds the fourth-largest coal reserve in the world. Since it has limited reserves of oil and natural gas, it remains highly dependent on imported petroleum. Seven major ports along India's 7,000-kilometer coastline serve the Indian Ocean trade routes.

India has 18 official languages—each spoken by more than 10 million people—and more than 650 dialects. Hindi is most prevalent, spoken by perhaps 30 percent of the population. English, the language of business, is spoken by just 2–3 percent of the population. Hindu is the largest religious affiliation, accounting for about 81 percent of the population. Islam is the second largest, accounting for about 12 percent of the population. Buddhists, Jains, Sikhs, Christians, and a few smaller affiliations account for the remaining 7 percent of Indians.

Hinduism, a polytheistic faith, is the most deeply rooted religious faith in India's culture. Hindus have no messianic or textual touchstone—no Jesus, no Old Testament, no Koran. Hindu philosophy grew organically over many centuries, absorbing diverse tribal and village customs. The oldest known texts are the four *Vedas*, explaining rites and rituals of various gods; the

Upanishads, or "divine revelations" of ancient seers; and the *Bhagavad Gita,* an epic poem that offers philosophical views about relations between men and between men and the gods.

The caste system evolved within Hinduism as a set of human and social relationships. "To be born a Hindu," writes one scholar, "is to have a caste place, however notional, in Hindu society." In rural India, even today, "Proper rela-

---

FIGURE 5-1

Map of India

tionships within a family between young and old, male and female, husbands and wives; legitimate marriages, births, adoptions, inheritances; appropriate behavior within a caste, among its members and between castes, among their members; right deportment, occupation and exchanges of goods and services within a village—all are prescribed."[3]

Varna Dhama, the religious philosophy of Brahmanic Hinduism, divides mankind into four *varnas*, or "categories," ranked by religious purity. At the top, unsurprisingly, are Brahmans, a priestly caste responsible for prayer. Next comes Kshatria, the warrior class, responsible for protecting others. Third, is Vaishya, the merchant class, responsible for commerce and agriculture. And fourth, supporting this structure, is the Sudra—a peasant class responsible for most manual labor. Over time, each caste was subdivided into hundreds of subcastes with different local status, functions, and relationships. At the bottom are the Dalit, or "untouchables." This underclass, responsible for the most menial jobs, has traditionally been destined to a life of poverty and discrimination. Others will not share food, water, or even space with the untouchables. They live in segregated communities, performing the least desirable tasks.

Dalits themselves, numbering about 170 million, deny any relationship between untouchability and sacred Hindu ideology. So does the Indian government, for which untouchability is a national disgrace. It is explicitly abolished by the constitution, which prohibits any public agency or establishment from discriminating against anyone based on their membership in a "scheduled caste." Moreover, the Indian government has engaged in an extensive affirmative action program. Fifteen percent of seats in Parliament, and in the state legislative assemblies, are reserved for Dalits. Likewise, places are reserved in educational institutions, including the best universities, with relaxed admissions criteria and scholarship schemes. Finally, there are a variety of antipoverty programs for scheduled castes, including the reservation of 27 percent of government jobs, established by Congress in 1990.

Growing at 1.5 percent annually, India's population had reached 1.08 billion by 2004. At the current growth rate, it will likely surpass China's population by about 2025. The Indian government, under Indira Gandhi, had made a brief effort to slow population growth by forced sterilization. This unpopular program, however, was soon abandoned. Because of the male orientation of Indian family life, however, feticide, neglect, and more recently ultrasounds and abortion have led to a significant gender imbalance, with just 933 females to every 1,000 males.

Life expectancy, meanwhile, had reached sixty-two years by 2002, up from thirty-two years at independence. The country's literacy rate had also risen to 65 percent but varied greatly by region, gender, and caste. The state of Kerala, for example, had attained a literacy rate of 91 percent by 2001, with only a small gap between males and females. At the other extreme was Bihar, with literacy of just 47 percent and an imbalance of 50 percent between men and women.[4]

Perhaps the sharpest distinction was the gap between rural and urban Indians, with regard to development, religious fervor, education, and income. About 72 percent of the population was still rural and largely dependent on agriculture. And although India had enjoyed an extraordinary "green revolution" in the 1970s, its agricultural output was highly variable, according to the monsoon weather patterns. Although India could generally feed itself, and indeed maintained a reserve of 35 million tons of grain, a bad monsoon such as that in 2002–2003 was severely damaging to the rural economy.

Income in India was inequitably distributed, and growing more so. Using the $1 poverty line, the World Bank estimated that 36 percent of the world's poor—433 million people—lived in India. Although this number had shrunk some by 2004, the per capita GDP was still only $610. When adjusted for purchasing power parity, this number grew by a factor of five—to about $3,000. But again, distribution was skewed toward the well-educated urban and upper classes. There was also a sharp regional imbalance. States like Bihar, with a population of 83 million, were barely above $114 per capita (per year); Uttar Pradesh, with 166 million, was at $216. At the other end were Goa and Delhi, with average incomes five to ten times as high.

A final characteristic that needs to be tied to the maldistribution of wealth is corruption. India, by almost any standard, was corrupt. In 2005, Transparency International ranked India eighty-eighth on its Corruption Perceptions Index, with a score of just 2.9. This index, which reflects the views of businesspersons doing trade and investment internationally, ranks countries from 10 (best) to 0 (worst). India, tied with Iran and Mali, had slipped below China (seventy-eighth), Saudi Arabia (seventieth), and Mexico (sixty-fifth), much less developed stars like Singapore (fifth). This degree of corruption affected all levels of society but, of course, hit the poor the hardest. While some of the poor received insect-infested food subsidies, for example, 40 percent of India's famine relief stock ended up for sale on the black market.[5]

Income distribution was both a cause and a result of corruption. But worse still was the Permit Raj—a huge bureaucracy that controlled virtually every aspect of the economy through a complex system of licensing. Everything from the registration of a document and repair of a telephone to the admission of a student to an educational institution entailed bribes. One estimate alleged that 20 percent of the members of Parliament had criminal backgrounds. As Manmohan Singh explained, "It [the Permit Raj] was inevitable, because in an economy where resources are scarce [and] demands are too many, you need rationing, you need controls, and therefore you need permit license rights. In the initial stages, these controls were introduced in the name of introducing greater rationality into the allocation process. But after a period of time, they became instruments of corruption."[6]

All these imbalances, combined with the sharp religious differences, obviously created severe social and political pressures.

Modern India

Less than three years after independence, India declared itself a republic. Its constitution established India as a secular, parliamentary democracy modeled after the British system. Run by a large bureaucracy, India was divided into twenty-eight states and seven union territories. Executive, judicial, and legislative branches governed India at both the central and state levels. States also had the exclusive right to directly tax agricultural income and land, and to regulate property ownership. Given that agriculture made up most of India's GDP, the central government was thus denied a large source of revenue.[7]

India's executive branch is represented by a president (currently Abdul Kalam) elected through an electoral college for a five-year term, a prime minister, and a cabinet. The president has no constitutional powers. The Rajya Sabha (Council of States) and the Lok Sabha (House of the People) serve as a bicameral parliament. The Rajya Sabha has 245 members, of which 12 are appointed by the president and 233 are elected by members of the lower house and the state assemblies. The Lok Sabha has 543 elected members (with 79 seats reserved for scheduled castes and 40 for scheduled tribes).

Led by the Gandhi-Nehru (Jawaharal) dynasty, the Congress Party held uninterrupted control of India's government for thirty-three of the forty-four years following independence. After repeated scandals came to light, however, the party's grip on power began to weaken. The first involved Indira Gandhi's declaration of a state of emergency in 1975, imprisoning her opponents. A second scandal linked her son Rajiv, who later served as prime minister, to corrupt activities involving kickbacks from foreign contracts.

Four wars punctuated the Congress Party's rule of India. The first, with Pakistan in 1948, disputed the partition of Kashmir, India's northern-most state. The UN stepped in, establishing a "line of control" that gave Pakistan control over the northern part of the region. Another border dispute with China led to war in 1962, which India lost. Disagreement over Kashmir led to a third war, with Pakistan, in 1965, which ended inconclusively. And in 1971, India defeated Pakistan, leading to the secession of East Pakistan, now Bangladesh.

India also suffered from a variety of religious and political disputes internally. In the early 1980s, Indian troops fighting Sikh separatists in the Punjab invaded the Golden Temple in Amritsar, killing five high priests. In 1984, Sikhs got revenge when two Sikh bodyguards assassinated Indira Gandhi in her garden. Violence against Sikhs spread throughout India, leaving four thousand Sikhs murdered and ten thousand homes burned. Far to the south, Tamil Tigers, seeking independence from Sri Lanka, caused Rajiv Gandhi, then prime minister, to send twenty thousand Indian troops—who were eventually withdrawn, after considerable indeterminate violence. In 1991, a young Tamil Tiger approached Gandhi with flowers during the political campaign and blew herself up, along with the prime minister.

In 1992, in the northern India town of Ayodhya, Hindu zealots wrecked a mosque, the Babtri Masjid, believing it was built atop a Hindu temple that was the birthplace of Lord Ram. Communal violence following its destruction led to two thousand or more deaths. Ten years later, a group of Muslim militants firebombed a train, killing fifty-eight Hindu activists returning from Ayodhya. Communal violence again erupted, in which some two thousand Muslims in Gujarat were killed and thousands left homeless. Today, occasional violence persists in the west, where independence movements bubble in Nagaland, Manipur, and Mizoram.

After the assassination of Rajiv Gandhi in 1991, the Congress Party lacked a prominent successor. Indecisively, they chose the aged P. V. Narasimha Rao to lead a government coalition. Surprisingly, not only did this coalition last for five years, but it successfully introduced most of India's free-market reforms. After the party's defeat in 1996, however, Sonia Gandhi, the Italian-born widow of Rajiv, entered the political arena as the new leader of the Congress Party. Sonia Gandhi's foreign origin clearly limited her popularity among nationalist groups. "The more educated and urban the crowd," observed Jairam Ramesh, an adviser to the Congress Party, "the greater is the salience of the foreign factor . . . [I]t is the educated elite who are more against her on the grounds that they figure we should be able to find at least one good candidate out of our one billion."[8]

The Bharatiya Janata Party (BJP) first appeared as a major party in 1991 when it won control of four states. Initially, the BJP served as the political wing of the traditionally Hindu religious group Rashtriya Swayamsevak Sangh (RSS). The RSS was criticized for its fundamentalism (among its famous members was the assassin of Mahatma Gandhi). To gain majority control, the BJP had to join with twenty-five other parties, forming a coalition: the National Democratic Alliance. Although the sheer number of disparate interests moderated the extremist elements of the BJP, efforts to reform the government proved difficult. In one account, "Opposition members sabotaged proceedings by crowding round the speaker's chair and shouting slogans until an adjournment was granted for the day." Reporter Edward Luce estimated that almost half of Parliament's sessions were forced to adjourn for reasons of parliamentary rowdiness.[9]

In 1999, the BJP dominated elections, winning a five-year term for Prime Minister Atal Bihari Vajpayee. His government weathered the 2001–2002 downturn and got India's economy growing again in 2002. Although it did not interfere with the immense success of high-tech firms in southern India, it bore responsibility for a quasi-war with Pakistan, in which nearly a million Indian troops were posted to the border and a nuclear exchange was feared. In 2004, the BJP was surprisingly routed in national elections, returning a Congress Party coalition to power.

Swadeshi

Shortly after independence, Jawaharlal Nehru took control of India's economic development. A "democratic socialist" and admirer of the Soviet Union, Nehru believed that state planning should allocate scarce investment resources. In 1948, the government issued its Industrial Policy Resolution, giving government exclusive authority over railroads, telecommunications, power, and the postal system. Nehru himself chaired the Planning Commission, which issued the first of what would eventually become nine five-year plans. The commission made two key decisions: (1) what was to be the size of the investment (presumably backed by domestic savings), and (2) how the investment was to be allocated among alternative uses.[10]

India's second five-year plan (1956–1961) sought "to rebuild rural India, to lay the foundations of industrial progress, and to secure to the greatest extent feasible, opportunities for weaker and underprivileged sections of our people and the balanced development of all parts of the country." In its Second Industrial Policy Resolution (1956), the government expanded its control to twelve sectors, including commercial banking, insurance, fertilizer, mining, steel, chemicals, and oil. It also established a complicated system of industrial licensing, monitoring each sector to prevent "unnecessary" competition or duplication of efforts.

While this approach to development produced some growth (3.7 percent per year), it also produced a spurt of imports (both capital equipment and consumer goods) and, by 1957, a foreign exchange crisis. The government promptly raised capital barriers to limit the outflow of foreign exchange and tried to accelerate domestic production of previously imported goods. "Buy Indian," a rallying cry during the independence movement, now became national strategy.

A combination of high tariffs and quotas were placed on all goods coming into the country. Tariffs ranged up to 350 percent. The administration allocated foreign exchange according to its priorities; the highest was foreign debt repayments, followed by embassies, defense, and imports of food, fertilizer, and petroleum. Capital goods were divided into "restricted" and "open general license" (OGL). Obtaining permission to import a restricted good required sixteen separate procedures, involving a variety of ministries and officials. No license was required for an OGL capital good, unless it led to an increase in capacity. The system for intermediate goods was still more complex, involving four categories (e.g., banned, restricted, limited access, and OGL). Obtaining a license for the first category was impossible; the next two required licenses. In 1973, Indira Gandhi got Parliament to enact the Foreign Exchange Regulation Act, placing a 40 percent limit on foreign equity ownership.

In addition to controlling industrial capacity and production, the government set prices for many goods and services. Transportation costs were regulated to prevent backward areas of the country from suffering a price disadvantage. The annual fertilizer subsidy to farmers cost the government approximately $1.9 billion per year in the 1980s. Government also regulated prices for such goods as coal, steel, pharmaceuticals, sugar, cooking oils, electricity, and lightbulbs.

When a company was in difficulty, the government also played a role. "Sick unit" regulation prevented companies from going bankrupt, subsidizing them through state-owned banks. In the 1980s, there were some ninety thousand sick units, for which layoffs of workers required approval under this exit policy. One hundred separate rules explicitly ruled out financial difficulty as a basis for layoffs.

Regulating and implementing this degree of government control required a great many bureaucrats. This colossal Indian bureaucracy—which I mentioned earlier was nicknamed the Permit Raj—not only created a complex, inefficient system but a channel for the corruption about which Manmohan Singh had spoken. By 1991, some 49 percent of industrial output was directly controlled by government. One hundred percent of the capital markets (banking and insurance) was in government hands.

Obviously, there were many, many problems with swadeshi. But perhaps the limiting factor was oil, in the wake of the first (1973–1974) and second (1979–1980) oil shocks. India simply lacked sufficient oil for any sort of industrialization. When the price of oil jumped to $12 per barrel, India's burden of importing oil became unsustainable. Why? Swadeshi had prevented the development of any globally competitive exports. Thus, as India imported more and more high-priced oil, it had to begin borrowing dollars to pay for it. In table 5-1, one can see the growing burden of oil. Imports doubled between 1972 and 1974, and again between 1978 and 1980. The current account turned negative, reaching $7.6 billion by 1980. Long-term capital inflows, almost zero in 1972, rose annually until reaching $6.7 billion in 1988.

By December 1984, when Rajiv Gandhi was elected, it was obvious that India needed reform. "A poor country," said Gandhi, "cannot afford to carry on billing the poorest people for its inefficiency and call itself socialist. It is ridiculous."[11] In his 1985 budget, Gandhi exempted sixteen industries from the Monopolies and Restrictive Trade Practices system, abolished the license for manufacturing investments in consumer goods, and introduced "broadbanding" in capacity licensing (allowing companies with thirty thousand units of output to upgrade capacity without a license). The government also cut personal income taxes and simplified the structure of indirect taxes. More liberal regulations of FDI encouraged joint ventures, including Pepsi's return to India and an expansion of Suzuki's equity involvement.

These reforms led to a spurt of productivity growth (3.6 percent annually) and economic growth (5.7 percent annually), leading some economists to cite the 1980s, not the 1990s, as the time of India's turnaround.[12] Nonetheless, by 1991, the costs of debt service were overwhelming. The Soviet Union, meanwhile, had collapsed, leaving India short of fuel imports and without a protected export market or a source of subsidized weapons. With its reserves

TABLE 5-1

India's deteriorating balance of payments, 1970–1990 (billions of U.S. dollars)

	1970	1972	1974	1978	1980	1983	1988	1990
Goods exports	1.9	2.5	4.0	6.8	8.3	9.1	14.2	18.5
Goods imports	−2.3	−2.8	−5.2	−9.0	−5.9	−4.8	−23.8	−27.2
Net services	0.0	0.0	0.2	0.7	1.4	1.1	0.8	0.8
Net factor income	0.1	0.0	−0.2	0.0	0.4	−1.1	−3.0	−3.9
Current account	**−0.4**	**−0.3**	**−0.5**	**−2.8**	**−6.9**	**−5.7**	**−9.6**	**−8.7**
Net direct investment	0.0	0.0	0.0	0.0	0.0	0.1	0.3	0.3
Net long-term loans	0.6	0.5	0.9	0.6	1.4	1.9	4.4	2.9
Other	0.0	0.0	0.1	0.0	0.3	0.9	2.3	1.6
Short-term flows	−0.2	−0.1	0.6	0.9	−0.9	−0.7	1.3	1.7
Capital account	0.4	0.4	0.3	1.5	0.9	2.2	8.3	6.5

Source: Compiled by author with data from International Monetary Fund, *International Financial Statistics Yearbook*, 2002.

dissipated to less than $1 billion, India had no choice but to turn for assistance to the International Monetary Fund (IMF).

Washington Consensus—Gradually

The *Washington consensus* is a sometimes pejorative term used to describe the set of policies that western powers (e.g., the IMF, the World Bank, and the U.S. Department of the Treasury) impose on developing countries faced with structural adjustment. The term, originally coined by economist John Williamson, refers to ten policies that usually dominate the "conditionality" associated with a structural-adjustment loan from the International Monetary Fund: fiscal discipline (deficit reduction), tax reform, interest rate liberalization, a competitive exchange rate, removal of barriers to trade and barriers to foreign investment, privatization, deregulation, secure property rights, and increased public expenditures on health and education.[13]

Rao and his finance minister, Manmohan Singh, gained some flexibility by airlifting twenty-five tons of gold to the Bank of England as collateral for an emergency loan if they could not reach an agreement with the IMF. Over the next several months, they introduced an aggressive program of stabilizing the economy and initiating microeconomic reforms. These policies generally matched the Washington consensus, albeit gradually.

First, Rao and Singh slashed subsidies to reduce the deficit, while widening the tax base. To get inflation under control, the Bank of India ceased its practice of monetizing deficits. Interest rates were raised to attract Indian investors to government debt. The rupee was devalued by 22 percent, after which it began a guided float downward. Tariffs were lowered and simplified. The average rate fell from 87 percent to 33 percent; the highest rate, from 350 percent to 65 percent. In an effort to attract foreign capital, procedures governing foreign direct investment were simplified.[14] The 40 percent ceiling on foreign ownership was lifted to 51 percent (except in a few strategic sectors). Approved foreign institutional investors were licensed, and controls governing takeovers were relaxed. Public sector enterprises were allowed, for the first time, to form joint ventures with private firms, and the licensing of capacity was abolished.

Consensus Reforms—Successful?

"In hard economic terms," said Palaniappan Chidambaram, now India's finance minister, "the growth rate has moved up to a 6 percent path. This is significant, but not dramatic. I would use the word dramatic once we moved to an 8 percent path."

While perhaps sounding harsh, in that India had avoided financial collapse and reentered a healthy growth trajectory, Chidambaram knew only too well the structural problems that remained:

> The result is that many sectors of India's economy are still not opened. The unreformed sectors are as large as the reformed sectors and this is what is holding back growth. But clearly a 6% growth is a sharp improvement on a 3.5% growth or a 5% growth, and at least for about five or six years in the '90s, we were generating a large number of jobs. Inflation had been at a historical low for many, many months in this decade, compared to the average of 8% or 10%. The average has been only about 5% or 6% here. And today, there is a sense of hope and confidence about the future among the young generation. And we no longer penalize efficiency or enterprise; in fact, we reward it.[15]

Indeed, as shown in figure 5-2, India's performance was impressive, especially given the backdrop of the Asian economic crisis (1997–1998). Even in 2002, when western economies slumped, India's growth merely slowed to 4.4 percent, before surging back toward 8 percent by 2004. Perhaps no sector was more responsible for this surprising performance than information technology and outsourced services in the southern states of Karnataka and Andhra Pradesh.

Information Technology and Outsourcing

While India's tenth five-year plan (2002–2007) took steps to improve primary education, the focus on education in India has long been higher education. Rooted in its efforts to industrialize, the government promoted engineering

FIGURE 5-2

Economic growth and inflation in India, 1985–2005

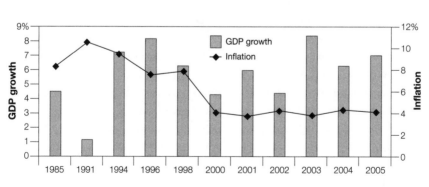

Source: Compiled by author with data from International Monetary Fund, *International Financial Statistics,* various years.

colleges to build India's technical knowledge base. And, with sixteen national universities and more than twelve thousand colleges, the state produces a huge number of educated, trained professionals—so many, in fact, that the *2001 UN Development Report* commented on an income loss of $2 billion due to emigration (mostly to the United States). Although questions were continually raised about the quality of higher education, there was little doubt that 7 million students, 100,000 engineers graduating annually, and limitless lawyers and accountants provided a deep base of skilled workers. In Chennai, in Mumbai, in Hyderabad, and most of all, in Bangalore, these graduates had begun making their mark. Two phenomena had developed simultaneously as a result, beginning in the mid-1980s.

First was the phenomenon of information technology. Encouraged by the loosening of restrictions on the import of technology, the absence of taxes on software exports, and the unique ability of software to avoid infrastructural bottlenecks, Indian entrepreneurs began building their own IT service firms, often after having done a stint of work in the United States. Years of hard work have now yielded results—several firms such as Wipro, Infosys, and Tata Consultancy Services exceed $1 billion of revenue annually. And a dozen other firms, growing at 30 percent or more annually, are not far behind. "The IT industry is not impeded by government policy issues," explained Nandan Nilekani, Infosys's CEO. "Ninety-eight percent of our revenue comes from the global markets. Our business does not exist in the physical world so we don't have to worry about such factors as ports, roads, airports, etc. We do not have labor problems. We are a unique set of businesspeople."[16]

The second was outsourcing. Taking advantage of the tech-savvy English-speaking workforce, American companies began outsourcing back-office operations to India. By 2002, more than 40 percent of the world *Fortune* 500 companies had outsourced a portion of their service operations to India. Often answering the phones with assumed American names, college-educated customer service agents replaced U.S. counterparts for a fraction of the cost. Plus, with a nine-hour time difference, Indian operations made twenty-four-hour service possible. Ernst & Young, for example, had begun outsourcing tax return services to India in 2002. "We hire fresh-out-of-college graduates with bachelor's degrees in accounting or math," explains Sharda Cherwoo, Ernst & Young's CEO of shared services. "On the average, we pay them from US$3,000 to US$5,000 per year, including benefits." And the tax returns travel to Bangalore via satellite (or the Internet), without infrastructural delays.[17]

Perhaps the best-known foreign employer is General Electric, with more than twelve thousand employees in India. GE employed thousands processing credit cards, placing internal orders, and performing insurance functions and a host of other back-office operations. GE had gone so far as to outsource some of its research, with a huge $80 million research campus in Bangalore that works on plastics, jet engines, wind turbines, and refrigerators. Late in 2004, GE spun off 60 percent of its international services business, hoping to develop outsourcing work as an independent entity—yet another GE Capital business with the promise of great success.

One encouraging result of this growth in technology and services was India's positive current account. That is, after years of deficits, growth of software and IT service exports had risen to nearly $9 billion by 2003. And although the goods deficit continued to rise toward $38 billion by 2005, the services surplus reached $6.6 billion. When added to India's huge inflow of $23 billion in private transfers (from Indians abroad), India enjoyed current account surplus from 2001 to 2004, only returning to a deficit of about $12 billion in 2005.

Persistent Structural Problems

Foreign direct investment remained thin in India, right through 2005. In comparison to the $30 billion to $60 billion annually invested in China, India's net inflow of FDI peaked at about $4.7 billion. Although many multinational companies had entered the Indian market, most limited their investment presence through joint ventures. There were several reasons. India had thus far failed to provide adequate power, transportation, or communications infrastructure. The highway system was totally inadequate. Truck travel from Delhi to Mumbai, a mere fourteen hundred kilometers, took eight days. When trucks arrived at the Port of Mumbai, entry required another wait in line of up to forty-eight hours. Continuing regulations at the federal and state level, export taxes, and high tariffs were also discouraging. As one investor noted, "Companies can't take advantage of the low-cost labor if the free trade and necessary infrastructure are not available to support it."[18]

Dabhol was still a particularly discouraging incident. In the mid-1990s, Enron, GE, and Bechtel led a consortium that financed construction of a two-stage gas-fired power plant, for $2.9 billion, on the coast in Maharashtra. Political controversy led to a temporary holdup in construction, eventually solved by a senior Enron executive. But when the second stage was virtually complete, the state utility board decided it could not pay the high rates agreed to (for electricity generated by liquefied national gas). So construction was again halted, and the new plant still lay idle through 2005, despite India's continuing need for electricity. Obviously, other would-be investors in infrastructural projects remain wary.

Another barrier to foreign direct investment has been the slow progress of privatization. To most members of India's elite, privatization was prerequisite to both reducing corruption and improving economic growth. "You only have to worry about corruption," observed Aroon Purie, the chief editor of *India Today*, "when you have to interact with the government. Corruption is a function of regulation . . . [I]t is a factor of the current infrastructure. The less you have to do with the government, the less that corruption is a problem."[19]

Despite efforts of government to reduce its control, 43 percent of India's capital stock was still in government hands. India's tenth five-year plan had focused on privatization to gain $20 billion in revenue. However, only about $3 billion had been received from privatization receipts by 2004. "Our privatization policy is clear," said Pradip Baijal, secretary of disinvestment. "Other than defense, railway and atomic energy, all sectors are being privatized."[20] But this was late in 2002, under the BJP government. Of the forty-eight companies that had been privatized, most were relatively small firms. Government often retained a "golden share," and none of the equity was sold to foreigners.

In 2002, the government had appointed Arun Shourie, a public economist and journalist, to head the Divestment Ministry. Shourie privatized thirteen companies in 2002, raising $2.2 billion. But the political opposition to privatization of big companies was intense. Many politicians feared that their parties would lose the electoral support of special-interest groups if they pushed necessary reforms. Protests by politicians, unions, and the media stalled Shourie's privatization plans. "I'm disposing of bleeding ulcers," a frustrated Shourie told me, "but the allegation is that I'm selling the crown jewels." He was intensely concerned with the slow pace: "Through privatization, the state institutions are weakened, but society is made healthier. We need to transfer power from the state to society."[21]

Without the revenue from significant privatization, government found it even more difficult to mitigate its worst economic problem—the huge fiscal deficit. The central government had been running significant deficits (5–6 percent of GDP) for decades, financing them through foreign borrowing before 1991 and domestic borrowing since then. During the early 2000s, the federal deficit was about 5.9 percent of GDP, but the states also ran deficits, funded by domestic borrowing. These deficits ran to about 4.5 percent, leaving a combined deficit of more than 10 percent of GDP.

India's tax base was rather small for several reasons. The formal economy only included about 30 million people, and many of them didn't pay taxes (either they were too poor, or they avoided taxes). Thus, personal income taxes delivered only 10 percent of expenditures (3.9 percent of GDP). Corporate taxes, which were likewise often avoided, contributed 11.7 percent of expenditures. "Our tax base has gone up, but so has tax avoidance," observed a deputy governor of the central bank. "In many cases, it is the rich who are not paying."[22]

These sizable deficits caused several problems. First is the debt service. With debt at nearly 85 percent of GDP by 2002, interest payments had risen to about half the government's expenditures. This burden obviously detracts from government's ability to invest in infrastructure or spend on needed social welfare. Second, such deficits result in higher real interest rates, as it draws so much capital from the domestic savings pool. And third, this burdensome deficit crowds out private investment by absorbing national savings and driving up interest rates. Thus, gross fixed capital formation, as a percent of GDP, has risen above 23 percent only once (in 1995) and currently stands at about 22.9 percent. While this number looks reasonable to an American or a European, it is 50 percent lower than that of most of the Asian superstars, including China.

Reining in expenditures has proved particularly difficult. Due to frictions with Pakistan, defense expenditures were nearly 25 percent of revenues. Natural disasters, ranging from droughts to the 2001 earthquake in Gujarat, absorbed additional expenditures. Agriculture and energy subsidies, at 11 percent of the budget, were difficult to reduce without loss of political support. As the finance minister commented in 2003, "What am I left with?"

Social and Political Conflict

In late May 1999, a quasi-war erupted between India and Pakistan over the disputed state of Kashmir. After on-and-off conflict, a Pakistani militant group stormed the Indian Parliament building in December 2000, killing twelve. Although Pakistani president Pervez Musharraf promised to crack down on terrorists, troop emplacement by both sides rose to more than 1 million. By 2002, western governments became concerned with the threat of nuclear war, because Delhi was scarcely four hundred miles from Pakistan and both sides had short-range nuclear delivery systems. Yet when I asked Yashwant Sinha, minister of external affairs, about the chances of war, he responded with distain . . . "total bunkum!"[23]

Making matters worse, at least for foreign direct investors, religious tensions boiled to the surface in India. In March 2002, the firebombing of Hindu activists by Muslim militants caused another outbreak of communal violence that resulted in more than two thousand deaths. When the BJP chief minister of Gujarat dismissed the violence, observing that people had "shown remarkable restraint," investors had to wonder when the time would be right to take a significant position in India.

Return of the Congress Party

On May 13, 2004, Atal Bihari Vajpayee surprised the world by resigning his position as prime minister. After nine years on the backbenches, the Congress Party was back with a huge upset victory in the national elections. Congress had won 219 seats (out of 539), over the BJP coalition's 188. There had been many issues, but a sense that the BJP had not done much to help rural India was the largest. In towns and villages throughout the country, voters rejected the BJP's slogan, "India Shining," complaining of high unemployment and inadequate investment in electricity, roads, and water. The religious issues associated with Hindu nationalism seemed to have died out.

Sonia Gandhi, the head of the Congress Party, chose to neutralize objections to her Italian nationality by refusing to accept appointment to prime minister. Instead, the party brought back Manmohan Singh to head the government and appointed Palaniappan Chidambaram, a Harvard Business School graduate, to serve as finance minister. But to create a majority coalition, the Congress Party had to join with various left-of-center parties, including India's Communist Party.

In June, the coalition published its Common Minimum Programme (CMP), announcing significant concessions to the Congress Party's partners. Privatization, anathema to Communists, was put on hold. The CMP also went easy on needed labor law reform and deregulation of the power sector. But it did provide more spending to farmers and the rural poor, education, and health. Perhaps the most aggressive proposal was an "employment-guarantee act," which would guarantee one member from each poor family one hundred days of employment at the minimum wage. Assuming a wage of $1.10 per day, and perhaps 50 million recipients, this program could cost the government as much as $5.6 billion.

Despite these initiatives, Chidambaram proclaimed that the country needed investment and that he would act as "investment minister." But if investment were to rise (either domestic investment or foreign investment), the government would have to reduce deficits, make labor laws more flexible, and reduce bureaucratic regulatory intervention in the economy.

To encourage investment, the government also knew that it had to reduce foreign policy tensions with Pakistan. Shortly after his victory, Singh commenced negotiations with Pakistan. In November, just before visiting

Kashmir, Singh announced a unilateral troop reduction and proposals for a $5 billion development package for Kashmir.

On the Move?

Indians were optimistic in 2006. Prime Minister Singh and Finance Minister Chidambaram were proving to be practical yet still committed to their reform ambitions. Regulatory and tax reforms were continuing, albeit slowly, encouraging the business environment. Privatization, although limited, was continuing through the sale of minority stakes. The 2006 budget proposed to expand rural and infrastructural spending, while still reducing the federal budget deficit to 3.8 percent. Economic growth, which had just reached the extraordinary level of 8.1 percent despite high oil prices, was expected to moderate a bit. Inflation was steady, and the rupee was depreciating gradually. Some analysts saw a further huge potential for the growth of information technology and IT-enabled services, with manufacturing likewise beginning to improve.

Yet problems did remain. India's labor costs were still higher, by 20–30 percent, than those of China. And educated Indians all recognized that China would be India's major competitor in goods and, perhaps increasingly, in services. Poverty (and worsening income distribution) remained a significant structural problem, which the new government was actively combating. Unemployment, still at 10 percent, could only be mitigated by rapid growth—probably in excess of 8 percent annually together with some liberalization of work rules.

The biggest short-term problems remained the fiscal deficit of the central and state government, inadequate infrastructure (especially power), scarce foreign direct investment, and relations with Pakistan. With government debt at 86 percent of GDP, debt service crowded out private investment and absorbed government revenues that could better be used to improve the infrastructure. If the infrastructure were improved—roads, ports, power systems, and telecommunications—it would increase productivity and enhance India's attractiveness to foreign investors.

If those issues could be ameliorated over the next two or three years, and relations with Pakistan stabilized, then India might see foreign direct investment grow—perhaps to $10 billion or even $20 billion annually.

In the spring of 2006, India was growing at about 9.3 percent—about the same as China! Consumer spending was surprisingly strong. Construction, finance, transportation, and communications were leading this growth, with manufacturing (growing at 8.9 percent) just behind.

Yet Finance Minister Chidambaram remained frustrated at the rate of market overhaul and institutional reform. "More reforms are necessary," concluded Chidambaram, "to sustain this growth."[24] Chidambaram knew the importance of good government. He new that India's government had managed too much in the past, too ineffectively. Swadeshi had clashed with globalization, especially after the oil shocks of 1973 and 1979. Once the Soviet Union collapsed in 1991, India had no choice but to liberalize—gradually. Yet liberalization of India's institutional potential still has a long way to go if India is to continue integrating with the global economy.

For sure, government in India will not go away. But good government and good governance will be absolutely crucial to effective development for decades to come.

PART II

The Difficulties of
Structural Adjustment

—— m ——

Mexico

INCOMPLETE TRANSITION

AT 11:06 P.M. on June 2, 2000, President Ernesto Zedillo went on television to address the Mexican people. "Today," said President Zedillo, "we have shown for all to see that ours is a nation of free men and women who believe in the means of democracy and law to achieve progress and resolve our problems." Then he announced: "Vicente Fox Quesada will be the next President of the Republic."[1]

The political transition begun in 1968 appeared to be complete. Vicente Fox represented the Partido Accion Nacional, a minority party that had overturned seventy-one years of corrupt and authoritarian rule by the Partido Revolucionario Institucional. It had taken thirty-two years of growing political resistance and eighteen years of adjustment to debt crisis. But now it seemed that the people of Mexico were ready to realize the benefits of reform.

The macroeconomy was more or less stable. And the microeconomy had been partially deregulated, privatized, and opened. In 1994, Mexico had embraced globalization by entering into the North American Free Trade Agreement (NAFTA). But cultural and institutional legacies persisted. The population of more than 100 million was poorly educated, urbanized, and for the most part, impoverished. Sharp regional differences separated northern Hispanics from Southern Indians.

"It is certainly valuable," said President Fox, "not to have to talk about a financial crisis; but it is sad to have to speak of a much more important and deeper crisis, the human crisis of the people sunk in poverty; the social crisis of those who have been excluded from development."[2] Thus, Fox set out an extraordinary program to purge government of the corruption and inefficiencies that plagued the Mexican political system. He and his talented team of ministers would work around the clock to reform Mexico's social system.

It would be great to look at all of Latin America—or at least Brazil, Argentina, and Chile, as well as Mexico. But Mexico will have to suffice. Almost all the countries in Latin America pursued import substitution to develop, incurred foreign debt to get through oil shocks, and then experienced debt crisis in the 1980s. They struggled, under IMF conditionality, to correct macroeconomic imbalance and reform their microeconomic policies. Economic liberalization, moreover, led to democratization. Thus, Mexico's story, notwithstanding particulars, represents the broad sweep of Latin America's.

Mexico's Revolutionary Legacy

Hernando Cortes, a Spanish explorer, landed in Mexico in 1519. Within two years, the conquistador's few hundred troops had laid waste to scores of cities and defeated the Aztec empire. Ending more than a thousand years of Indian autonomy, Cortes made Mexico a colony of Spain.

Conquest was followed by three hundred years of death from European diseases, slavery, Catholic evangelization, mining exploitation, and the development of huge agricultural estates, or haciendas. Income distribution became painfully imbalanced as Spanish haciendas encroached on peasant farms. Led by a Catholic priest named Miguel Hidalgo, revolution finally erupted in 1810. After several years of violent turmoil, General Agustín de Iturbide led revolutionary forces to victory in 1821. Mexico declared independence.

Independence, however, did not ensure peaceful development. During the next ninety years, Mexico was ruled by a series of *caudillos*, or "strongmen," mostly from military backgrounds. Americans are most familiar with Antonio Santa Anna, who ruled from 1833 to 1855. Although he overpowered Texan revolutionaries at the Alamo, Santa Anna was eventually defeated by Sam Houston and gave Texas its independence. Ten years later, Santa Anna lost a war with the United States, ceding California, Arizona, New Mexico, and parts of three other states in the Treaty of Guadalupe Hidalgo.

Santa Anna was succeeded by Benito Juárez, whose presidency was briefly interrupted by the conquest by French troops and the Austrian rule of Archduke Maximilian. In 1867, when Juárez liberated Mexico, he eliminated the privileges of the Catholic Church and initiated the rule of law, codified in the Constitution of 1857. Shortly after the death of Juárez, power struggles gave way to the rule of Porfirio Díaz—a violent dictator who nonetheless unified Mexico. Revolution erupted again in 1910, driving Díaz from office but leading to decades of violence. Famed revolutionaries Poncho

Villa and Emiliano Zapata rallied peasants in their fight against more traditional generals and landowners who sought to restore constitutional order.

Midway through this prolonged revolution, in 1917, Mexico produced a new constitution that mandated a formal separation of church and state; articulated social, agrarian, and labor rights; and confirmed the existence of a strong presidency, restricted to a one-term (six-year) *sextenio*. The ruling party, the National Revolutionary Party, was organized in 1929. Agrarian reforms were fulfilled by Lázaro Cárdenas in 1934, distributing small holdings—*ejidos*—to millions of peasants. And in 1938, Cárdenas nationalized foreign oil companies, creating Petroleos Mexicanos (PEMEX), and instituted the *dedazo*, the process of picking a presidential successor. In 1946, the party changed its name to Partido Revolucionario Institucional (PRI).

During this period of political consolidation, most of Mexico's key political institutions emerged. Public employees and teachers were represented through their unions, in the Confederation of Mexican Workers. Peasants were organized in the National Peasants' Confederation. And business organizations were represented indirectly by interests within the PRI. From its founding in 1929, the PRI had utterly dominated the political system, controlling all thirty-one governorships and sixty-four senate seats until 1988.

Postwar Growth

After World War II, Mexico followed a deliberate policy of import substitution to reduce its dependence on raw materials exports and imported manufactured goods. The fledgling manufacturing sector was protected from foreign competition by tariffs and quotas on imports. In the 1950s, those restrictions covered about 10 percent of domestic production, rising to 60 percent in the 1970s and 100 percent in 1982–1983.

The government provided low-interest, long-term loans to industry through state investment banks. The public sector also invested directly in infrastructure and basic industries such as steel, transportation, and energy. In spite of revolutionary constraints (and unlike India), foreign investors responded well to the import substitution policies. From 1950 to 1970 FDI increased fivefold, with the United States investing—by far—more than other countries.

From 1954 to 1970, Mexico also followed a macroeconomic policy it termed *desarrollo estabilizador*, or "stabilized development." This involved relatively tight fiscal policies and government restraint using unsupported central bank credits to finance increased spending. As a result, the average growth in per capita income often exceeded 3 percent. Low inflation persisted with a fixed exchange rate regime.

By the mid-1960s, however, underlying problems in this system were becoming apparent. Growth rates were slowing, especially for agricultural production, and exports of manufactured goods stagnated. As the United States rapidly modernized, Mexico's economy became even more dependent on imported capital goods. Between 1965 and 1970, its current account deficit ballooned from $367 million to $946 million. (The current account balance represents net trade in goods and services, plus net investment income and unilateral transfers.)

With this emerging economic stagnation came social unrest. It began haltingly, in the summer of 1968, when some high school students, in a brawl after a touch-football game, were clubbed and arrested, along with their teachers. Protests ensued, followed by further repression. President Gustavo Díaz Ordaz had little patience with youthful protestors.

High school protests and police action eventually led to student strikes at UNAM, Mexico's premier university. By August, student protests precipitated a downtown march by two hundred thousand people disaffected by the PRI's corrupt and ineffective rule. Marches, demonstrations, and spreading violence between students and police worsened during September. President Díaz Ordaz became increasingly agitated with Mexican students who threatened to disrupt the Olympic Games in October.

On October 2, the dam broke. Late in the day, the army sealed off a demonstration at Tlatelolco Plaza. When shots rang out and people panicked, the army opened fire with automatic weapons. Several hundred students died, with nearly a thousand injured. Octavio Paz, awarded the 1990 Nobel Prize in Literature, drew the following conclusion at the time: "Without democracy, economic development makes no sense. On October 2, 1968, the student movement in Mexico came to an end. So did an entire period in Mexican History."[3]

Following this violent turn, Mexico's next president used government spending to accommodate competing claims on the political system. Luis Echeverría Alverez increased spending on health, education, and infrastructure. He imposed restrictions on foreign direct investment in 1973 and began borrowing to bridge the gap between expenditures and lagging revenues. The inflation rate rose steadily. By 1976, Mexico's foreign debt had reached $18 billion, with debt service of nearly $1 billion. As capital flight intensified and foreign exchange reserves neared depletion, Echeverría was forced to devalue the peso, from 12.5 to 20 pesos per dollar, and turn to the International Monetary Fund for a short-term bridge loan.

His successor, José López Portillo, imposed austerity, briefly, and terminated the IMF stabilization agreement. Announcing his intention to develop oil, agriculture, and tourism, Portillo inaugurated the "Mexican miracle."

The year before Portillo's inauguration, Mexico was a net oil importer. Its proven reserves, with oil valued at $2–$3 a barrel, were a mere 6 billion barrels. But in 1976, with oil prices at $14 per barrel, PEMEX expanded exploration and immediately announced a 76 percent increase in reserves. During the next four years, proven reserves grew from 11 billion to 16 billion, to 40 billion, to 50 billion, and then to 60 billion by December 1980.[4]

Thus, soon after taking office, Portillo announced a development program to push daily production from 900,000 to 2.25 million barrels of oil. To finance it, Portillo borrowed from western banks, where interest spreads (the difference between the cost of capital and a bank's loan rate) had reached all-time lows. Over his six years in office, he ramped up Mexican foreign debt from $20 billion to $82 billion! Oil development alone required more than $40 billion. Then too there were subsidies for agriculture, for infrastructure, for state-owned enterprises, for education, and for the poor. There was, as well, massive corruption as state funds leaked out to labor leaders, affluent business executives, and politicians of all stripes.

In the "miracle" that ensued, public sector outlays boomed, rising from 25 percent to 42 percent of GDP by the early 1980s. Mexico began growing at a rate of nearly 8 percent annually. Gross domestic investment (both public and private) reached 30 percent of GDP in 1981. Imports, however, grew even faster at almost 18 percent annually. Mexico needed capital equipment, and with the peso becoming increasingly overvalued at its fixed rate, consumers likewise expanded their imports. Thus, even as oil revenues began to pour in, Mexico was overwhelmed by import expenditures. The current account deficit grew from $1.5 billion to $12.5 billion between 1976 and 1981. Mexico merely financed it.

The central bank did nothing to mitigate inflation. The money supply, which had generally grown at 21 percent annually, now expanded to 33 percent. Inflation jumped from 15 percent to 25 percent annually. Yet as prices in Mexico escalated more than twice as fast as those in the United States, the peso-dollar exchange rate held firm. Banks were lending, and the prospect of Mexico's future stream of oil revenues seemed to undergird the value of the peso, at least until February 1982.

But as the economy boomed and money flowed, smart Mexicans were beginning to have doubts. As the fiscal deficit grew, from 5 percent in the mid-1970s to 17.6 percent by 1982, these Mexicans began to wonder how the government could continue to service its debt. By early 1980, some Mexicans began converting their huge peso incomes to dollars and investing those dollars in U.S. bonds and savings accounts, and real estate in Colorado Springs, San Diego, and Miami. In 1981, this capital flight increased to more than $8 billion, and in the first eight months of 1982, it reached $6.6 billion.

Thus, Mexico's dollar reserves were diminished by nearly $15 billion in less than two years.

The "miracle," meanwhile, had not reached everyone. At the end of the 1970s, 35–40 percent of all households earned a total income below the prevailing minimum wage; approximately 20 percent of the population in 1979 was suffering from malnutrition; 45 percent did not receive adequate health care. About 50 percent of all homes lacked running water and sewage services, and 25 percent had no electricity. The lowest 20 percent of all households held 3 percent of the national income while the top 20 percent held 41 percent of that income.[5]

In the spring of 1981, shortly after Ronald Reagan took office in the United States, oil prices eased a bit, dropping from $36 to $31 per barrel. At the same time, Paul Volcker, head of the Federal Reserve, raised interest rates to get inflation under control. As he did so, the U.S. economy plunged into recession. U.S. demand for oil (as well as other Mexican exports) eased, and tourist flows to Mexico dropped sharply as American's struggled with rising unemployment. With revenues from oil exports and tourism falling, with high interest rates pushing up Mexican debt service to $14 billion, and with capital flight intensifying, the Mexican central bank no longer had sufficient dollar reserves to maintain the peso exchange rate.

In February 1982, after vowing publicly to "defend the peso like a dog," Portillo was forced to devalue, but it was not enough. By summer, capital was pouring out of the country. Jesus Silva Herzog, Portillo's finance secretary, began discussions with U.S. Treasury Secretary Donald Regan and Paul Volcker in Washington. When Regan said to Silva Herzog, "Mr. Secretary, you have a big problem," Silva Herzog replied, "No, Mr. Secretary, I'm sorry to tell you but *we* have a problem."[6]

All together, the central bank's foreign exchange reserve had fallen short by perhaps $25 billion. Thus, on August 15, Mexico announced it could not meet its interest payment obligations. The peso collapsed.[7]

Two weeks later, Portillo nationalized the banking system, accusing bankers of profiteering from speculation. He called in the International Monetary Fund to negotiate a standby agreement. But Portillo would leave it for his successor, Miguel de la Madrid, to sign the agreement and take the heat.

Until the crisis of 1982, Mexico's political system had relied on its capacity to maintain order and increase living standards, even in the face of rapid population growth and highly unequal distribution of wealth. The government had maintained equilibrium in the short run by spending and borrowing but was unable to prevent long-term decline. Debt crisis necessitated those serious adjustments, and it was de la Madrid's lot to implement them.

Miguel de la Madrid was a new kind of president. A forty-seven-year-old lawyer with a master's degree in public administration from Harvard's Kennedy School of Government, de la Madrid had worked for more than a decade in Mexico's treasury and budget secretariats. When Portillo chose him by dedazo, de la Madrid had virtually no experience in Mexico's political trenches. Yet in many ways he was right for the job. No sooner had he been inaugurated in December 1982 than de la Madrid would sign a harsh IMF stabilization plan, pledging to reduce the fiscal deficit, restrict growth of the money supply, devalue the peso, restrain wages, and open the economy to international trade and investment.

De la Madrid promptly appointed an ideologically cohesive cabinet, with Silva Herzog remaining at the treasury and Carlos Salinas becoming secretary of planning and budget. The new president's first task was repairing relations with the private sector, yet he could "not reverse the [bank nationalizations] for political reasons and because nationalization was already introduced into the constitution."[8] Although his administration did indemnify stockholders for those nationalizations, there was no effective capital market for the remainder of the decade.

Budget cutting was intense during the first two years of de la Madrid's presidency. Subsidies were cut and public sector prices increased; the value-added tax was raised. These efforts helped reduce deficits from 17.6 percent to 8.7 percent by 1984. Unfortunately, the largest cuts were in public investment, which did not recover in real terms until a decade later. To curb inflation, the central bank raised interest rates as high as 100 percent, undermining private investment as well. Inflation moderated somewhat for a couple of years.

The real exchange rate and the real wage were the administration's principal instruments for balancing the external sector (and generating enough foreign exchange to meet debt-service obligations). Under de la Madrid, the peso depreciated from 57 to 637 per dollar by 1986; the real peso dropped about 50 percent. This immediately cut imports by almost two-thirds and eventually helped non-oil exports grow.

As for real wages, de la Madrid quietly changed the indexing of minimum wages to inflation. From 1983, minimum wages were indexed to "expected inflation," which during his administration was severely underestimated. Thus, real wages fell more than 40 percent. Essentially, this event meant that a Mexican worker making $1.94 per hour in 1982 was earning but $1.51 by 1988. That decrease would obviously help curtail demand for imports. And on the other hand, it made Mexico an increasingly attractive site for foreign direct investment. The *maquila* sector, and its in-bond assembly facilities, began to boom (a *maquiladora*, or *maquila*, is a foreign-owned assembly plant).

Finally, de la Madrid pushed Congress to join the GATT and eventually lower Mexican tariffs by almost 50 percent. Under a loophole in Mexico's FDI law, de la Madrid's administration allowed a few high-tech companies to make wholly owned investments—including IBM's $1 billion computer facility in Guadalajara. And de la Madrid even began to privatize—some 116 state-owned firms netting $422 million. Late in his term, de la Madrid privatized Aeroméxico for $300 million.[9]

But de la Madrid's management of structural adjustment was interrupted by two exogenous developments—the earthquake that struck Mexico City in 1985 and the collapse of oil prices in 1986. The earthquake that struck on September 19 registered 8.1 on the Richter scale. It destroyed more than 370 buildings and disrupted infrastructure for months. De la Madrid's government was slow to respond, only acknowledging the crisis some thirty-six hours later. With thousands dead and nearly a hundred eighty thousand left homeless, the government and the PRI were overwhelmed. For the first time, citizens formed their own nongovernmental organizations to cope with the disaster, and some of the media actually exhibited independent reporting.

Less than a year later, oil prices plunged, from more than $27 per barrel in 1985 to just over $8.54 per barrel in July 1986; Mexico's export revenues dropped from $13.3 billion to $5.6 billion in that single year. Mexico's response to both these crises was, logically, to increase spending and borrowing sharply. The government deficit doubled, to 16 percent of GDP. External debt jumped to 58 percent of GDP and internal debt to 32 percent. The central bank, accommodating this burden, expanded the money supply rapidly (129 percent) in 1987, thus pushing inflation to 140 percent. In October, the Mexican stock market collapsed and the peso fell to 1,405 per dollar.

Miguel de la Madrid, now seriously worried about the prospects of default, adopted an unorthodox solution—the Pacto. He called together representatives of business, organized labor, agriculture, and government to agree to reduce deficits, coordinate wages, and set prices. These efforts would be necessary to curb inflation and especially expectations of more inflation. The peso was devalued by another 22 percent. The maximum tariff on imports was reduced from 40 percent to 20 percent. Government expenditures were cut, revenues increased, and credit growth slowed by 55 percent.

By 1988, the de la Madrid administration had reestablished control of the economy. Growth had turned positive, exports were growing again, and inflation had dropped by more than half. Interest rates and the fiscal deficit were dropping, as were foreign and domestic debt (as a percentage of GDP). Yet "our greatest success," according to de la Madrid, "was maintaining social peace in the country. It was a constant preoccupation in my government to maintain peace, avoid violence, avoid social conflicts, and I believe that we were successful . . . One has to remember that during my government real wages fell by 40 to 50 percent. In other countries, this would have provoked a revolution."[10]

Government policies had begun eliciting institutional responses. The left organized, and leftist parties began to make some electoral gains. And as the PRI failed to deliver economic benefits, hundreds of independent nongovernmental organizations were also formed. Their ranks included political parties and business, labor, peasant, mass media, and human rights groups. The political right also grew more organized, uniting within the Partido Accion Nacional (PAN). PAN and its presidential candidate, Manuel Clouthier, campaigned for even greater economic liberalization and for the democratization of the electoral process.

The most serious electoral challenge to the PRI came from within its own ranks. Tension was growing between the traditional dominant politicos and the *técnicos* (technical, rather than political bureaucrats) who had come to dominate national policymaking under de la Madrid. Many old-guard politicos viewed reform measures such as privatizing state-owned enterprises and reducing subsidies as a betrayal of their party's revolutionary heritage. Those who favored traditional economic solutions were frozen out of power.

In October 1987, some of these elements left the party to form an opposition movement under the leadership of Cuauhtémoc Cardenás and Porfirio Muñoz Ledo. Cardenás criticized the administration for abandoning the PRI's commitment to social justice and national self-determination and argued that these views were not getting sufficient representation in the selection process of de la Madrid's successor. Cardenás was essentially purged from the party, but the split within the PRI allowed the fragmented opposition social movements to organize politically. Cardenás declared himself a candidate for president under the umbrella of the National Democratic Front.[11]

Miguel de la Madrid, using dedazo one more time, chose Carlos Salinas Gotari, his own successor in the budget secretariat, as president-elect. The forty-one-year-old Salinas, with a PhD in political economy from Harvard University, shared his predecessor's commitment to free-market economic policy. But this clever political strategist, with an owlish appearance, evinced little appeal with voters.

Salinas's election, on July 6, 1988, was a mess. Mexicans remember the day as the day in which *se cayo el sistema*—"the system crashed." The phrase refers both to the computer system that aggregated ballots and the political system by which the PRI had traditionally controlled the electoral process. Historically, presidential elections had been a ritualistic ratification of candidates chosen behind closed doors by the PRI's political elite. For the first time the PRI's candidate, Salinas, faced organized opposition parties from the left and right. On election day, many traditional PRI voters abstained or joined the opposition.

When the early returns showed Cardenás in the lead, the government's computers went silent for six hours. Although the PRI declared victory at 2 a.m., it took another week, during which Cardenás ballots were found "floating down rivers and smoldering in roadside bonfires,"[12] before the official results were released: Salinas had won 50.7 percent of the vote, the narrowest margin of victory in the PRI's history. The opposition gained almost half the seats in the Chamber of Deputies and four seats in the Senate.

Nicknamed the Atomic Ant, Salinas approached his job vigorously. A workaholic, he made intense use of the *gira*—the "presidential tour." He traveled throughout Mexico, opening schools, kissing babies, and attending conferences. And he used the media to advertise his work, his plans, and his views. He promised both economic and political reforms, although the former would take priority.

Scarcely a month after his inauguration, Salinas grabbed headlines by going after one of the most corrupt of Mexico's oligarchs—"La Quina"—Joaquín Hernández Galicia, the president of the Oil Workers Union. Salinas sent the army to La Quina's house, demolished the front door with a bazooka, and hauled him off to jail. Before long, Salinas had jailed Miguel Felix Gallardo, a notorious drug dealer, and Eduardo Legorreta, a financier who had contributed to the Salinas campaign! And when Ernesto Ruffo, the PAN candidate for governor of Baja California Norte won his election in July 1989, Salinas attended Ruffo's inauguration. This was the first governorship to fall to the opposition, and Salinas was emphasizing his commitment to an open political process. Mexicans were thrilled!

Over the next five years, Salinas strengthened and deepened de la Madrid's strategy of fiscal and monetary restraint, debt restructuring, privatization, investment liberalization, and free trade.

With the economy (and thus tax revenues) growing again, Salinas restrained spending to drive the fiscal deficit down from nearly 15 percent of GDP to a small surplus by 1992. (Some creative bookkeeping appeared to help.) The Pactos were renegotiated seven more times, controlling wage gains and price hikes. With high interest rates falling gradually from 69 percent to 15 percent, Mexico's central bank succeeded in lowering inflation to 7.4 percent in August 1994.

In May 1989, the government announced a sweeping liberalization of foreign investment regulations. It revoked remaining restrictions of minority ownership and opened new areas to foreign investment. The new rules allowed 100 percent ownership in the tourism sector and in maquilas, hopefully to generate jobs and foreign exchange.[13]

Fortune chose Salinas as one of its twenty-five top business leaders for 1989. His reforms were labeled "Salinastroika." A poll by the *Los Angeles Times* revealed that while only a quarter of Mexico's population believed that Salinas had actually won, 79 percent gave him a positive presidential approval rating.

Salinas began privatizing Mexico's larger state-owned enterprises, including the banks. Some two hundred firms were privatized by 1994, netting the government some $22 billion. Foreign direct investment picked up, both to acquire privatized firms and to open maquilas. By the time Salinas left office, FDI amounted to more than $4 billion annually.

Debt forgiveness was also on Salinas's agenda. With the debt at about $102 billion, debt service was nearly $8 billion, leaving the current account in deficit and necessitating additional borrowing. Mexico negotiated a $3.6 billion loan from the IMF in 1989 just to build foreign exchange reserves. But only when U.S. Treasury Secretary Nicholas Brady had leaned on creditor banks to renegotiate did Mexico finally make progress.

The agreement, signed in February 1990, involved some debt forgiveness and some injections of new lending. The deal's main feature was conversion of bank debt into so-called Brady bonds. These were thirty-year zero-coupon bonds guaranteed by the U.S. Department of the Treasury on the collateral of Mexican oil revenues. The agreement, covering $48 billion, required no servicing before maturity, when a single balloon payment would be due. Mexico's foreign debt, reduced to $79 billion, freed up resources to apply to growth.[14]

NAFTA

In the winter of 1990, Salinas traveled to England and France to pitch Mexico to potential foreign investors. He was greeted politely, but with little interest. The same happened in Davos, Switzerland, at the World Economic Forum. It was there that Salinas decided to approach the Americans to discuss a free trade agreement. This was an attempt by Salinas to cement his reforms and ensure Mexico's competitiveness in the world economy.

After two years of negotiations with Canada and the United States, the North American Free Trade Agreement was initialed by Prime Minister Brian Mulroney and by President George H. W. Bush, shortly before he left office. Yet it fell to Bill Clinton to build political support and push the agreement through both houses of Congress. After renegotiating the environmental and labor provisions in 1993, the House and Senate ratified the treaty in the fall, and it took effect on January 1, 1994.

Tariffs on approximately 50 percent of the nine thousand traded items covered by the treaty would disappear immediately, tariffs on another 15 percent within five years, and tariffs on all remaining goods over the following ten years. Mexico would immediately eliminate any remaining licensing requirements and quotas, except for agriculture, automobiles, energy, and textiles. Sectors most sensitive to import competition were granted fifteen-year transition periods, and procedures were established to allow countries to reinstate tariffs in response to damaging import surges.

For textiles and apparel, duties would be phased out over a ten-year period and NAFTA would take precedence over the existing Multifiber Agreement. To prevent other countries from using Mexico as an export platform to the United States or Canada, rules of origin required that all goods be produced from yarn made in North America; for cotton and synthetic-made fibers, the fiber itself had to originate in one of the three countries. The United States would immediately remove import quotas on goods that met the rule-of-origin standard from Mexico and would gradually remove import quotas on Mexican goods that did not meet the rules of origin. For automobiles, the rule of origin was set at 62.5 percent. After ten years, 62.5 percent of the value added in a car had to be sourced in North America to attain a zero tariff. In addition, Mexico's trade-balancing requirements would be phased out, and its domestic-content requirements would fall to 29 percent of value added in ten years.

In agriculture, tariffs would be lowered over ten years, except for corn and soybeans in Mexico and for orange juice and sugar in the United States— all of which would be lowered over fifteen years. Salinas knew this would indeed be hard on Mexico's 10 million ejidos but could think of no other way to force modernization.[15]

NAFTA eliminated barriers to trade and investment in automotive parts, government procurement, services (including financial services), land transportation, air services, and telecommunications. "National treatment," where investors were guaranteed equal rules in all three countries, was guaranteed. Intellectual property would be protected. Only in the energy sector, where PEMEX was a historic legacy of difficult intercountry relations, was there no significant opening.

On New Year's Day 1994, President Salinas and his advisers gathered to celebrate the crowning achievement of his presidency. And at the time, indeed, Salinas's reforms were popular. Under his administration, social spending rose substantially, even as the overall budget deficit was reduced. Between 1988 and 1994, spending on education more than doubled; spending on health care and social security rose by 82 percent and on urban development by 51 percent. Thirteen and a half million more people were provided with potable water, 11.5 million with sewage services, and 4 million with electricity. And NAFTA had realigned Mexico's fundamental economic interests and forced Mexicans to rethink their historic preference for isolated nationalism.

The Fall

But there was still a year to go. No sooner had the celebration begun than word reached Los Pinos (Mexico's Presidential Palace) of a revolution in the south. A band of guerillas, calling themselves the Zapatista National Liberation Army (EZLN), had assaulted and captured four cities in the Los Altos region of Mexico's southernmost state, Chiapas. For twenty-four hours, rebels held the city of San Cristóbal. Disaffected and disenfranchised, the poor agrarian economy of the south stood to gain little from the introduction of free trade.

This rebellion had been developing for several years. In the two and a half decades before the uprising, a variety of groups had been active in promoting peasant organizational activities. The reasons for disaffection were many. Though Chiapas was a rich land containing fertile farmlands, pastures, and forests, and was a major source of the nation's coffee, its wealth was severely maldistributed. According to available statistics, a little more than a hundred people controlled 12 percent of the coffee lands. Some six thousand families held more than 3 million hectares of cattle land. Meanwhile, a third of the households in Chiapas at the time were without electricity, 41.6 percent were without drinking water, and 58.8 percent lacked drainage.[16]

The government responded to events in Chiapas with uncertainty. The Salinas administration tried to downplay the situation and deflect criticism by declaring the rebellion to be the work of external forces trying to destabilize Mexico. The government blamed Central American guerrillas, the drug cartels, and even the Catholic Church. On January 12, President Salinas declared a unilateral cease-fire in the region. By that time the Mexican army's presence had swelled from approximately two thousand soldiers to over fourteen thousand—more than enough to cordon off the Zapatistas' stronghold in the Lacandona jungle. By mid-January Congress passed an amnesty decree, clearing the way for peace negotiations.

The economy, meanwhile, was not working as the president had hoped. Growth (and thus job creation) had slowed to almost zero by the end of 1993. The central bank had stabilized the peso, allowing it to fluctuate in a narrow band at just over 3,000 pesos per dollar. With Mexico's inflation averaging 10–11 percent higher than American inflation, it appeared that the peso was once again becoming severely undervalued. Imports boomed, as consumers rushed to take advantage of lower prices north of the Rio Grande. The trade deficit jumped to $18 billion, and the current account deficit, with $9 billion in debt service, to $28 billion.

To maintain the level of reserves, Pedro Aspe, the minister of finance, raised interest rates and began borrowing more dollars from abroad. To do so, Mexico assumed the exchange rate risk on capital inflows that was previously borne by foreign—particularly American—investors. The vehicle for this borrowing was the issuance of *tesobonos*—a short-term Mexican government bond indexed to the dollar. As the year passed, the government shifted its borrowings from medium-term *cetes*—the traditional domestic treasury bills—into short-term tesobonos at ever higher interest rates.

On March 23, Luis Donaldo Colosio, the PRI candidate for president—Salinas's handpicked successor—was gunned down at a campaign rally in Tijuana. Colosio had vowed during the campaign to continue Salinas's reforms and continue the Pactos. His assassination was thought to be a conspiracy among those in the PRI who opposed reform. Suddenly, economic reform seemed in jeopardy. Foreign confidence was severely jolted, and the inflow of foreign capital dried up and began to reverse. To protect themselves from the financial consequences of possible devaluation, Mexicans again moved their savings off shore to safe dollar accounts in Miami and elsewhere.

The peso began to fall.

Drug-related violence and corruption, meanwhile, further muddied the waters of recovery. By 1993, roughly a dozen major drug lords and several minor ones were in control of drug cartels, and they were increasingly engaged in turf wars. During the first five months of the year more than eighty people were killed in Culiacán, a city that had acquired the nickname Little Medellín, and most killings were believed to have been drug related. In May, Cardinal Juan Jesús Posadas Ocampo and several other people were gunned down at point-blank range at the Guadalajara airport during a shoot-out between rival gangs. The government maintained that the cardinal's murder was a case of mistaken identity, but critical questions remained unanswered. At the time, unidentified officials had ordered the delay of a Tijuana-bound Aeroméxico passenger jet, allowing eight of the gunmen to board. Even after it became apparent to investigators on the ground that some of the killers had escaped by plane, Mexican officials made no effort to halt the jet or meet it in Tijuana. Upon arrival, the gunmen simply walked away. None of this inspired confidence in the peso.

In June 1994, I asked President Salinas whether he intended to devalue. No, he responded; they would squeeze inflation so hard that the value of the peso would rise up to meet the value of the dollar. Groan! One month later, José Francisco Ruiz Massieu, general secretary of the PRI, was assassinated. Massieu had been expected to play a crucial role in brokering the reforms planned by the president-elect, Ernesto Zedillo. Subsequent investigations led to the arrest of Salinas's brother, Raúl, and the resignation of the victim's brother, Deputy Attorney General Mario Ruiz Massieu, who had presided over several high-profile drug raids. As figure 6-1 illustrates, exchange reserves continued to flee the country.

Late in November, outgoing President Salinas met with president-elect Zedillo; Pedro Aspe; Jaime Serra Puche, the trade secretary; and Miguel Mancera, head of the central bank. What to do about the peso? Salinas and Aspe did not want to devalue; Zedillo and Puche did. In the end, the group did nothing, except that Aspe resigned and Puche took over as finance secretary.

Three weeks into Ernesto Zedillo's presidency, the Mexican economy collapsed. Foreign exchange markets had waited eagerly for a plan, but no plan was forthcoming. On December 21, panic seized the markets, and Mexico lost $4 billion in exchange reserves. With $23 billion in short-term tesobono liabilities but only $6 billion remaining in reserves, the government—in fact, the country—had lost credibility. The next day, the peso dropped 20 percent, from 3.2 to 5.3 *new* pesos (with three decimals taken off) . . . and to 7.6 the following year. This marked the beginning of the "tequila crisis."

The Zedillo administration now faced one of three painful alternatives. The government could push interest rates sky-high in a bid to attract capital to Mexico; this would, of course, cause a deep depression. It could default, which would not only cause a depression but would probably trigger massive capital flight from other developing countries and leave Mexico a pariah state. Or it could go to New York, hat in hand, and beg for a bailout.

FIGURE 6-1

Mexican foreign exchange reserves, 1994

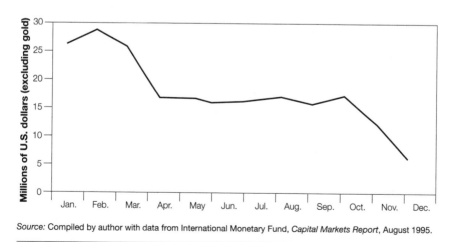

Source: Compiled by author with data from International Monetary Fund, *Capital Markets Report*, August 1995.

On January 5, Guillermo Ortiz Martínez, Mexico's new finance minister, flew to Washington to discuss a bailout with Robert Rubin, President Clinton's treasury Secretary, and Rubin's undersecretary, Lawrence Summers. After the U.S. Senate declined to help, the Clinton administration drew on outdated laws and several international institutions to amass a $52 billion bailout package by March. Ortiz spent much of 1995 removing billions of dollars of bad loans from the balance sheets of banks and restructuring programs for mortgage holders and small debtors. Mexico, meanwhile, plunged into a deep recession during the remainder of the year. But the bailout worked. The peso stopped dropping, and Mexico came roaring back with NAFTA-led growth of 5.5 percent annually for the next five years. Mexico repaid all of its U.S. loans ahead of schedule.

Political Reform

Ernesto Zedillo, a Yale PhD and secretary of planning and budget, was a political outsider. He believed in free markets, deregulation, and global commerce. He opposed big government, social patronage, and much that the PRI had stood for.[17] Zedillo had pledged to defend democratization by distancing the government from the PRI and curbing the powers of the presidency. The state's massive assistance to the party, he said, would be ended, and the PRI's candidate-selection process would be opened up by the introduction of primary elections. In his inaugural address Zedillo had criticized the Salinas administration for tolerating graft, lax law enforcement, and neglect of the nation's poor. He promised to fight poverty and to reform the corruption-ridden judicial system.

Corruption had long been a problem for Mexico, where government functionaries, like those in India, were paid little but had significant power. This was true on the street, where police officers making $700 a month had power; in government agencies, where environmental inspectors made $400 per month; and in the office of the president (Raúl Salinas, the president's brother, had acquired hundreds of millions of dollars). While Zedillo abhorred corruption, he found it almost impossible to reform. It was endemic and institutional. In 2005 Mexico was ranked sixty-fifth by Transparency International—worse even than Brazil and Colombia.[18] Government functions were operated like businesses—garbage collection, taxi licenses, electric power, and prostitution are just a few examples of the government services enmeshed in the shadow economy.

By July 1996, Zedillo had succeeded in convincing Congress to adopt new election rules. Seventeen constitutional amendments created an entirely new framework for electoral politics. When the new rules were first tested in the July 1997 midterm elections, the PRI lost its majority in Congress. Perhaps more surprising was the victory of the Democratic Revolution Party's (PRD) twice-defeated candidate, Cuauhtémoc Cárdenas, as mayor of Mexico City. The PAN, meanwhile, captured governorships in the important states of Querétaro and Nuevo León.

The PRI's loss of a majority affected politics in two ways. First, it meant that the president no longer exercised unlimited authority. And second, party discipline among PRI members eroded. During Zedillo's terms, the Mexican supreme court was strengthened, and fiscal spending was decentralized, giving governors more power relative to the president.[19]

Unfinished Agenda

Vicente Fox had worked for Coca-Cola México, starting as a route supervisor and eventually becoming CEO. In 1979, he returned to his family ranch in Guanajuato, where he managed a large vegetable farm. In 1988, he entered politics as a member of the Chamber of Deputies. Nine years later, as a popular PAN governor of Guanajuato, Fox blithely announced his intention to run for president. Fox was viewed by all as a maverick—someone with no obligations to the system, someone who would bring change. Fox ran on a platform of change. Surprisingly, some of Mexico's business leaders who were sick of business as usual secretly funded the Fox campaign. On June 2, 2000, Fox stunned the political establishment by defeating Francisco Labastida, the PRI candidate.

After his inauguration on December 1, Fox unveiled a cabinet that included technocrats and liberals committed to reform. As finance minister, Fox chose Francisco Gil Díaz, a University of Chicago–trained economist and former CEO of Avantel SA. Luis Derbez, a former World Bank executive and economics PhD, became economics minister. Other key appointments included Carlos Abascal as labor minister, Ernesto Martens Rebolledo as energy minister, and Josefina Vázquez Mota as social development minister.

The macroeconomy seemed relatively strong in the early months of 2001. GDP during the previous year had grown at 6.9 percent—a rate not seen since the "Mexican miracle." Investment was a healthy 21 percent of GDP, while trade (exports and imports) had grown to an amazing 70 percent of GDP. Inflation, while still high at 9.5 percent, was declining steadily. So was unemployment. Real wages, after the "tequila crisis," had dropped 33 percent and had only come back by about 7 percent. Thus, unit labor costs were down sharply, producing booming exports to the United States. But it was the budget where Zedillo had really made improvements. As a percentage of GDP, the deficit was down to 1 percent and had not exceeded 2 percent since 1992. As a consequence, net public debt had fallen from 39 percent to 23 percent, and the external portion had shrunk to just half of that. The exchange rate appeared to have stabilized at about 9.5 pesos per dollar.

For sure, there were still problems. There were several "off-budget" deficits, including the Institute for Protection of Bank Savings' liabilities (these were government obligations incurred when the banking system was bailed out in 1996–1997) and some oil and gas subsidies known as Pidigregas. Savings were still low, and while nominal interest rates had fallen substantially, the real rates at 6 percent were still too high for financing domestic business. The current account of the balance of payments was negative by nearly $17 billion—partly because of a trade deficit of $7.8 billion, but mostly due to the outflow of net income (dividends and interest) of nearly $13 billion. Temporarily, at least, this was being financed by $13 billion of incoming foreign direct investment.

Thus, in Fox's first one hundred days in office, his administration could focus either on finishing the political reform or on attending to the pressing social problems that plagued the Mexican people. Unfortunately, the president no longer had the power necessary to control the legislative agenda. Although Fox had run against the presidential system, he did not realize how much the system had already changed. He thought that everyone in Congress would jump to implement his programs. Yet while he was a charismatic leader, Fox really had few political skills. He knew next to nothing about negotiation. He might have avoided criticizing the past and negotiated with the PRI. Instead, he ridiculed the PRI, eventually leaving himself (and the PAN) isolated in the political process.[20]

In his campaign, Fox had promised to improve education, health care, and infrastructure; to deal with the deteriorating environment and an energy sector approaching crisis; and above all, to improve the lot of migrants, Indians, and the poor. He had convinced himself that social reform rather than political reform should thus be the administration's agenda.

Indeed, nearly half of Mexico's population lived in poverty. According to the World Bank, 50 million Mexicans were poor, with incomes of less than $2 per day, while 24 million were extremely poor, with incomes of less than $1 per day. The top 20 million, however, received more than 60 percent of total income. This maldistribution (a Gini coefficient of 0.55) had a geographic component as well. Most of the relatively affluent Mexicans lived in northern Mexico or the Federal District. The poor, including some 10 million Native Americans, lived mostly in the south—in Chiapas, Oaxaca, Tabasco, and Veracruz. One-third of Mexican workers made less than the minimum wage of $4 per day; some 42 percent of the workforce made just twice the minimum.[21]

There were a host of reasons for this severe inequity—land inheritance, underdeveloped financial markets, gender discrimination, (perhaps) globalization, and (for sure) education. In 2000, the average Mexican child received only 7.7 years of schooling. And this varied sharply by region—it was much higher in the north and lower in the south, far worse in rural communities than in major cities. Many low-income families had too few resources to finance the costs (transportation, food, books, and clothing) even of public schools. And the public schools were generally substandard, with poorly trained and underpaid teachers, few books, no computers, and overcrowded and decrepit classrooms. Anyone who could afford to send their children to private schools did so.

For both the poor and the poorly educated, the Fox administration intended to expand resources. The Zedillo administration had begun a successful program called Progressa, which increased welfare payments to poor families according to how long their children stayed in school. In 2001, Social Development Minister Vázquez received a 4 percent increase in her budget and expanded the program further—renaming it Oportunidades. Enrollment rates expanded, and the government moved the cutoff for mandatory schooling to nine years. Some progress was made in retraining teachers and refurbishing classrooms, and educational spending was retargeted from 5 percent to 8 percent of the federal budget.[22]

Another key area of social reform was labor. While the formal labor force had experienced declining unemployment, this effect was partly due to the growth of informal labor—people working outside the formal economy, who received no benefits and paid no taxes. Informal underemployment was thought to be 15–18 percent.

Yet even among the formal workforce there were problems. Decades of strong and corrupt unionism had led to increasing labor costs, restricted work hours, all sorts of mandatory benefits, and absolute rigidity in firing rights. By one calculation, the base salary of Mexican workers was less than 45 percent of compensation.

Carlos Abascal, the labor minister, proposed replacing the Pactos with a Council for Productive Sector Dialogue, which would help maintain low wages, improve productivity, and build support for reform of Mexico's labor law, enacted more than two decades earlier when Marxist sentiments were rampant. The Fox administration was proposing a reform that would introduce probation periods, during which newly hired workers could be fired; more flexibility in working hours, making part-time work more attractive; simplifications of bureaucratic requirements; and measures to reduce corruption. Political progress, however, had been slow. There were fewer strikes, but wage increases barely exceeded the inflation rate. A somewhat watered-down version of this labor initiative was expected to pass in December 2004.[23]

Environmental degradation was a third key area of reform. Not only was the air in Mexico's cities polluted, but the water supply was experiencing severe losses. Desertification was destroying arable land, and 50 percent of Mexico's drinking water supply was lost through leaky pipes. Industrial wastes and sewage contaminated much of the supply. Too many farmers and mining concerns were subsidized, absorbing 70 percent of the water supply at no cost. A third problem was the loss of six hundred thousand hectares of southern forests annually. Illegal logging and slash-and-burn practices were destroying biodiversity and eroding topsoil through deforestation.

Victor Lichtinger, a Stanford economics student and previous administrator of NAFTA's Commission for Environmental Cooperation, was appointed minister of SEMARNAT—the environmental ministry. While Mexico's environmental laws were reasonably strong, they were simply not enforced. The ministry had too few resources and was plagued by corruption. Although Lichtinger announced a national crusade for waters and forests, with plans to induce local communities to get involved, progress was slow, to say the least. Although he made some progress with forests, water remained a huge problem as long as it bore no price. A frustrated Lichtinger resigned in 2003 and reentered the private sector.

PEMEX was a fourth major problem that Fox wanted to repair. As noted earlier, this huge state-owned company had expanded rapidly in the 1970s as the Portillo administration poured foreign capital into exploration, production, refining, and petrochemicals. But the oil giant, now producing more than 3 million barrels daily, was the government's chief source of funds. Thus, for nearly two decades, it was left with too few retained earnings to reinvest. Its oil reserves were depleting, its producing fields were becoming inefficient, and its refineries and petrochemical plants were decrepit. Natural gas, moreover, was largely wasted, and PEMEX imported from the United States. The electric sector, which burned oil and gas, was likewise inefficient, subsidizing residential consumers and agriculture, and the price for industrial users.

The Fox administration appointed Raúl Muñoz Leos, the former DuPont México CEO, as director general of PEMEX. Muñoz was charged with cutting costs, reducing the workforce (by one hundred and twenty thousand), and reinvesting. But without reform in the labor laws, reform in the electric sector, or fiscal relief, Muñoz was able to make little headway. Indeed, he could scarcely control the four major operating units—exploration and production, refining, natural gas, and petrochemicals—of this vast state-owned enterprise. He actually told me that when he called the four executive vice presidents to a meeting at headquarters, he could not compel them to come. Muñoz too announced his resignation, in October 2004.

To finance his social, environmental, and energy reforms, President Fox proposed a major tax reform, removing exemptions and standardizing the value-added tax at 15 percent on everything—even food and clothing. Mexico's tax-to-GDP ratio was not only the lowest in the OECD but among the lowest in Latin America. Without PEMEX revenues, taxes dropped to 15 percent of GDP. Too few people and too few companies paid taxes, and here again, corruption was an issue. Fox was determined to relieve the budget's reliance on the retained earnings of PEMEX, allowing the company to modernize and expand. Thus, a tax hike was crucial to raise government revenues and realize the social agenda.

But to get it through the Chamber of Deputies, Fox would need the PRI or the PRD to support his party, the PAN. The PRD considered the tax reform regressive and refused to help in any way. The PRI, likewise, had opposed the legislation for political, as well as ideological, reasons. Thus, nothing had happened during the succeeding four years. There was some hope for a compromise early in 2005, but Mexico could not wait indefinitely.

Mexico and the Global Economy

While fiscal and social reform hung in political limbo, events in the global economy swirled about Mexico unremittingly. The U.S. slump combined with 9/11 threw the Mexican economy into recession. Not until 2004 did Mexico really recover. That, combined with rising Chinese competitiveness, severely damaged Mexico's maquilas and added to Mexican unemployment. By the end of 2003, nearly three hundred maquilas had closed their doors, laying off three hundred thousand workers. Ten years of NAFTA had made Mexico an economic appendage of the United States, which absorbed 88 percent of its exports. (See table 6-1 for details on Mexico's performance during these years.)

The effect of this slump, however, was to shake Mexico's inertia. Some Mexicans had finally begun to realize the pressure from international competitiveness. That is, waiting for another sextenio to see the completion of political transition and real progress with economic reforms would not work. The world—Singapore, Brazil, South Africa, Turkey, and especially India and China—would not wait. So the modernization of Mexico's institutions that affect competitiveness, the improvement of secondary and technical education, perhaps the targeting of its strongest industries (electronics and automobiles), and the simplification of unnecessary regulation were among the targets of opportunity identified by the president's office.

Somehow, this realization of a few technocrats had to be extended to all Mexicans—workers and labor unions, students and teachers, parents, business leaders, and legislators. They needed to see that $6,000 per capita was not only inadequate for a decent life, but it was not sustainable in the face of overwhelming global competition. They needed to realize that Mexico's development strategy had passed through three phases—import substitution, resource and debt-leveraged growth, and structural adjustment. But phases four and five—resuscitating the poor, rural, and uneducated population and modernizing the institutions that business needed—still lay ahead and could not wait.

After the election of 2006, Mexico's new president will need a political coalition capable of legislating—to implement a strategy for development. And he or she will need to finish modernizing Mexico's institutions—especially in finance, law, infrastructure, energy, and the environment. Mexico needs to leverage its relationship between the United States and South America to develop the supply side of its economy—petroleum and natural gas, productivity, and above all, education. If it can become a midrange competitive supplier of value-added goods—better than China and cheaper than the United States—it can grow. And if it grows at 4–6 percent annually and alleviates corruption, Mexico can use the revenues to fix its social problems.

Mexican business, however, needs to be more involved in the economic strategy of government. And of course, I mean "involved" in an upright, unself-interested manner. Large Mexican corporations, together with foreign investors (like GE, Citicorp, and DaimlerChrysler) wield substantial re-

TABLE 6-1

Mexico's economic performance, 2001–2005

	2000	2001	2002	2003	2004	2005
Real GDP	6.6%	−0.1%	0.7%	1.3%	4.0%	3.0%
Customer price index	9.5%	6.4%	5.0%	4.5%	4.5%	4.0%
Exports (billions of U.S. dollars)	166.5	158.5	160.8	164.9	184.7	213.7
Imports (billions of U.S. dollars)	175.4	168.4	168.7	170.5	192.5	221.3
Exchange rate (pesos/U.S. dollars)	9.46	9.34	9.66	10.79	11.29	10.90

Source: Organisation for Economic Co-operation and Development, *Economic Survey of Mexico*, January 2004; Economic Intelligence Unit, *Mexico Country Report*, March 2005.

sources. They need to actively support good government—participating in policy discussions, acting to prevent corruption, and facilitating policy so that it doesn't end in legislative gridlock. If a sufficient block of Mexican leadership would take responsibility for Mexico's development strategy, I am certain that the country's performance would benefit—significantly.

Mexico has great promise, but it is time to realize that promise—now.

———w———

South Africa

GETTING IN GEAR

"THE TIME TO BUILD is upon us," commented Thabo Mbeki just before Christmas 2004. Although he was speaking about racial harmony, he could as easily have meant the economy. While much had been accomplished in South Africa during the ten years since the end of apartheid—a peaceful transition, structural adjustment to global competition, and fiscal probity—economic growth remained mediocre and unemployment was still unacceptably high. Almost certainly, thought Mbeki, it was time for a new strategic initiative.

Mbeki's remaining three years in office would no doubt be judged by his administration's success in stimulating economic growth while mitigating the AIDS epidemic and facilitating the transition to black economic empowerment. To do this, the government had made significant adjustments to its strategy. It would now ramp up its fiscal stimulus, spending for infrastructure, education, and health care. It would forgo further privatizations, relying instead on improvements to public service. And it would aggressively pursue black economic empowerment. Externally, Mbeki would continue to foster a peaceful self-policed southern Africa and an increasingly cooperative South African Development Community.

Whether these initiatives would work—that is, accelerate South Africa's economic growth, reduce unemployment, and enhance international competitiveness—depended in part on the social, political, and economic investments of the previous ten years.

An Extraordinary History and Geography

The cone of South Africa occupies 1.2 million square kilometers, bordered by oceans on two sides and five countries to the north—Namibia, Botswana, Zimbabwe, Swaziland, and Mozambique—and completely surrounding Lesotho. It is divided into two main regions—a relatively arid inland plateau and coastal plains—by an escarpment dominated by the Drakensberg Mountains. Climatically, it is divided into a winter-rainfall area in the southwest and a summer-rainfall one in the east.

These zones were sufficiently different that for more than two thousand years, relatively little interaction occurred between the pastoral people of the west (the Khoisan) and the Iron Age cultivators (the Bantu tribes) that occupied the east. However, archeological research in the past ten years has provided significant evidence of *Homo sapiens* occupation for at least a hundred thousand years by hunter-gatherers in South Africa. (Indeed, many biologists believe that *Homo habilis* and *Homo erectus*, the predecessors of modern humans, likely originated in southern Africa nearly 2 million years ago.)

Among the Bantu tribes in the Limpopo Valley, there is evidence of sophisticated material and political culture in the third or fourth century AD—a tribal life with dialects of the same language, the modern forms of which are Xhosa and Zulu. Sorghum was the primary crop and cattle the primary source of protein. Iron, copper, and gold were mined from surface deposits for simple tools and jewelry.[1]

Europeans, representing the Dutch East India Company, arrived at Table Bay (the harbor at Cape Town) in 1652, establishing a fort and refueling station. For the remainder of the century, immigrants gradually spread north of Cape Town, encroaching on the grazing lands of Khoikhoi herders. Slave labor was imported from elsewhere in Africa and from India. As colonial farmers (*trekboers*) penetrated northward, conflict between the Dutch and Khoikhoi became widespread. By the middle of the eighteenth century, the Dutch had begun exerting control over indigenous laborers, imposing travel passes on "bastard Hottentots" (*Hottentot* was another name for the Khoikhoi) and indenturing women. The language of the Dutch settlers, a simplified version of Dutch, evolved into Afrikaans.

When the British captured the Capetown region in 1795, they inherited a thinly settled, loose-knit territory. Until driven out in 1819, Xhosa farming people overran the territory far to the west of the Fish River. Trekboers periodically rebelled, and Khoikhoi were trying to maintain some degree of autonomy. The British cared about the Cape mainly as a stepping-stone to India, where the British East India Company engaged in highly profitable trade.

Autocratic British governors were forced by the Crown to abandon the slave trade in 1806 and slavery altogether in 1828. Ordinance 50 was intended to make "Hottentots and other free people of colour" equal before the law. Enforcement, however, by both British and Afrikaans settlers, did not curtail discrimination or usurp the entrenched domination of whites.

As British colonists expanded throughout the southeast, they came increasingly into conflict with Xhosa, who had occupied the land for centuries. A series of battles, disease, and cattle slaughters eventually broke the back of Xhosa resistance, pushing the Xhosa northward where they ran into Zulus and the powerful forces of Shaka.

Meanwhile, the Afrikaners, who could not tolerate British domination in the south, were migrating northward in the Great Trek, between 1836 and 1854. Similarly, these migrants faced repeated conflicts with elements of the Zulu kingdom, more or less ending victoriously in 1838, when European rifles killed more than three thousand Zulus at the Battle of Blood River. Thereafter, Afrikaners formed semi-independent states of Natal, the Orange Free State, and Transvaal.

A British census in 1865, anticipating the racial distinctions of apartheid, reported a Cape population of one hundred eighty thousand whites (British and Afrikaners), two hundred thousand Hottentots and others collectively called "colored," one hundred thousand Kaffirs (black Africans), and a few thousand Asians.[2]

In 1867, Shalk van Niekerk, a farmer in Hopetown, on the border of the Cape Colony, was engaged in buying an adjacent piece of land. While visiting the prospective farm, he noticed children playing klip-klip, a game of five stones and pebbles. One of the children held a large crystal, in which van Niekerk expressed interest; the mother said he could keep it. A friend, to whom he showed it a few months later, thought it looked like a diamond. When it was assayed by a geologist, it proved to be a 21-karat diamond—the Eureka—which van Niekerk sold in London for five hundred pounds. Two years later, when a shepherd brought him a similar stone, he paid five hundred head of sheep and immediately had it assayed—the Star of Africa weighed 83.5 karats. The rush was on!

Over the next two decades, Kimberly became the world's center of diamond mining. And less than twenty years later, about five hundred miles northeast, gold was discovered in what would soon be Johannesburg. These immense discoveries inspired massive immigration, changing the face of South Africa forever. Cecil Rhodes acquired control of the Kimberly mines, consolidating them under the name De Beers. And eventually, platinum, chrome, and a half dozen other rare minerals were discovered, making South Africa the world's leading producer of precious minerals.[3]

But the mines also changed South Africa for the worse. The British high commissioner issued rules that *de facto* excluded black persons from owning mines. Gradually, a two-tiered, racially segregated workforce and migratory social system emerged. The gold-mining area was organized in the quasi-autonomous Transvaal Republic, governed by Paul Kruger. Kruger's efforts to expand the Transvaal's autonomy eventually clashed with Cecil Rhodes, by then governor of the Cape Colony. When negotiations failed in 1899, the Boer War ensued. Britain adopted a scorched-earth policy, leaving thousands of Afrikaners dead and placing women and children in concentration camps.

British victory and the Peace of Vereeniging led to the establishment of British colonial rule. South Africa, in the words of High Commissioner Alfred Milner, would be "a self-governing white community, supported by well-treated and justly-governed black labour from Cape Town to the Zambesi."[4] Yet black Africans were disenfranchised and ruled by "pass laws" enforced by the military. Colonial elections in 1907 were won by Afrikaners Louis Botha and Ian Smuts, who assumed control of the Union of South Africa when it gained independence three years later.

Apartheid

The United Party, led by Botha and Smuts, dominated an era of formal segregation from 1910 to 1948. While racial discrimination prevailed in many countries, including the United States, in South Africa race and class coincided. Whites dominated the capitalist economy, while blacks were poor, unskilled, and uneducated. Race mattered even in industrial relations. Unionized white mineworkers, for example, earned eleven to fifteen times as much as black mineworkers. Not surprisingly, the income gap between whites and blacks was huge. Thus, by the 1990s, the top 10 percent of South Africa's population earned sixty-seven times that of the bottom 20 percent. South Africa scored 0.58 on the Gini index—worse than Mexico (although not quite as bad as Brazil).[5]

Under Botha and Smuts, South Africa was ruled as a gradually tightening racial state. In 1911, the Mines and Works Act granted white workers a monopoly on skilled jobs. In 1913, the Native Lands Act prohibited black Africans from purchasing land outside racial reserves. A 1922 law authorized urban governments to enforce locations of black residence.

Black South Africans resisted, of course, but gradually adapted. They formed various political organizations, the most important of which was the African National Congress (ANC) in 1912. Headed by lawyers, clergy, and journalists, the ANC sought constitutional means of opposing racism, but to no avail. More radical organizations, such as the Industrial and Commercial Workers Union, were ruthlessly suppressed. Eventually, a group of young ANC radicals published a platform against segregation—*African's Claims in South Africa*. Among this group were Oliver Tambo, Walter Sisulu, and Nelson Mandela.

As blacks migrated to cities, the Afrikaans establishment became increasingly worried about race relations. The word *apartheid* was coined by an Afrikaner intellectual to mean "apartness." When the National Party won the election in 1948, the prime minister appointed Hendrik Verwoerd to be minister of native affairs. Over the next sixteen years, the last eight of which Verwoerd was prime minister, apartheid was implemented in its most brutal form.

According to historian Leonard Thompson, four ideas were at the heart of apartheid. First, the population was composed of four racial groups—white, colored, Indian, and African—each with its own culture. Second, whites, the most civilized, were entitled to absolute control over the state. Third, white interests should prevail over black interests. And fourth, whites composed a single nation (of British and Afrikaners), while blacks belonged to ten geographically distinct groups, eventually organized in reserves.[6]

These ideas were written into a series of laws: the Prohibition of Mixed Marriages Act, the Immorality Act, and the Population Registration Act. Under the Group Areas Act of 1950, cities were divided into zones where members of only one race could live. An estimated 3 million blacks were forcibly resettled. "If the native in South Africa today," testified Verwoerd in 1953, "is being taught to expect that he will live his adult life under a policy of equal rights, he is making a big mistake."[7]

Repressive laws just kept coming: the Riotous Assemblies Act (1956), the Unlawful Organizations Act (1960), the Sabotage Act (1962), the Internal Security Act (1976), and so on. To enforce apartheid, the bureaucracy was expanded and a large security force created, operating with increasing impunity. Under the combined weight of repression, poverty, and forced resettlement, black community eventually broke down. By the 1980s, millions lived in Soweto, Crossroads, and other segregated ghettos—in one- or two-room shacks, without plumbing, fresh water, or electricity. Uneducated children stole to survive until they eventually acquired arms.

Resistance persisted. As early as 1955, the ANC organized a huge meeting in Kliptown near Johannesburg. Thousands of delegates, assembled as the Congress of the People, adopted the following charter: "We the People of South Africa declare for our country and the world to know that South Africa belongs to all who live in it, black and white, and that no government can justly claim authority unless it is based on the will of all the people."

Violence escalated. In Sharpeville, as 5,000 people demonstrated peacefully in 1960, the police killed 69. Three years later, the ANC leadership was arrested. Nelson Mandela and Walter Sisulu received life sentences at the prison on Robben Island. In 1976, when black schoolchildren demonstrated in Soweto, a police crackdown killed 575 people. Another leader, named Steve Biko, formed the South African Student Organization but was beaten to death in police detention in 1977.

Finally, that same year, the world intervened. The UN Security Council imposed an arms embargo on South Africa, and Vice President Walter Mondale told Prime Minister Vorster that the United States supported majority rule. As western firms withdrew their investment, the South African government invested in oil, power, minerals, and manufacturing to duplicate imported sources of capital goods. In 1985, Chase Manhattan precipitated a financial crisis when it refused to roll over its loans to South Africa. And faced with intensive citizen pressure, the U.S. Congress, over President Ronald Reagan's veto, passed the Comprehensive Anti-Apartheid Act, imposing an economic boycott on South Africa.

Transition

GDP growth had long since begun to slow; by 1986, it reached zero. Given the incredibly inefficient investments by government to ensure autonomy, total factor productivity had actually turned negative. South Africa was losing ground. And it certainly did not help that when gold prices rose to $800 per ounce, the real exchange rate of the rand strengthened, making South Africa less competitive than ever. As the current account turned negative, unemployment rose even further. Income per capita actually peaked in 1981, long before sanctions were applied.

As the domestic situation worsened, groups of British and even Afrikaners began organizing for reform, holding meetings outside of South Africa and searching for some way out. Botha, meanwhile, tried to substitute an ideology of survival for one of white solidarity—any way to hold Afrikaners' nationalism together. With the United States and Europe clearly opposed to apartheid, the Soviet Union too began making noise about a negotiated settlement. The ANC, previously opposed to anything except a unilateral solution, now indicated from Lusaka, Zambia, that if Nelson Mandela were released, a negotiated settlement was possible. The break came in 1989, when Botha, the rancorous "Old Crocodile," stepped down due to ill health and was replaced by a far younger Frederick de Klerk.[8]

Although appearing as a loyal nationalist apparatchik, de Klerk saw the handwriting on the wall. On February 2, 1990 in a speech to Congress that stunned the nation, de Klerk lifted the bans not only on the ANC but on all of South Africa's opposition institutions, suspended capital punishment, and freed political prisoners. Nine days later, after twenty-seven years and a round of secret discussions with de Klerk, Nelson Mandela stepped out of prison. Later that year, the basic apartheid laws were repealed. Two more years of talks produced an interim constitution endorsed by de Klerk, Mandela, and eighteen political parties.

All South African citizens went to the polls for the first time in April 1994. In a surprisingly free and peaceful election, they gave the ANC 63 percent of the vote. Nelson Mandela was inaugurated as president on May 19, 1994. It took two more years to write a new constitution.

South Africa would have a federal government with a two-house parliament and nine provinces—each with a premier, regional legislature, and significant local authority. The Parliament consisted of the 400-seat National Assembly and the 90-seat Senate, directly proportionate to democratic elections. President Mandela and Deputy President Thabo Mbeki represented the dominant party—the African National Congress—with 252 seats. The National Party, with 82 seats, was represented by Deputy President de Klerk. Twenty-seven cabinet ministers ran the executive branch. The constitution contained several distinctive features, including a bill of rights, a council of traditional leaders, a commission on human rights, and recognition of eleven official languages.[9]

As part of his effort to create a peaceful and unified South Africa, Nelson Mandela took a number of early steps toward racial reconciliation. He visited ex-president Botha at Botha's home and dined with the administrator of the prison at Robben Island. When South Africa defeated New Zealand in the largely white sport of rugby, Mandela donned a Springbok shirt and walked out onto the field to congratulate the team; the Afrikaans audience went wild!

One of South Africa's most distinctive institutional decisions was Mandela's creation of the Truth and Reconciliation Commission, headed by Archbishop Desmond Tutu, the Nobel laureate. The objective of this multiracial commission was to investigate the human rights abuses that had occurred under apartheid. Beginning in December 1995, the commission heard horrific stories of violence. Under its amnesty program, the worst criminals of apartheid came forward and apologized for their crimes. Despite its many critics, both white and black, the Truth and Reconciliation Commission was generally credited with achieving racial healing by the time it concluded in 1998.

The New South Africa

The end of apartheid brought new changes to the division of South Africa (see figure 7-1). Gauteng was the smallest of the nine new states but had the largest, most urban population in Johannesburg, Soweto, and Pretoria. The Western Cape, where Cape Town is located, held a concentration of business. KwaZulu-Natal, where the city of Durban is located, was the third-largest province by population and disposable income. The country's infrastructure, due to apartheid's legacy, was bifurcated. Eskom, the state-owned utility, generated forty thousand megawatts of electric power at 2.3 cents per kilowatt-hour (compared to 7 cents, for example, in the United States). Similarly, the country had twenty-one thousand kilometers of railroads, fifty-eight thousand kilometers of highways, and 5 million telephone connections; modern radio and television broadcasters; port facilities; and air

FIGURE 7-1

Republic of South Africa

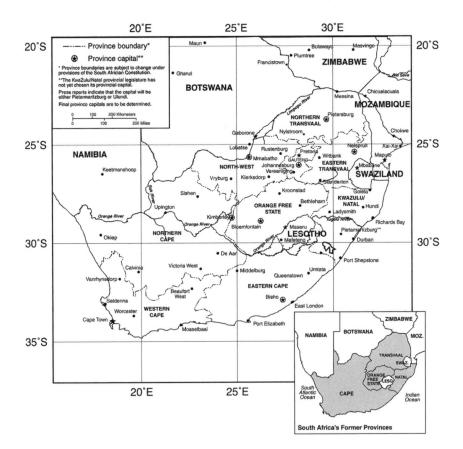

Source: Courtesy of the University of Texas Libraries, The University of Texas at Austin.

transportation. State-owned medical and industrial laboratories yielded a first-world health-care system and a globally competitive weapons industry. All of this made parts of urban South Africa look European. Yet for 30 million to 35 million black people, this infrastructure meant little. It neither serviced them nor benefited them financially.

Because of South Africa's apartheid-driven investments, its business structure was highly concentrated. Corporate acquisitions had resulted in a number of interlocking conglomerates. These were dominated by a few huge financial institutions—Old Mutual, Sanlam, Standard Bank, Absa, First National Bank, Nedcor, and Investec (each with more than R50 billion in assets). Among mining houses, Anglo American, Gencor, Gold Fields of South Africa, Anglovaal, and Johannesburg Consolidated Investment (JCI) were the leaders. South Africa's industrials included the Rembrandt Group (tobacco and mining), Anglo American, South Africa Breweries, Sappi (paper), Sasol (synthetic gasoline and chemicals), and a half dozen other large firms with assets in excess of R10 billion. Eskom was the third-largest electric company in the world. Two dozen other financial houses and nearly fifty other firms had assets in excess of R4 billion. Foreign firms—such as Royal Dutch/Shell, Siemens, and Volkswagen—were also major investors in South Africa.

Unbundling and black economic empowerment were structural phenomena that proceeded hand in hand after 1994. *Unbundling* referred to the restructuring of business ownership by selling off the diverse operating units owned by large conglomerates. *Black economic empowerment* was an effort, at first voluntary but eventually mandated, to encourage the rise of black managers and owners. Through the use of pension funds from black unions, bank debt, and leveraged buyouts, a series of increasingly large mergers had resulted in eighteen black-controlled firms listed on the Johannesburg Stock Exchange by 1997. Led by the spin-off of Johnic from Anglo American, more and more black-owned groups catapulted into the financial limelight. MetLife, New Africa Investments Ltd., and a dozen other firms controlled about R35 billion in assets by 1997. A new black business leadership—led by Cyril Ramaphosa, Dikgang Moseneke, and others—was emerging.

South Africa also had a well-developed (some would say too well-developed) system of labor organizations. There were more than two hundred unions representing more than 3 million workers. These were organized into several federations, the largest and most powerful of which was the Congress of South African Trade Unions (COSATU). These unions lobbied successfully for the Labor Relations Act of 1995, redefining the basic relationship between employer and employee. The Basic Condition of Employment Act of 1997, amended again in 2000 and 2002, created bargaining councils for wages, workplace forums for plant-level issues, maximum hours, vacations, sick time, and maternity leaves, and a Commission for Conciliation, Mediation and Arbitration.

Social Challenges

Decades of apartheid had created an array of social challenges that demanded immediate attention if a democratic state were to survive. Among these were crime, education, unemployment, infrastructural expansion (housing, electricity, and water), immigration and emigration, and AIDS. All of these issues were made more difficult by the racial issues that encompassed them.

Crime

Poverty combined with a lack of education and nearly two decades of revolutionary resistance had made crime endemic in South Africa. It had long since become acceptable for armed teenage dropouts to attack the systems that had oppressed them. Criminal syndicates eventually emerged to organize the drug trade, auto theft, and truck hijacking.

The most serious problems were murder, rape, motor vehicle theft, and robbery. When crime statistics were last released, the number of violent crimes had risen 7.8 percent between 1994 and 1998, to more than 2 million (5,065 per 100,000 people). People worried little about the 100,000 car thefts, compared with more than 13,000 hijackings (theft when the driver is in the car)! The number of murders stood at 2,000 a month, with nearly 30,000 burglaries and auto thefts monthly. [10]

Fear of crime had become palpable in some areas, such as Johannesburg, to the point where people changed their daily behavior. Homes were surrounded by high walls with barbed-wire fencing and elaborate alarm systems. Affluent neighborhoods hired guards on their streets and kept large dogs inside their residential compounds. At first, the South African Police Service was undereducated, underfunded, and understaffed. The governments of Mandela and Mbeki made strident efforts to change this, increasing budgetary support for training and salaries. A new specialized unit called the Scorpions was established to fight crime at the highest levels. In the government's ten-year review, violent crime is reported to have declined about 33 percent, with some other crimes dropping as much as 50 percent. [11]

Education

The start of the school year in 1996 made history in South Africa. For the first time in decades, school began for all children, regardless of race. Compulsory education was required for all children to age fifteen. A new national education department would shape the curricula, build two thousand new schools (sixty-five thousand new classrooms), educate teachers, and rectify the huge gap between per-pupil spending for blacks and whites.

New enrollments increased from one hundred fifty thousand to two hundred eighty thousand, and class sizes reduced from forty-five to thirty-eight. Secondary enrollment was up to 85 percent or more of the eligible population, and the numbers going to college, or junior college, exploded. Education is now the single largest item in South Africa's budget.

Infrastructure

At the outset of democracy, water, sewage, and power had been inequitably provided for the benefit of whites. Only 54 percent of South African homes had running water, and even in cities some 15 percent lacked plumbing. Electricity was a similar story—only 73 percent of urban dwellings and 15 percent of rural ones had power. Housing was perhaps the most pressing shortage. With an estimated 8.3 million households, South Africa apparently contained little more than 3.4 million homes, of which only 1.5 million were "formal housing units," that is, other than shacks. Several million new units were needed if people were to live with any sort of dignity.

The governments of both Mandela and Mbeki sought to improve all these elements of inadequate infrastructure as quickly as possible. But money was the limiting factor. Nonetheless, over the next five to seven years, the government got fresh water to an additional 3.7 million households and provided sanitation to 63 percent of all dwellings. Eskom, the state electric company, installed more than 1.5 million new connections, raising the portion with electricity to 70 percent. The government, meanwhile, built nearly a half million new homes, with subsidies of more than R22 billion. In some ways, this largesse actually outstripped the culture's ability to absorb. Many people who did not understand mortgages actually lost newly acquired homes, and private banks ended up with far too many repossessions.

Unemployment and Immigration

Unemployment, constantly fueled by immigration, was South Africa's largest economic—indeed structural—problem. Years of racially segregated development had left the black population severely underemployed. When the economy broke down during the 1980s, even the inferior jobs for which blacks were eligible stopped growing. Meanwhile, poor and uneducated immigrants from mid-African countries poured into South Africa, where income opportunities, however grim, were superior to those at home. Thabo Mbeki estimated that 2 million to 3 million illegal immigrants were in South Africa in 1996, but the police suggested a number as high as 5 million. The reported population, despite AIDS, swelled from 39 million to 45 million during the postapartheid decade.

Once the economy was freed of apartheid, companies began laying off extra employees as they sought to reinvest and lower costs. Thus, the unemployment rate in the formal economy, at 25.9 percent in 1994, quickly rose to 31 percent by 1998. As shown in figure 7-2, during the next few years, it shrank again, although this was mostly due to discouraged workers dropping out of the unemployment ranks and entering the informal economy. As of mid-2004, the unemployment rate was still 27.8 percent.

AIDS

The most severe problem facing the new South Africa, and certainly the most mismanaged one, was AIDS. During the 1980s, South Africa was relatively free of AIDS. But by 1992, the government had recognized the problem and created the National AIDS Committee of South Africa. The ANC subsequently put in place a plan to deal with AIDS as one of South Africa's twenty social priorities.

Unfortunately, the implementation capacity of the new government was exceedingly weak, while the AIDS epidemic grew quickly. The combination of poverty, violence, mass resettlements, refugees from other parts of Africa,

FIGURE 7-2

Population, workforce, and unemployment in South Africa, 1994–2005

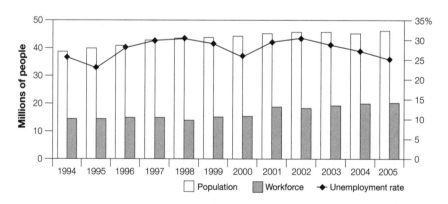

Source: Compiled by author with data from International Monetary Fund, *International Financial Statistics,* various years.

migrant truckers, miners away from families, women's subordinate economic status, and the propensity for women to engage in sex early and for males to have a number of sexual partners (without condoms) all led to the rapid expansion of HIV. By 2004, the United Nations reported that 5.3 million South Africans were infected with HIV—the largest number of individuals in any country. Infection among pregnant women was 28 percent.[12]

In the late 1990s, South Africa's health minister announced that she would permit neither AZT nor NVP antiretroviral therapy to be provided to pregnant HIV-positive women in public health facilities. To make matters worse, in 2000, President Thabo Mbeki publicly questioned the link between HIV and AIDS. Despite international outcries from the medical profession and nongovernmental groups inside and outside South Africa, Mbeki and his health department dragged their feet until 2003. Only after the province of Western Cape defied the government, and leading firms began providing treatments for sick workers, did the South African government finally begin providing antiretroviral therapy to HIV-positive patients.

More than a million South Africans have already died of AIDS-related illnesses, and the long-term consequences of the epidemic will be severe. Life expectancy will fall by about twenty-seven years, from sixty-eight to forty-one years. The government has already increased medical expenditures by a factor of one hundred, and the entire society will long be struggling with dying workers, orphans, reduced family incomes, and the sadness of untold additional deaths.

Growth, Employment, and Redistribution (GEAR)

Planning South Africa's growth for a postapartheid world began in 1986, when Anglo American, the huge mining conglomerate, first generated its high-road/low-road scenarios. In the early 1990s, a team from Royal Dutch/Shell and Harvard University offered a "Change of Gears" strategy, followed in 1994 by the ANC's Program for Reconstruction and Development. Despite its pro-Communist background, the ANC faced the realities of a globalizing post-cold-war world. It laid out plans for rebuilding the infrastructure, creating jobs, reducing trade barriers, privatizing state enterprises, and attracting foreign direct investment.

After two years of slow growth, in the face of wildly optimistic popular expectations, it became clear that South Africa could not afford to implement this plan. Unemployment was actually rising as companies began to lay off workers to structurally adjust. And with gold prices falling, South Africa's current account balance had swung sharply negative, which in February 1996 resulted in a run on the rand. President Mandela abolished the

Program for Reconstruction and Development and authorized a technical team, supervised by Trevor Manuel, the new finance minister, to come up with a more workable plan. That new strategy, called Growth, Employment, and Redistribution (GEAR), committed the government to still more trade and investment liberalization, while adopting a more realistic macroeconomic strategy of tight money and fiscal austerity.

GEAR had seven parts. First came fiscal reform, with the tax base broadened and expenditures cut to reduce the deficit from 5.6 percent to less than 3 percent of GDP by 2000. Monetary reform came second, with a gradual relaxation of capital controls and continuing tight money. Further trade liberalization combined with an active industrial policy was the third part. Public sector restructuring, with better governance and regulation of public corporations, was fourth. The fifth policy, continuing from the reconstruction program, was infrastructural investment. Sixth—a key provision—was to achieve greater flexibility within the collective bargaining system, which would allow globally competitive wages in labor-intensive sectors. And the seventh part was a social pact between business, labor, and government, to facilitate wage and price moderation and thus attenuate the inflation that was weakening the rand.[13]

To achieve the deficit reduction, Manuel's budget relied on increased use of the value-added tax, while curtailing defense expenditures and selling some public assets. To reduce inflation, Chris Stals, governor of the central bank, raised interest rates to 18 percent with the goal of maintaining a constant real exchange rate. The sharp decline of the rand, which had already occurred, threatened to raise import prices and thus contribute to inflation. The high interest rate, while killing domestic investment, at least helped attract foreign reserves—thus keeping the South African Reserve Bank (barely) liquid.

The industrial policy and the labor policy were designed as a package. The minister of trade and industry (MTI) conceived a two-part policy that would encourage both high-tech and low-tech sectors. For the competitive sectors—agriculture and wine, synthetic fuels, mining and metals beneficiation, defense electronics, and financial services—the ministry fostered lower tariffs and structural adjustment. These sectors, it was thought, could compete directly with the EU and the United States. But to encourage job creation, the MTI needed to help low-value-added sectors as well. Encouraging industrial "clusters" and free-trade zones, the minister tried to foster the development of industries such as textiles that could compete with Asia and India for markets in Africa and the Indian Ocean rim.

GEAR's labor policy was also two-pronged. Unions, which provided the political backbone for the ANC, were too entrenched politically to reform.

Thus, for the advanced sectors, in which the unions were strong, the government hoped to hold wage increases to small annual gains in real terms. But for the less value-added sectors, the government sought to encourage a two-tiered wage system, starting new workers at far lower than unionized wages. This would not only encourage job creation and growth, but it would also help keep South Africa competitive with low-wage Asian countries.

Public sector asset restructuring was also important, both to fiscal policy and competitiveness. The government controlled all sorts of assets—ports, railroads and airlines, electric power, oil and gas, and telecommunications, among others. Most of these were inefficient, needing subsidies from the budget. If the government could divest some of these, while creating effective regulatory and governance systems, it could strengthen the budget and induce substantial productivity growth.

The National Economic Development & Labour Council—a tripartite institutional mechanism for conducting discussions between business, labor, and government—was the final optimistic creation of GEAR. As early as 1997, however, this organization was already functioning ineffectively, as COSATU had opted out of participating.

Delivery, not strategy, as one economist put it, was the key to South African success. Over the next several years, the team headed by Manuel and his chief of staff, Maria Ramos, delivered on some of these commitments—deficit reduction, disinflation, stabilizing the rand, and delivering a positive current account. By 2002, the fiscal deficit was reduced to 1.4 percent of GDP, a feat that stabilized the debt and finally reduced inflation to about 6 percent. Interest rates fell from a high of 25 percent to less than 14 percent, and the rand weakened substantially in the wake of the dot-com bubble, reaching a low of R13 per dollar before recovering to 8 and eventually strengthening (against the dollar) to 5.6.

Partly as a consequence of the weak rand, but also because of the restructuring efforts of firms, the trade balance improved substantially, leading to a current account surplus in 2002. Economic growth had recovered, but only to 3 percent annually—not really enough to create the jobs that South Africa so desperately needed. Labor productivity had also increased substantially, but so had real wages—leaving unit labor costs on a gradually upward path. Personal savings, meanwhile, had continued to shrink as newly liberated blacks eagerly sought to consume the fruits of freedom. This, of course, kept up the pressure on real interest rates, which remained extraordinarily high (at about 8 percent).

The real problem was that corporate restructuring, combined with slow economic growth, had hindered the government's efforts to create jobs.

Employment generation had dropped 3.7 percent through 1999, sustaining a 30 percent unemployment rate through 2004. More than half a million employees had lost their jobs as corporations reinvested and struggled to gain competitiveness. Only in 2003 were net new jobs created for the first time in nearly two decades.

Privatization, meanwhile, was disappointing. Although President Mbeki had pledged to accelerate it, announcing divestitures of the South African Forestry Company Ltd., Denel (aerospace), South African Airways, and twenty of Eskom's power plants, nothing had happened. When similar pronouncements were made in 2002, COSATU staged general strikes in opposition to any sort of privatization.

Although Thabo Mbeki had been elected in 1999 with 66 percent of the vote, his economic plans did not seem to be working, at least for growth and job creation. Accordingly, in February 2001, Mbeki began to rethink the government's strategy of fiscal austerity: "We have decided that this year the government itself," said Mbeki in his state of the nation address, "must make a decisive and integrated contribution towards meeting the economic challenges the country faces."[14] He planned to concentrate increased spending on weak areas of infrastructure and target government efforts on exports, tourism, agriculture, and information and communications technologies.

For the next three fiscal years, the South African government began to increase spending—carefully—on infrastructure and social programs (e.g., education and health services). For these stimulative purposes, it added R63 billion to the budget in 2002, R105 billion in 2003, and R44.5 billion in 2004. This had the effect of raising the fiscal deficit from 1.4 percent of GDP in 2001 to 3.1 percent. The treasury ministry viewed these deficits as tolerable if they stimulated growth. Net government debt, which had shrunk to 36 percent, was expected to drift back up toward a tolerable 39 percent by 2007.

With this fiscal policy in place, with policy on AIDS having been resolved, and with Thabo Mbeki taking a leadership role in NEPAD—New Partnership for Africa's Development (an initiative for regional cooperation and using "quiet diplomacy" to deal with Zimbabwe)—the government was ready for elections. In April 2004, the ANC, in a tripartite alliance with the South African Communist Party and COSATU, won a resounding victory with 69.7 percent of the vote and control of all nine provinces. Despite a first term of mixed results, Thabo Mbeki received a mandate for four more years.

Mbeki shuffled his cabinet, while keeping the economic team intact. Trevor Manuel remained in finance, and Alec Erwin moved from trade and industry to public enterprises. Jeff Radebe was moved from public enterprises to transport, with the job of restructuring Transnet (ports and rails) going to Maria Ramos, Manuel's effective assistant. Mandisi Mpahlwa, from finance, would take over trade and industry, and Tito Mboweni would remain at the helm of the South African Reserve Bank.

In addition to the expansionary fiscal policy, two other initiatives would apparently dominate government policy: restructuring state assets and black economic empowerment (BEE).

Privatization seemed dead, not withstanding Alec Erwin's assurance that strategic equity partnerships and outright sales of government assets would continue. But COSATU was adamantly opposed, and many in the government, including President Mbeki, were disappointed that existing privatization had failed to deliver any jobs. Since some of the assets, such as Eskom and Sasol, were incredibly valuable, many bureaucrats believed they should be strengthened and improved, so that their efficient revenue generation would benefit government directly. At organizations like Transnet (railroads) and South African Airways, corporate governance needed strengthening as the first step toward efficient management.

The government's Black Economic Empowerment Act took effect in April 2004. This law represented the black majority's frustration at the slow pace of change in economic equity over the previous ten years. It was true that the income differential between blacks and whites had dropped somewhat. But the gap between middle-class blacks and poor blacks had actually increased substantially with empowerment—resulting in an even higher Gini coefficient of 0.63 by 2002 (up from 0.59 in 1995). Although several laws had been enacted during the late 1990s, requiring varying degrees of affirmative action and preferential job training, the results were still incredibly frustrating to the huge black majority.

Accordingly, the government had proposed a more radical empowerment program in 2002, which was enacted midyear in 2003. The BEE Act called for significant initiatives in hiring, training, promotions, ownership, and control. With broad guidelines stated as goals, the law called on each microeconomic sector to negotiate its own charter—a voluntary commitment to achieve BEE objectives over the next ten years. By the end of 2004, several sectors had agreed to charters, of which the mining, financial, and information technology sectors were certainly the most important.

The Financial Sector Charter, by way of example, was formally signed in the fall of 2004 after two years of extensive negotiations. It is an amazing document! It starts out with a blunt admission: "There are low levels of black participation, especially of black women, in meaningful ownership, control, management and high-level skilled positions in the sector [e.g., banking, insurance, brokerage, and investment banking]." It goes on to acknowledge the long history of discriminatory practices and laws in the workplace that undermine efficiency, competitiveness, and productivity.

The remedies are laid out in careful, extraordinarily precise commitments:

1. HUMAN RESOURCE DEVELOPMENT: investment in training of black managers with the goal of getting 25 percent black people into senior management (4 percent of them women) and 50 percent black people into junior management by 2008

2. PROCUREMENT: striving to develop black-owned suppliers for 50 percent of all procurement by 2008 and 70 percent by 2014

3. ACCESS TO FINANCIAL SERVICES: committing to expand transactional products and services to 80 percent of the population by 2008

4. EMPOWERMENT FINANCING: established quantitative targets for BEE transactional financing and investment

5. OWNERSHIP: targets of a minimum of 25 percent black ownership at each financial institution by 2010

6. CONTROL: a target of 33 percent black people on boards of directors by 2008[15]

Suffice it to say, this is an extraordinary commitment for an entire industry to make, certainly never matched anywhere else on earth. Implementation, however, remains to be seen.

Looking Forward

It must by now be obvious that South Africa is a very complicated place. Thabo Mbeki has his hands full. At this point, I would identify five issues (although there are no doubt many more) that are key to South Africa's success in transforming itself to a nonracial state and succeeding in the global economy.

First, as I have just indicated, is the institutional mitigation of racism through a successful experience with black economic empowerment. The fact that industry sectors are committing to charters that they construct for themselves is an unusually good start. Rebuilding institutions to fit the racial composition and preferences of the populace is necessary. Hopefully, South Africa is strong enough to absorb the costs of this structural adjustment.

Second is government's response to AIDS. The epidemic has already happened, so South Africa at this point can only respond as effectively as possible. Above all, it needs to arrest the growth rate of HIV—currently at about sixteen hundred cases daily. An intensive education campaign—involving all segments of government, schools, the health profession, and nongovernmental organizations (NGOs)—is crucial. Additionally, the government, together with other countries and global NGOs, must do its best to treat AIDS victims with medicines that will mitigate the worst effects of the disease. And its unions, schools, firms, and bureaucracy must work in a timely fashion to replace the experienced workers whom they will lose. This too entails institutional adjustment to difficult circumstances. And this adjustment must be made now—regardless of cost.

Third, South Africa must stimulate savings and investment. Household savings, at less than 2 percent, are totally inadequate to provide resources for the investments that the nation needs. Savings should be encouraged in every way possible, including mandatory savings in a sort of Singapore-style Central Provident Fund. Private investment must also be encouraged. At 17.7 percent of GDP, South Africa's gross fixed investment is less than half the level of its Asian competitors. Given the improvement in tax recovery by internal revenue, perhaps some tax breaks can be used to push investment into the range of 25 percent. This much, at least, is needed if this country is to succeed in global competition.

Fourth, the country needs to maintain low unit labor costs if it is to be competitive. This goal can be accomplished in two ways: reduce nominal wage increases or encourage productivity. Both are easier said than done. The term of wage bargains might be stretched to three or four years, and the level must be preserved at or below the inflation rate. Again, South Africa could take a lesson from Singapore and develop a productivity board to help stimulate productivity in every way possible.

Finally, the South Africa Reserve Bank must keep close control of inflation (currently 4 percent), so that real interest rates can fall to encourage domestic (and foreign) investment. Inflation targeting can be aggressively pursued to get the rate to less than 3 percent.

As President Mbeki knows well, South Africa has incredibly rich resources—natural, human, and institutional. Yet these were grotesquely misused during the decades of apartheid and have only recently recovered through a decade of reform. Now it is time to build on those resources, to push South Africa toward the ranks of developed countries. "South Africa is not going to be a welfare state," Jabu Molaketi, the new deputy finance minister observed; "it needs to be a developmental state."[16]

Well, if South Africa truly is to be a developmental state, its government must craft and implement an effective strategy, resting on a structure of institutions now emerging. South Africa can be a global competitor and continue to develop, but this will take years of hard work and sacrifice by both whites and blacks. Whites must help and indeed encourage the black population to take more and more political and social responsibility, and they will have to be content with a smaller share of the pie. Black leadership, on the other hand, must work intensely and defer consumption if their children are to have a better life.

And above all, South Africa's government must play the leader in establishing these new norms and policies—quickly—as South Africa's competitors around the world won't wait.

—ᴍᴍ—

Saudi Arabia

MODERNIZATION VERSUS WESTERNIZATION

EARLY IN THE TWENTY-FIRST CENTURY, the Kingdom of Saudi Arabia struggled with changes imposed by globalization. For more than thirty years, since the first oil shock in 1973, Saudi Arabia had been modernizing rapidly. Its oil reserves, reported at 261 billion barrels, represented one-fourth of the world's proven reserves. Over three decades, the House of Saud had built a modern infrastructure, several modern cities, eight national universities, huge ports, and some of the world's largest petrochemical complexes. In 2005, it was producing 10 million barrels of petroleum per day. With oil prices approaching $70 per barrel, Saudi Arabia's export revenue would reach $175 billion by year's end.

Yet because of this largesse, the kingdom had been unable to reduce its dependence on oil. More than 90 percent of trade, 88 percent of the government's revenues, and 51 percent of GDP came from petroleum in 2005. Oil was like a drug that effectively drove out other economic opportunities. It kept the exchange rate strong and made Saudi Arabia's non-oil exports uncompetitive. It provided huge government revenues that propped up the monarchy, resulted in maldistribution of wealth, and discouraged reform. And perhaps worst of all, it had done little to stimulate economic growth. For twenty-four years, since 1981, the economy had grown but 1.9 percent annually—substantially lagging behind most other developing countries as well as Saudi Arabia's own birthrate of 3.3 percent.

King Abdullah, the reigning monarch, had adopted a strategy of diversification and development. Yet much of his time was taken by domestic political challenges from liberals, women, and radical fundamentalists. Since 2003, the government had been repeatedly threatened by terrorism and violence.

It had strengthened its domestic security, prosecuted and executed scores of terrorists, and was trying hard to ensure domestic safety. "The killing of the innocent," observed Adel Al Jubeir, the foreign affairs adviser to Crown Prince Abdullah, "regardless of the reason, is a violation of the teachings of all religions, including Islam. The individuals who commit these crimes are outside the bounds of their faith."[1]

Yet for Saudi Arabia, the faith—Islam—is the touchstone and the starting place of the country's long history.

Saudi Arabia's Evolutionary History

The Arabian Peninsula is the result of relatively recent tectonic forces that split off a shield from the African plate. About the size of Europe, the peninsula is bordered by seas on three sides, with mountains in the west on the Red Sea and a huge desert (Rub al-Khali) in the southeast. Saudi Arabia occupies about 80 percent of the peninsula, bordered by Yemen and Oman in the southeast; the United Arab Emirates, Qatar, and Bahrain in the east; and Kuwait, Iraq, Jordan, and Egypt in the north. It was first inhabited just after the last Ice Age, perhaps twenty thousand years ago, by Neolithic hunter-gatherers.

As the region warmed, its population gave way to more advanced civilizations in Dilmun (Bahrain), Magan (Oman), and Babylonia (in adjacent Mesopotamia). The oldest known piece of literature—the Epic of Gilgamesh (1300 BC)—told the story of the great flood that occurred in Dilmun. Eventually, the Sabaean civilization came to dominate southern Arabia while the northwest was controlled by Nabataea. Between these two civilizations were "Arabs," described by biblical and Assyrian texts as nomadic desert dwellers.

Arabs eventually developed as both sedentary and nomadic populations—the former residing in villages and towns associated with oases and wells, the other (Bedouins) breeding livestock and moving about to graze in the sparse desert lands. Commerce was conducted by caravan, from Persia in the east to Egypt and Europe in the northwest. Religion consisted of Judaism, Christianity, and mixes of pagan polytheism. Mecca was an important interior city already venerated by Arabs as the home of the Kaaba—a stone building where Ishmael, Abraham's son, reputedly stamped his foot and a spring appeared.[2]

This was the environment into which Muhammad was born, in Mecca in about AD 570. After growing up as an orphan and working as a shepherd and caravan attendant, Muhammad was a respected member of the Quraysh tribe in Mecca. He eventually married his employer, a widow named Khadija, who bore him six children. Only one daughter, named Fatima, both survived and had children.

In his late thirties, Muhammad had developed an antipathy for the pagan practices of Mecca. After spending much time praying and fasting, he told his wife of a vision he'd had on a retreat to a cave near Mount Hira. He had seen the angel Gabriel, standing aside the horizon. Gabriel told him that he was an apostle of God and directed Muhammad to spread the Koran—a heavenly book—through recitation. This revelation marked the beginning of Islam.[3]

Throughout the remaining twenty-three years of his life, the prophet Muhammad continued to experience revelations that were written down in Arabic in a collection of lyrical passages. The Koran consists of 6,348 verses, organized in 114 chapters. Unlike other religious tracts, there is a single Arabic translation—which is deemed perfect by Muslims: "This (Book) is a clear exposition (of the truth) for mankind (to follow) and a (means of) guidance, and an exhortation to those who guard against evil (and are dutiful to God and mankind)" (3:138).[4]

Islam, the name of the prophet Muhammad's religion, means "submission"—submission to Allah, the supreme being. Islam was monotheistic and rejected the pagan idols that were worshipped in Mecca. Islam recognized heaven and hell, the Judeo-Christian prophets Abraham and Moses, and the Christian Jesus (whom Islam deemed a prophet and explicitly not divine). The Old and New Testaments were recognized as revelations, anticipating the final prophet, Muhammad, and the ultimate revelation, the Koran. Thus, Jews and Christians were deemed People of the Book and tolerated by Muslims, at least initially.

The prophet Muhammad preached his new faith in Mecca, gaining a small group of followers and substantial opposition from established commercial and political interests. Eventually, Muhammad and his followers were forced to leave Mecca, making the *hegira*, or "journey," to Yathrib, an oasis city more than two hundred miles to the north. Muhammad eventually converted the Arab clans of that city, which was renamed (in Arabic) Medina—the City of the Prophet.

In 623, the prophet Muhammad began a campaign to conquer Mecca. After seven years and several major battles, Muhammad and his Muslims entered Mecca peacefully, had the idols in the Kaaba demolished, and established an Islamic state. During the remaining two years of his life, Muhammad expanded his empire across most of the Arabian Peninsula. He died in 632.

Islam

Today there are more than 1 billion Muslims worldwide. As both a religious and sociopolitical system, Islam is based on five devotional tenets, known as the Five Pillars of Islam: (1) testimony of the core tenet, that "There is no God but God [Allah], Muhammad is his Messenger"; (2) praying five times daily; (3) giving alms (the *zakat*) to the poor of one's own clan or the larger community; (4) fasting during *Ramadan*, the ninth month of the Muslim calendar; and (5) the pilgrimage, or *hajj*, to Mecca once during one's lifetime. Islam also includes Six Pillars of Faith: the one God, the angels, the sacred books, the messengers, the day of judgment, and the divine will.

Another Islamic concept is that of *jihad*, or "struggle." There are at least two definitions of jihad. The *greater jihad* refers to a spiritual struggle for moral perfection. The *lesser jihad* refers to a war fought against non-Muslim faiths. It is this concept of lesser jihad that has been misused by extremists to justify acts of terror against non-Muslims.

Muslims follow Islamic dogma called the *Sharia*, meaning "right path," which is based on the Koran; the sayings of the Prophet, which are compiled as the *Hadith*; the studies of Islamic scholars, called the *fiqh*; and the interpretations of Koranic verses, called *tafsir*. There are no priests in Islam, but those who specialize in Koranic studies, called *ulema*, lead the organization of the religion. In Saudi Arabia, the Council of Senior Ulema consults frequently with the king, and during times of controversy, the ulema can issue *fatwas*, or "opinions," on any points in doubt. Fatwas can cover trivial issues, like the sending of flowers to a hospital patient or the banning of the children's video game Pokémon, or more serious issues like the U.S. military's involvement in the Gulf War or Iran's death warrant for the author Salman Rushdie.

The Golden Age of Islam

In the 120 years after Muhammad's death, Islam spread quickly out of Arabia into Persia, Afghanistan, the Ukraine, Iraq, Iran, and Turkey, and through Egypt, across northern Africa, into Spain and Portugal. Islam, meanwhile, had split into two sects: Sunni and Shia. The Sunni, the vast majority in Saudi Arabia, believed that any prayer leader could be an *imam*—or "holy man." Shia, which came to dominate Iran and Iraq, believed in the hereditary divinity of imams from Muhammad's grandson, Ali, down through a series of caliphs (that separated from the Sunni leadership after the fourth imam). While the religious differences between these two groups are minor, the political issues—as in Iraq today—can be significant.

For four centuries, this Islamic empire was ruled by caliphs in Baghdad. This was a golden age for Islam—a time when Islamic culture and scholarship dominated the known world. In astronomy, chemistry, zoology, literature, and the arts, Islamic achievements during these years would eventually become the basis for the Renaissance. The science and literature of Greece was translated into Arabic and thus preserved for the rebirth of scholarship in Europe nearly seven centuries later. This extraordinary interlude in the Dark Ages ended in 1258, when Mogul hordes defeated the Muslims and razed the city of Baghdad.

Saudi Arabia quickly reverted to a hodgepodge of fragmented tribes and clans. Not until the mid-1700s, near Diriya in central Saudi Arabia, did the al-Saud family begin to consolidate power. In 1744, Muhammad ibn Saud formed a pact with a local religious leader named Muhammad Abd al-Wahhab. Al-Wahhab was a strict constructionist of Islam who intended to purify Islam, eradicate cults, and spread his Wahhabi version of Islam far and wide. "You are the settlement's chief and wise man," Wahhab told Ibn Saud. "I want you to grant me an oath that you will perform *jihad* against the unbelievers. You will be *imam*, leader of the Muslim community and I will be leader in religious matters."[5]

Through jihad, the Saud-Wahhabi alliance succeeded in reuniting Saudi Arabia. Town after town fell to Muhammad ibn Saud's invading forces and would thereupon be converted to the teachings of Wahhabi Islam. By 1818, when their forces were defeated by Egyptian soldiers and Ottoman Turks, Saudi Arabia had again become a single state. Various emirates would rule on behalf of the Ottoman empire until the early twentieth century, when once again a descendant of Muhammad ibn Saud—Abdul Aziz ibn Abdul Rahman al-Saud—emerged to unify the country.

Emerging in 1902 from exile in Kuwait, Ibn Saud surprised and conquered the garrison of Riyadh with but forty warriors. From there, Ibn Saud's fighting forces turned to adjacent towns in the Najd. In 1912, he formed the Ikhwan (Brotherhood)—a fierce fighting force that embraced Wahhabi teachings. By the mid-1920s, the brotherhood had conquered most of the Hijaz—the western region that embraced Mecca and Medina. With financial support from the British, Ibn Saud finished his consolidation in 1932, when he proclaimed the Kingdom of Saudi Arabia.

The Al-Saud Dynasty

When Ibn Saud died in 1953, he left forty-three sons and more than fifty daughters. Ibn Saud had used the Islamic provision of four wives liberally, both to expand his family's connections and to satisfy his own voracious lust. A more favorable interpretation credits this exogamous behavior to a clever political strategy of cementing alliances and ensuring the survival of the al-Saud dynasty.

This strategy worked. Today there are some seven thousand to eight thousand members of the ruling family, who control much of Saudi Arabia's wealth, many of the important businesses, and a significant share of government. Since Ibn Saud died, four of his sons have been king—Saud, Faisal, Khalid, and Fahd. Saud was deposed in 1964 on the grounds of incompetence. Faisal was assassinated in 1975, and Khalid died in 1982. King Fahd succeeded Khalid and named his half-brother Abdullah crown prince. To reassert his power and express his deep commitment to Islam, Fahd assumed the title of the Custodian of the Two Holy Mosques.

Fahd, who faced declining oil prices, tried to liberalize the Saudi economy and boost non-oil revenues. The business community, however, resisted many of his proposed reforms. Turning his attention to regional politics, King Fahd helped orchestrate a cease fire between Iraq and Iran in 1988 and acted as a mediator in the Lebanese civil war. And he played a key role in the formation of the Gulf Cooperation Council, a coalition of six Arabian Gulf states to foster regional economic cooperation and development. In 1995, however, Fahd suffered a debilitating stroke. Since then, Crown Prince Abdullah has been the de facto ruler of the kingdom. Popular among Saudis, Abdullah has been committed to economic and social reform.

Until 2005, when he became king, Abdullah struggled to rule under the shadow of King Fahd and the constraints imposed by the Sudairi Seven—the seven sons of Ibn Saud's favorite wife. King Fahd is one of these, together with Princes Sultan, Abdel Rahman, Nayef, Turki, Salman, and Ahmed. Several of these princes hold important positions, including ministers of defense, interior, and foreign affairs. Each would have liked his own family, rather than that of Abdullah, to succeed King Fahd. The 1992 Basic Law of Government authorizes the reigning king to nominate his heir, choosing the "most upright" of Ibn Saud's descendants.

Oil and Development

During the early years of King Saud's reign, the Great Depression had sapped pilgrimage traffic, the principal source of Saudi Arabia's revenues. With the monarchy deep in debt, any source of revenue seemed attractive. Although earlier oil exploration efforts had not paid off, Standard Oil of California (SOCAL) signed an agreement with King Saud in May 1933, giving the company a sixty-year concession for five hundred pounds annually. After two years of promising exploration, SOCAL struck oil at Dammam No. 7, which eventually produced fifteen hundred barrels daily. In 1939, the first tanker with Saudi oil left Ras Tanura.

Recognizing the importance of Saudi oil, the U.S. government provided lend-lease aid to King Saud during World War II. In February 1945, Ibn Saud and President Franklin Roosevelt met on the Navy cruiser USS *Quincy*. A secret agreement, supplanting Great Britain's traditional imperial role, allowed the United States to build an air base at Dhahran in exchange for light weapons and continuing support of Saudi Arabia's oil development. The Arab American Oil Company (Aramco) was formed to produce in Saudi Arabia. It was owned jointly by Exxon, Mobil, SOCAL, and Texaco—four of the largest American oil companies.[6]

By the early 1970s, Saudi Arabia was producing more than 7 million barrels per day. Europe, Japan, and the United States were all net importers. Oil prices stood at about $2.14 per barrel, and by March 1972, spare production capacity in the United States (unused oil production held off the market to support prices) had virtually dissipated. When Libya put price pressure on the United States, a leapfrogging dynamic took hold—with Saudi Arabia, Iran, and then Libya repeatedly raising prices. In October, eleven days after the outbreak of war between Israel and several Arab states, President Nixon chose to rearm Israel. Saudi Arabia decided to use its "oil weapon," declaring an embargo on the United States. Within weeks, oil prices jumped from $3.00 to $11.65 per barrel—the first oil shock.[7]

A second oil shock began late in 1978, with the outbreak of the Iranian Revolution. When Iran's production of 3 million barrels per day went down after October, oil prices jumped once again to about $28 per barrel. When Iraq invaded Iran, prices increased further, stabilizing at $34 (with the spot market price more than $40). In 1981, Saudi Arabia's revenue from its oil exports reached an astounding $113 billion.[8]

Saudi Arabia had become the "swing producer"—the country that dominated the pricing policies of the Organization of the Petroleum Exporting Countries (OPEC) by dint of its large proportion of OPEC capacity and its own production options, thanks to spare capacity. The Saudi oil minister—most famously Ahmed Yamani and more recently Ibrahim al-Naimi—was thus the most influential minister in OPEC, shaping quotas and occasionally pushing ahead with capacity to keep rising oil prices under control.

Still, oil markets are global, and supply and demand both respond eventually to price. Thus, Saudi Arabia had experienced difficulty stabilizing global oil markets. After the second oil shock, high prices sparked new production capacity and conservation. As one can see from figure 8-1, price began falling in mid-1981, reaching a low point in 1986 of about $12 per barrel. Yamani was fired. After a brief recovery during the Gulf War, prices again fell

FIGURE 8-1

Real and nominal crude oil prices, 1970–2005

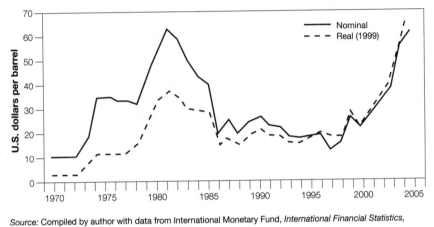

Source: Compiled by author with data from International Monetary Fund, *International Financial Statistics,* various years.

and only began to recover in 1999, once OPEC established a "price band" and made the cuts necessary to balance supply with demand.

With the immense revenues earned in the late 1970s and early 1980s, Saudi Arabia decided to modernize. It let contracts, both foreign and domestic, build a modern infrastructure—power, roads, airports, railroads, ports, and telecommunications. It expanded its cities, its mosques (especially in Mecca and Medina), and built thousands of schools and a handful of universities. And it invested in defense—building a modern air force and a mobile army of two hundred fifty thousand.

The Gulf War

On August 2, 1990, Iraq invaded Kuwait and threatened Saudi Arabia. Iraq quickly conquered Kuwait, declaring it Iraq's nineteenth province. As Iraqi soldiers massed on Saudi borders, King Fahd grudgingly asked for U.S. military assistance. The United States responded by sending six hundred thousand troops with substantial air and naval support. Sheikh Abd al-Aziz ibn Baz, the country's supreme religious leader, issued a fatwa permitting jihad against Saddam Hussein with the help of infidel forces.

Desert Storm commenced with an air campaign on January 17, followed by the rapid invasion of one hundred sixty thousand U.S. troops. The Iraqis, overwhelmed, surrendered on February 28. Kuwait was liberated, Hussein defeated, and the Kingdom of Saudi Arabia protected, although not neces-

sarily from itself. Fundamentalists, including Osama Bin Laden, were out-
raged with King Fahd's "submission" to westerners. Bin Laden wrote: "The
presence of the USA Crusader military forces on land, sea and air of the states
of the Islamic Gulf is the greatest danger threatening the largest oil reserve
in the world. The existence of these forces in the area will provoke the people
of the country and induce aggression on their religion, feelings and pride."[9]

The Economy

The souring of the global economy coincided with the 9/11 terrorist attacks, lowering the demand for oil and driving oil prices down in the fourth
quarter of 2001. The downturn left Saudi Arabia with growth of but 0.5 percent for 2001 and even less—0.1 percent—for 2002. Although the government had run an unusual surplus in 2000, it returned to deficits in 2001 and
2002. Debt, which the government financed domestically, had reached 109
percent of GDP.

Saudi Arabia had no income taxes. Most of the government's revenues
came from oil exports, excise taxes, and the revenue from state-owned enterprises. Its largest expenditure was defense and security (about 37 percent of
the budget), followed by education, debt service, health, water, infrastructure,
and social subsidies. And often outlays exceeded the budget, leaving actual
deficits far larger than planned.

Saudi Arabia's central bank, the Saudi Arabian Monetary Agency, conducted a monetary policy that aimed to maintain the stability of prices and
the exchange rate of the Saudi riyal. The country's inflation rate remained
low—generally less than 0.5 percent. "Monetary conditions are sound and
well managed—liquidity is ample in the banking system, money supply
growth is supportive of GDP growth, inflation is in check, and interest rates
are low," reported the Saudi American Bank.[10] Since June 1986, the Saudi riyal
had been pegged against the U.S. dollar at a rate of SR3.75 per dollar. Whether
or not this was overvalued, however, is of considerable importance.

Saudi Arabia has generally run a trade surplus and a current account
deficit—except for the years since 2000 when high oil prices turned the current account positive. Table 8-1 summarizes the country's transactional relationship with the rest of the world. One can clearly see the reliance on oil
exports, oil's price volatility, and the huge current account surplus earned in
the past couple of years. Second, one notes that trade in services—like transportation, engineering services, IT, and financial services, among others—is
significantly negative. Third, the net transfers are outflows. This represents
the earnings of 6 million foreign workers that they sent home to their families. And finally, one sees that net income, which used to be a significant

TABLE 8-1

Saudi Arabia's balance of payments, 1990–2005 (billions of U.S. dollars)

	1990	1994	1997	2000	2002	2003	2004	2005
Trade balance	22.9	21.3	34.4	51.2	42.9	59.3	67.7	123.3
Export of goods	44.4	42.6	60.7	78.9	72.6	93.2	107.1	174.6
Of which oil was	**39.9**	**38**	**53.2**	**72**	**na**	**63.5**	**77.9**	**156.8**
Imports of goods	−21.5	−21.3	−26.3	−27.8	−29.6	−33.9	−39.4	−51.3
Net services	−19.4	−14.5	−21.7	−20.5	−19.8	−19.3	−23.2	−22.0
Net income	7.9	1.5	2.8	0.3	−0.2	3.0	4.3	0.3
Net transfers	−15.6	−18.7	−15.1	−15.5	−15.9	−14.8	−13.6	−17.4
Current account balance	**−4.2**	**−10.5**	**−0.3**	**15.6**	**11.9**	**28.0**	**51.9**	**87.1**
Net direct investment	1.9	0.3	3	−1.5	−0.6	−0.6	−0.3	0.4
Net portfolio investment	−3.3	8.2	−7.4	−9.4	7.6	na	na	na
Net other investment	0.2	11.5	0.7	−2	−16	−9.6	−17.9	−27.7
Overall balance	**5.4**	**0.1**	**−0.6**	**−2.7**	**−2.7**	**20.9**	**32.0**	**68.9**

Source: Compiled by author with data from International Monetary Fund, *International Financial Statistics Yearbook*, 2004; Saudi Arabian Monetary Authority, *Quarterly Economic Report*, January–March 2006.

source of funds, turned negative by 2002. Wealthy Saudis were earning less on deposits abroad due to low interest rates and have probably been holding those earnings abroad because of a lack of confidence in their own country.

On the capital account, foreign direct investment has generally been negative—Saudis are investing more abroad than foreigners invest there. Portfolio and net other investments bounce around, depending on fiscal deficits, oil prices, and the performance of the Saudi stock market. Overall, Saudi Arabia's foreign exchange reserves have risen, to $87 billion.

Abdullah's Reform Agenda

In the mid-1990s, Crown Prince Abdullah assumed responsibility for a stagnant economy, where per capita income had fallen from nearly $18,000 to less than $7,000. Savings was less than investment, implying a current account deficit. Political opposition and even domestic terrorism was on the rise.

Abdullah's brother had already begun liberalizing the process of political decision making. When Fahd had announced his plans to initiate reform in November 1990, a group of radical ulema had issued a petition entitled "The Letter of Demands." The document listed a set of political reforms that would increase the power of religious leaders. The demands included establishment of an independent consultative council, the repeal of laws and regulations that did not conform to Islamic law, and a requirement for all government officials to be moral. Public wealth was to be evenly distributed. Banks were to be cleansed of usury. And foreign policy could not rely on alliances that were not sanctioned by Islamic law.[11]

Two years later, another group, the King Saud University Committee for Reform and Advice submitted a second letter of demands, entitled "The Memorandum of Exhortation." This letter, which was signed by more than one hundred professors and ulema, listed grievances such as military overspending, government aid to non-Islamic governments, and the airing of television programs that glorified "decadent Western lifestyles." This time, the petitioners demanded that both the government and the ulema be released from their roles as the sole arbiters of Islam. They sought to return to the more decentralized religious system that had existed before Ibn Saud.

In response, King Fahd denounced the radicals but introduced some major reforms, including the Basic Law of Government. While the Basic Law reaffirmed the religious principles and monarchial rule, it clarified succession and created the Consultative Council of 60 members to review government reports and advise the government. The council was expanded to 90 in 1997 and to 120 in 2001. In 2005, Prince Sultan announced that it would expand again to 150 and eventually one-third or even two-thirds of the council's membership would be elected.

The kingdom's strategic planning took the form of five-year plans. Since 1970, these plans had formally laid out the government's development objectives, its major strategic initiatives, and the fiscal and policy objectives of each major cabinet ministry. The seventh plan, adopted in 2000, identified three sets of objectives:

1. SOCIAL OBJECTIVES: with emphasis on safeguarding Islamic values, developing a skilled Saudi workforce, and improving social welfare

2. ECONOMIC OBJECTIVES: focusing on diversification, balanced growth, and higher productivity

3. INSTITUTIONAL OBJECTIVES: including raising the efficiency of government services, privatization, improving administrative regulation, and reorganizing government[12]

In practice, this meant that Abdullah would try to restructure the kingdom's economy, making it more open to a global world. Business was becoming increasingly impatient—"we're becoming a nation of great talks and no action," complained one. "The rigid legal system hindered reform efforts," said another, "as outdated laws allowed no mechanisms of review."[13]

Foreign Investment

By decree in 1999, the crown prince created the eleven-member Supreme Economic Council to meet weekly and formulate new policies. In April 2000, this council approved the radical Foreign Investment Act, allowing 100 percent ownership of real estate by non-Saudis and creating the Saudi Arabian General Investment Authority to encourage foreign direct investment with soft loans, tax holidays, and a process of one-stop shopping.

To kick off interest in foreign investment, Crown Prince Abdullah proposed opening the kingdom's upstream natural gas sector to foreign companies. Saudi Arabia held the world's fourth-largest reported reserves of natural gas, at 204.5 trillion cubic feet. Yet Aramco, focused almost exclusively on oil, produced less than 2 billion cubic feet daily. In 2001, the government designated three core foreign ventures, with large blocks of the kingdom awarded to each of them. ExxonMobil would head two projects and British Petroleum the third, with Royal Dutch/Shell, Phillips, Occidental, Marathon, Total Fina Elf, and Conoco also participating. In exchange for the right to explore and produce, these major international companies would build petrochemical facilities, power plants, and desalination facilities. Together with gas production, this would require at least $25 billion of foreign investment.

After two years of negotiation over price and putative gas reserves, the project collapsed. The foreign companies were cautious and unwilling to commit such capital without better knowledge of reserves and higher guaranteed prices. Only late in 2003 did Royal Dutch/Shell and Total Fina Elf sign a $2 billion deal with the Saudi government.[14]

Diversification

Although the oil industry dominated Saudi Arabia's economy, the non-oil sector generally grew faster in the years leading up to 2004. Growth in agriculture, manufacturing, construction, and financial services all contributed. Subsidies to agriculture resulted in wheat exports and self-sufficiency in poultry and in some fruits and vegetables. This, of course, required huge amounts of free water—a scarce commodity in the desert kingdom. Large investments were made in petrochemicals, steel, rubber, plastics, and construction materials. With its emphasis on infrastructure, the government was the construction industry's biggest client.

Infrastructure Development

By the new millennium, Saudi Arabia's infrastructure was in need of repair and expansion. Population growth fueled the need for housing, electricity, telecommunications, ports, and airports—and above all, water. The seventh five-year plan, for example, identified growth in electricity demand over the period 2000–2004 of 4.5 percent annually. Generating capacity needed to expand from twenty-one thousand to seventy thousand megawatts. Eleven million new telephone lines and full digitization would be needed. Demand for municipal water would increase from 1.8 billion to 2.03 billion cubic meters. This would require investment in expensive desalination plants—again subsidized by the government, since it charges nothing for water.

Privatization

Continuing budget deficits also made privatization of state-owned companies a priority. Despite resistance from bureaucrats, Crown Prince Abdullah announced that he was "keen to progress with privatization in a way that would not negatively impact on the welfare of citizens, especially the less privileged."[15] Given a high unemployment rate, the crown prince hoped to avoid massive layoffs. Nevertheless, he urged privatization efforts to continue in telecommunications (the first one-third of which was sold in 2000) and to spread to electricity, airline, postal service, and railway sectors. In February 2000, Saudi Arabia's ten electricity companies were consolidated into a single joint-stock company, the Saudi Electricity Company. Eighty-five percent would gradually be divested. Saudi Arabian Airlines was also scheduled for privatization, but only after its profitability improved. And in 2005, the government appointed a new board of directors to the Saline Water Conversion Corporation, a step toward that organization's eventual privatization.

Judicial System

A huge backlog of commercial cases had built up over the previous ten years. Simple issues such as debt collection could drag on for six or eight years. Thus, on April 2, 2005, Abdullah issued a royal decree announcing sweeping reforms of the judicial system. He announced the creation of a supreme court, a network of provincial appeals courts, and new dedicated courts for commerce and labor. *Sharia* law, based on the Koran, however, would still serve as the touchstone.

Banks

Saudi Arabia's ten commercial banks operate in the markets for foreign exchange, interbank deposits, government debt, and equity. Three of these were wholly Saudi owned. The Al Rajhi Bank adhered to the Sharia, which outlawed the payment of interest. At the other banks, only a small but quickly growing portion of business was conducted along Islamic principles. Most banking was conducted along traditional lines, with payment and collection of interest. The banks, however, were not legally protected in recovering faulty loans on real estate—thus, mortgages were in short supply.

Tourism

Saudi Arabia had three types of tourists: pilgrims making the *hajj* to the holy cities of Mecca and Medina, business visitors, and recreational tourists from Saudi Arabia and other states in the Gulf Cooperation Council. In 2000, Abdullah established the Supreme Council on Tourism. "As the cradle of Islam," read the council's vision statement, "we the Kingdom of Saudi Arabia aim to develop sustainable tourism for the socio-cultural, environmental and economic benefit of all, reflecting our cherished Islamic values, heritage and traditional hospitality."[16] Statistics indicated that the number of tourists, at 3.3 million in 2000, was growing annually at 17 percent. The council's plan focused on family-oriented tourism, identifying ten thousand potential historical, cultural, and natural sites.

Fiscal Budget

Abdullah, intent on bringing the budget back into balance, experienced great luck in 2003 with the sharp rise in oil prices. Government revenues jumped 37 percent, from SR213 billion to SR293 billion; in 2004, they rose again by 34 percent to SR393 billion. Even the Saudi government couldn't increase spending quite that fast. Although it allocated $20 billion for capital projects, including schools, water, sewers, and other infrastructure, surpluses still emerged: 4.5 percent and 10.5 percent of GDP in 2003 and 2004, respectively. Government debt, already falling, declined further to 66 percent of GDP.[17]

Demographics and Unemployment

Saudi Arabia's official estimate of population is 23 million, including just more than 6 million foreign nationals. Saudi Arabia's fertility rate of 5.5 infants per woman was much higher than the world average of 2.7. By the end of 2001, more than 45 percent of the population was below the age of sixteen (view more recent population data in figure 8-2). To accommodate so youthful a population, the government needed to build more schools, increase spending on health care, and create employment opportunities.

The Saudi population is expected to nearly double to 30 million by 2020, increasing the Saudi labor force from 3.3 million to 8.3 million. Yet already young Saudis are having difficulty finding suitable employment. Estimates of unemployment vary but range from 8 percent to a high of 15 percent. Each year about one hundred sixty-three thousand Saudi males enter the labor force, while the private sector generates about fifty thousand jobs and the public sector generates about thirty thousand. Women make up a mere 15 percent of the workforce.

During the oil boom of the 1970s and early 1980s, Saudis had lived quite comfortably. After receiving a free college education (often in the West), Saudis were guaranteed a high-paying job in the public sector, where many worked less than a full eight-hour day. When oil revenues fell, some Saudis were reluctant to seek work in the private sector. Most of the unemployed Saudis were in their twenties. The younger Saudis longed for the laid-back lifestyle that their parents had enjoyed. But government salaries had changed little over the past fifteen years, and young Saudis could not afford to live extravagantly. Moreover, many of them believed that certain jobs,

FIGURE 8-2

Saudi population profile, January 2006 (Saudis only)

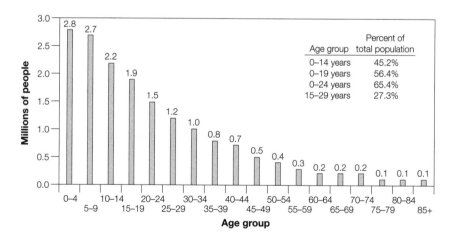

Age group	Percent of total population
0–14 years	45.2%
0–19 years	56.4%
0–24 years	65.4%
15–29 years	27.3%

Source: Saudi Arabian Central Department of Statistics, Samba estimates.

usually held by non-Saudis, were beneath them. "They do not want to get their hands dirty," commented one expatriate business manager. "Until young Saudis change their attitudes, the country is going to remain over-dependent on foreign labor."[18]

But many young Saudis lacked the specialized skills of foreign workers who made up more than a quarter of the population and two-thirds of the workforce. University graduates, who tended to major in Islamic or Arabic studies—programs that were not in high demand in the workplace—lacked practical experience. Employers argued that foreign workers were cheaper and more dependable. "Most Saudis are spoiled," explained one Saudi investment banker. "They won't work. They believe that by their birthright, they deserve this or that."[19]

In an effort to increase Saudi employment, the government introduced a policy of "Saudization." The goal was to replace foreign workers with Saudi nationals. Since 1995, the government had raised the administrative expenses of hiring expatriates. Moreover, firms with a minimum of twenty employees were required to "Saudize" 5 percent of their workforce annually. However, many firms avoided these requirements or paid special fees for expatriates. Relative salaries, which were three times higher for Saudis than foreigners, certainly discouraged effective Saudization.

Education

More than 60 percent of Saudi boys were enrolled in both primary and secondary school. For girls, enrollment rates were a little more than 50 percent. Saudi Arabia's ulema had substantial control over the state's education system. As a result, primary school, secondary school, and often even college curricula focused on Islamic studies. In the lower grades, one-third of the curriculum was dedicated to Islamic studies; one-third to Arabic; and one-third to other subjects, usually minimizing social sciences, math, and physical sciences. Many parents complained that the religion-intensive lessons, which were based on rote learning, bored students. Some were concerned that the education system encouraged Saudi youth to join radical Islamic fundamentalist groups.[20] "The educational system is a disaster," argued one parent. "Religious fanatics control the curriculum . . . It is very radical and anti-West."[21]

During the 1970s and 1980s, the government funded university education abroad for thousands of Saudis. By the 1990s, eight universities had been established in the kingdom. The government continued to pay for higher education, but generally for attendance at the domestic schools. Over 30 percent of university students were females who were allowed to enroll in six of the eight universities. Two were Islamic universities, and even at more technical institutions, religion dominated the curriculum. Crown Prince Abdullah sought to improve education, but not reform its content, by pushing government funding to 25 percent of the budget.

Women

The role of women in Saudi society is controversial. Saudi culture placed restrictions on where and how women traveled, worked, dined, studied, shopped, dressed, married, and divorced. Although Islamic law allowed polygamy, the practice had become less common. Women, including foreign women, were not allowed to drive and when traveling had to be escorted by a male relative. They could be admitted to hospitals only with the consent of a male relative. In public, women were required to wear the *abaya*, a black robe and veil that covered the entire body, exposing only the eyes. In 2002, when a fire at a girls' school in Jeddah left fifteen students dead, the religious police were accused of stopping the girls from leaving the burning building because they were not wearing the abaya. Although an investigative probe commissioned by Crown Prince Abdullah cleared the *matawwa* (religious police) from any wrongdoing, the incident fueled debate over the restrictions placed on Saudi women.

Although women were permitted to work, only 5 percent of them held jobs. Their pay was lower than that of males. Female workers were not allowed to have contact with their male coworkers; most women worked as teachers, physicians, or nurses. However, the arrival of the Internet helped some females create and run businesses without the need to interact in person with males.

Some progressive Saudis believed that women's rights should be expanded. "When will we start showing the trust that our mothers, wives, sisters and daughters justly deserve?" questioned Hani Yamani.[22] Others believed that women's rights were protected by the Sharia. "The Islamic faith has given women rights that are equal to or more than the rights given them in the Old Testament and the Bible," attested the crown prince. "There is no inherent discrimination against women and no limitation to how far women can go in our society."[23]

Over the years, Saudi women lobbied for increased civil rights. On November 6, 1990, more than seventy women drove through the streets of Riyadh protesting the ban on female driving. When Islamic fundamentalists condemned their behavior, the government fired the female demonstrators from their jobs. In December 2001, Saudi women's rights expanded when Interior Minister Prince Nayef agreed to issue female citizens their own identity cards. The new cards included a picture of the woman's unveiled face. Previously, women carried family identity cards that listed them as dependents of their fathers or husbands. "They don't want us to show our pictures," explained a Saudi woman. "It is not Islam; it is culture."[24]

Radical Fundamentalism

Those who believe, and those who follow the Jewish faith, the Christians and the Sabians, whoever believes in Allah and the Last Day and acts righteously shall have their reward with their Lord, and shall have nothing to fear, nor shall they grieve.

—Koran, 2.62

Do not take these Jews and Christians for allies; they are allies of one to another, and whoso from amongst you takes them for allies, is indeed one of them. Verily, Allah does not guide the unjust people to attain their goal.

—Koran, 5.51

As early as the 1920s, radical Islamic fundamentalists have challenged the ruling al-Saud family's legitimacy. The leaders of the opposition movement in Saudi Arabia were ulema. Some were angry at the monarchy for assuming control over political and economic reform. Some opposed Saudi's commercial and military relations with the United States. To appease these clerics, the al-Sauds accommodated their authority in religion, education, and the judiciary. Yet the ulema demanded a still greater role in political and economic decision making in order to preserve Islamic traditions. They objected to modernization and the severity of income distribution that separated rich and poor. "The Islamists are not angry because the airplane has replaced the camel," explained one Muslim scholar; "they are angry because they cannot get on the airplane."[25]

In 1979, Sunni Muslim extremists seized the Grand Mosque in Mecca. After several weeks, the Saudi military successfully removed the dissidents. But more than two hundred soldiers and radicals died in the standoff, while the remaining radicals were publicly executed. And when fundamentalists overthrew the shah of Iran, the revolution further mobilized Saudi fundamentalists. When oil prices (and per capita incomes) fell in the mid-1980s, radical ulema were able to recruit disgruntled, low-income youths to their cause. And for some, the alliance with the United States in the Gulf War was betrayal by the royal family.

Terrorism within Saudi Arabia took a turn for the worse in November 1995 when a bomb exploded outside U.S. Army headquarters in Riyadh, killing five Americans and two Indians. Seven months later, a car bomb near the air base in Khobar killed nineteen U.S. soldiers and wounded sixty-four others. A link to Saudi militant Osama Bin Laden was suspected, although U.S. investigators eventually blamed the attack on a senior member of the Iranian Revolutionary Guard Corps.

On September 11, 2001, nineteen Muslim terrorists hijacked four passenger jets and crashed them into the World Trade Center in New York and the Pentagon in Washington, D.C. Nearly three thousand people died. In the weeks following the 9/11 attacks, U.S.–Saudi ties weakened. Wary of strong anti-U.S. sentiment among Islamic fundamentalists, Saudi officials hesitated to join the international coalition against terrorism organized by the U.S. government. Crown Prince Abdullah was also reluctant to allow the United States to launch attacks against Afghanistan from its air bases.

In the United States, the press reported that the royal al-Saud family was guilty of funding terrorist organizations. With fifteen of the nineteen terrorists of Saudi origin, many Americans grew critical of Saudi Arabia's government and culture. In an editorial published in the *Wall Street Journal* in January 2002, one American wrote: "Anti-women, anti-meritocratic, anti-democracy, anti-education in any meaningful, liberating sense, racist and profoundly anti-freedom, Saudi-sponsored religious extremism, funded by all drivers of those oversized SUVs on American roads, is the most destructive vision in the world today."[26]

Upset by the U.S. media, Crown Prince Abdullah defended the regime and criticized foreign journalists for misinterpreting Saudi society. "It might seem paradoxical to Western observers that a royal family who denies democracy, basic freedoms, and accountability could enjoy widespread public support—but a paradox in the West is politics in the Middle East," wrote Nawaf Obaid. In his article, "In Al-Saud We Trust," Obaid compared Saudi Arabia with prerevolutionary Iran, concluding that the Saudi government was more stable and had greater popular support.[27]

Between 2003 and 2005, domestic terrorism in Saudi Arabia intensified. Shortly after the United States attacked Iraq, a terrorist bombing in Riyadh, linked to the terrorist organization al-Qaeda, killed thirty-five people—mostly Muslims. Another in November 2003 killed seventeen; four more died in an April bombing. In all, some five hundred Saudis have died in these and other incidents. The Saudi government responded forcefully, reportedly wiping out four of five al-Qaeda cells in the kingdom. In February 2004, the government hosted delegates from fifty-four countries at the International Counter-Terrorism Conference in Riyadh. Terrorism was also high on the agenda for talks between Crown Prince Abdullah and President George W. Bush in April, in Crawford, Texas.

Saudi Oil and America

Since 9/11, oil prices have tripled. The U.S.-led economic recovery and the miracle growth in China were primarily responsible for pushing up demand, while continuing difficulties in Iraq and exhausted refining capacity in the United States constrained supply. OPEC had allowed production quotas to increase, with Saudi Arabia producing 9.5 million barrels daily. The Saudi government, meanwhile, announced plans to increase capacity (from 10.4 million barrels to 11.5 million barrels a day). In April 2005, Abdullah assured Bush that Saudi would produce all the oil the market demanded.

Lurking in the background, however, was some concern among western-ers about Saudi's real oil reserves and ability to produce at more than 10 mil-lion barrels per day. Matthew Simmons, chairman of a Houston-based investment firm that focused on oil, had recently devoted his intellectual at-tention to Saudi's oil reserves. In 2003, he made a presentation to the Center for International and Strategic Studies in Washington. In that presentation, Simmons noted that most of Saudi's oil was produced from seven fields— five of which had been producing for nearly fifty years. Moreover, Aramco had never explained clearly why it changed its reserve estimates in 1979 from 100 billion to 160 billion barrels, and then raised them again in 1988 to 261 billion. After noting that lateral drilling and water injection were now necessary to keep production coming, Simmons asked rhetorically, what if the reserves are not real?[28] His question elicited intense interest in energy and defense circles.

Continuing violence in Palestine and Israel remained at the heart of U.S.-Arab relations. Many Saudis could not understand why the United States continued to support Israel. Arab media focused mainly on the horrific spi-ral of violence between Israelis and Palestinians since the outbreak of the *in-tifada* (uprising) in October 2000. Yet when the Arab League met in 2002, Crown Prince Abdullah proposed a normalization of relations. "I tell the Israeli people," he said, "that if their government gives up the policy of force and suppression and accepts genuine peace, we will not hesitate in ac-cepting the Israeli people's right to live in security with the rest of the people in the region."[29]

As the violence continued along with Israeli occupation of West Bank settlements, the Islamic world became more and more critical of U.S. policy. Many believed the United States tolerated Israeli military dominance of

Palestine because of Jewish political influence in the United States, combined with the evangelical Christian belief that Israel must prevail for Jesus to come again. When the issue arose in April, President Bush told Abdullah that he planned to deal with the conflict one step at a time.

Keeping the House in Power

Going forward, the House of Saud had its economic and political hands full. Although high oil prices assured economic growth and a balanced budget for the next couple of years, diversification of the economy remained elusive. The so-called Dutch disease was hard to cure—even for larger countries with more democratic governments. Getting Saudi businesses to invest in Saudi Arabia, to diversify, and to hire more Saudis in relatively labor-intensive jobs ran against many existing institutional arrangements. And the government had been slow to change. When Fahd died on August 1, 2005, Abdullah became king. After several months of consolidating his power and expanding government budgets fat with oil revenue, it remains to be seen what the new monarch will do.

In addition to modernizing Saudi Arabia's institutions and privatizing more of its infrastructural and resources businesses, Abdullah faces additional challenges of culture. His people are not used to working very hard nor engaging in entrepreneurial activities. Women remain virtually excluded from the economy. Even more serious, however, are the frictions within Islam—fundamentalism and the role of education.

"We are proud Arab Muslims," commented Prince Bandar Bin Sultan, the Saudi ambassador to the United States. "We'd like to modernize, but not necessarily Westernize, and we are different."[30] But really, is modernization without westernization possible in an increasingly globalized world? Can Saudi Arabia have a modern economy, with all the conveniences of modern life, and yet keep out the influences of western culture? Can the country remain conservatively Islamic, while still participating in the global political economy?

Malaysians have done it, as have Turks. But neither are desert Arabs, followers of Wahhabi, or protectors of the two sacred mosques of Mecca and Medina. And they certainly don't have the blessing or the curse of the world's largest reserves of oil. From this complicated, resource-rich amalgam of history and religion, King Abdullah must craft and implement a serious development strategy—one that gets the Saudi people to work, save, invest, and compete.

Institutional Collapse and Recovery in Russia

JUST HOURS BEFORE the new millennium, Russian President Boris Yeltsin surprisingly announced his resignation, passing presidential powers to his new prime minister, Vladimir Putin.[1] In his farewell address on December 31, 1999, Yeltsin said: "Today, on this incredibly important day . . . I would like to ask for your forgiveness. Forgiveness for your dreams that did not come true . . . I ask forgiveness of those who hoped that with one push we could transition from the dark, stagnated, totalitarian past into the bright, prosperous and civilized future."[2]

Yeltsin's regrets came at the end of a turbulent decade, during which the Soviet Union ceased to exist and Russia's own economy all but collapsed. During the late 1980s as the Soviet Union stagnated, Yeltsin's predecessor, Mikhail Gorbachev, had tried unsuccessfully to implement reforms. Gorbachev had undertaken *glasnost* (political liberalization) and *perestroika* (economic restructuring) gradually, and haltingly, in an effort to stanch a failing economy.

These unsuccessful efforts, swamped by defense spending and failing productivity growth, culminated in an attempted coup by hard-line Communists. When anti-Communist protesters led by Yeltsin prevailed, Gorbachev found himself leader of a country that no longer existed. When Gorbachev resigned in December 1991, Yeltsin and the leaders of the other Soviet republics dissolved the Soviet Union. The Russian Federation became one of fifteen sovereign states within the Commonwealth of Independent States.

This extraordinary development marked the beginning of a decade of disastrous economic performance. Under Yeltsin, Russia tried to implement radical economic reform—opening all at once a Communist economy that had been closed for seventy-four years. Prices were freed, trade and foreign investment liberalized, and thousands of firms were privatized—*all at once*. Without capitalist institutions, with no tradition of private property, and without any serious rule of law, Russia virtually collapsed into a free-for-all of greed, crime, and poverty.

Not until the end of the decade, when Vladimir Putin took over, did the Russian Federation begin to recover. An ex-KGB agent, Putin asserted the controls he thought necessary to begin rebuilding the state. With the good fortune of sharply rising oil prices, Russia recovered. Now, more than five years later, the world watches to see how Putin will balance authoritarianism and democracy in the pursuit of Russian growth.

Prerevolutionary Russia

Modern Russia, lagging the West in economic and social development, pretty much dates from the rule of Alexander II, 1855–1881. Alexander abolished the practice of serfdom, bringing his country out of feudalism. He established a central bank, procedures for the government budget, and commercial codes. He actually encouraged business and tried to facilitate foreign investment.

Toward the end of the century, Russia built railroads beyond the Ural Mountains into Siberia, which began to tie the huge country together. European and American entrepreneurs were encouraged to take advantage of Russia's population and land, in addition to its rich resources of gold and coal. Under Sergei Witte, minister of finance during the early years of Czar Nicholas II (1894–1917), the country began producing iron, steel, and petroleum. Industrial growth jumped to 6–8 percent. Czar Nicholas, however, proved unable to manage the turmoil that grew out of rapid industrialization. In January 1905, when a group of hungry workers and peasants demonstrated at the czar's winter palace in St. Petersburg, imperial guard ruthlessly opened fire in the massacre now known as Bloody Sunday. Russians were utterly demoralized by the loss of the Russo-Japanese War and its resolution at the Treaty of Portsmouth, orchestrated by American president Theodore Roosevelt.

Czar Nicholas took several steps to mitigate the rising opposition. He promulgated the October Manifesto, establishing the Duma (Russia's legislative body) and promising other political reforms, which he later often ignored. His prime minister, Pyotr Stolypin, launched a campaign against street crime, social unrest, and revolutionary terrorism, and pursued extensive agrarian reform. Yet he was assassinated in 1911. World War I caused 1.5 million Russian casualties, which together with economic difficulties at home and continuing diplomatic embarrassments, forced Nicholas II to abdicate in 1917. Thus ended the 304-year rule of the Romanov dynasty.

Within months, the Bolshevik Party, under Vladimir Lenin, staged a coup d'état. Bolsheviks promised a swift end to war, land for the peasantry, and food for workers. However, their first years in power were characterized by civil war and a series of arrests called the Red Terror. Lenin sought to destroy the aristocracy and the bourgeoisie. His Red Army murdered hundreds of thousands of civilians; among them were Nicholas II and his entire family. "Everything earned before the Revolution," proclaimed the Bolsheviks, "was stolen from the working class." Hence, everything was nationalized.

Marxism-Leninism and the Market

Marxism-Leninism was the ideological basis of the Soviet state. Vladimir Lenin was, philosophically, a student of Karl Marx, whose most important work, *Das Kapital*, was a critique of capitalism. Marx viewed capitalism as an essential but unsustainable stage of economic development. Capitalists, he believed, saved and invested to create productive assets that expanded material wealth. However, Marx did not believe that workers (the proletariat) received the full value of their contribution. Thus, he predicted increasing concentration of wealth, provoking a worker revolt that would inaugurate communism. "The theory of communists may be summed up in a single phrase," wrote Marx in his *Manifesto*: "abolition of private property."

Marx, however, did not view Russia, a largely agricultural country, as the likely object of a Communist revolution. He had England, or perhaps Germany, in mind. Thus, Lenin, trying to adapt Marx's ideas to Russia's conditions, developed the idea that the Communist Party would lead people directly from feudalism to socialism.

Rise of the Soviet Union

With the Soviet economy in chaos (hyperinflation, unemployment, and crime were rampant), Lenin initiated the New Economic Policy (NEP). Under the NEP, small manufacturing, retail, and wholesale trade and agriculture remained private, helping stabilize the Russian economy. But when Joseph Stalin took over after Lenin's death in 1924, he abolished the NEP and adopted a policy of industrial-led growth driven by state investment and a forced increase in the industrial labor force.

Stalin recognized that even a modicum of private business threatened the nature of the totalitarian state (a concern proven six decades later under Gorbachev). The most brutal aspect of his policy was collectivization. He moved to fight the so-called *kulaks*, or "wealthy peasants," forcing them to surrender their land to collective farms. Millions of peasants were mercilessly killed or sent to the Gulag, the system of Soviet labor camps, essentially reestablishing serfdom.

Stalin was in a hurry. "Do you want our socialist fatherland to be beaten and to lose its independence?" he asked. "If you do not want this you must put an end to its backwardness in the shortest possible time and develop genuine Bolshevik tempo in building up its socialist system of economy. There is no other way. That is why Lenin said on the eve of the October Revolution: 'Either perish, or overtake and outstrip the advanced capitalist countries.' We are fifty or a hundred years behind the advanced countries. We must make good this distance in ten years. Either we do it, or we shall be crushed."[3]

In this rush to industrialize, Stalin employed brutal conditions. Twelve-hour shifts, with no days off, were the norm. Penalties for complaints, or even tardiness, were extreme. Managers worked to achieve ambitious output guidelines, set by Gosplan (the state's economic planning agency) in its five-year plans. Fear was the motivation. Waves of purges continued throughout Stalin's twenty-nine-year rule, especially harsh in the late 1930s and again between 1948 and 1953. The average citizen never knew whether he would awaken in his own bed in the morning (the NKVD, renamed KGB after Stalin's death, usually made its arrests at night). Historians estimate that Stalin's victims number between 30 million and 40 million.

Central Planning

The system of planning in the USSR was complicated (see figure 9-1). Stalin organized the economy of this huge nation like that of a large capitalist firm. At the top of the organization was the politburo of the Communist Party—analogous to the board of directors. The politburo made strategic decisions, which cabinet ministers would implement. The important ministers were planning, finance, agriculture, and industry. The Soviet people, meanwhile, elected a parallel legislative body called the Supreme Soviet. The Supreme Soviet, in turn, enacted legislation and selected the Presidium to oversee the executive branch, called the Council of Ministers.

Gosplan produced five-year plans to achieve the politburo's goals. Analyzing the previous year's performance data, Gosplan officials tried to measure and allocate all the inputs needed for production of the entire Soviet economy. Once they had developed this information, they transmitted it to Gossnab, the agency responsible for distributing all inputs to the various ministries, which in turn allocated that information to the various enterprises. All of the enterprises were state owned. Each enterprise manager thus received a

FIGURE 9-1

Political organization of the USSR under Stalin

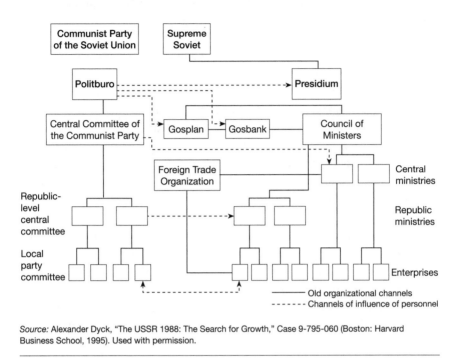

Source: Alexander Dyck, "The USSR 1988: The Search for Growth," Case 9-795-060 (Boston: Harvard Business School, 1995). Used with permission.

production target and an allocation of inputs. He was rewarded for meeting the target. Profitability was irrelevant, and prices passive.

In fact, prices were determined initially by Gosplan (and later by Goskomtsen), not as a means of reflecting scarcity, but to aid in measurement, accounting, and control. Prices were attached to inputs and outputs only after the quantity of goods to be produced was determined. For consumer goods, particularly necessities, retail prices were held below wholesale prices, reflecting political considerations. Wages were gradually increased, while prices were held constant for years at a time. Obviously, this created an economy of shortage. Only when subsidization of output imposed pressures on the state budget were prices raised, as in 1936, 1949, 1955, 1966, and 1982; otherwise, stability prevailed.[4]

Despite the irrationality of this system, Stalin's forced industrialization and collectivized farming did indeed make the USSR's huge economy grow. The Soviet Union was rich in resources—human resources, capital, and the immense natural wealth of petroleum, gas, coal, gold, diamonds, and virtually every raw material essential to industrial growth. Economic historians estimate that

Stalin's economy grew at a rate in excess of 5.5 percent annually, slowing to 3.7 percent in the early Khrushchev years and 2 percent by the 1980s. Given a slow-growing population, this yielded growth of GDP per capita of almost 3 percent, which certainly made Soviets feel that they were getting richer.

Total factor productivity, however, was a different story. While its measurement is uncertain, it appears that productivity not attributable to labor and capital inputs was growing very slowly—at a rate of 1.1 percent, slowing to zero by 1975, and thereafter turning negative. In other words, the USSR was growing because of increasing inputs, as Stalin and Khrushchev threw more and more resources at the economy. But its efficiency was disastrous, and getting more so. By the time Brezhnev was in power, growth had slowed, productivity was negative, and nearly 20 percent of GDP was devoted to defense. Performance like this was almost certainly unsustainable, regardless of Gorbachev's later efforts.

In 1956, three years after Stalin's death, Khrushchev began the difficult process of revealing the nature and extent of Stalin's crimes. During the Twentieth Party Congress, Khrushchev condemned Stalin's "cult of personality," urging the country to return to Leninist ideals. Khrushchev also struggled with diplomatic challenges. In 1956, he violently suppressed the Hungarian Revolution and then ordered the massacre of striking workers in Novocherkassk in 1962. Later that year, he engaged the United States in the Cuban Missile Crisis, bringing the world to the brink of nuclear disaster. He pushed Russian space exploration and took credit for the flight of Sputnik in 1957 and Yuri Gagarin's first human journey into space in 1961. But he also pounded his shoe on the table at the UN and engaged Richard Nixon in a series of "kitchen debates" during Nixon's visit to Moscow in 1959.

Frustrated with his anti-Stalin campaign, his foreign policy failures, the discouraging performance of the domestic economy, and his overall erratic behavior, the Soviet apparatchiks deposed Khrushchev in 1964. They replaced him with Leonid Brezhnev, a reactionary who shunned any major change or reform whatsoever on the economic, political, and social fronts. The eighteen years of his rule, 1964–1982, are known as *gody zastoya*, "the years of stagnation."

The Soviet Union had become a vast empire, dominating Eastern Europe and extending its tentacles to Africa, India, Asia, and Latin America. Military and foreign aid continued to sap the resources of the USSR. Free speech at home was further suppressed, as the Gulag's inmates numbered more and more dissidents. Andrei Sakharov was exiled internally in 1980, and Aleksandr Solzhenitsyn was exiled to the West in 1974. Both received the Nobel Prize (for peace and literature, respectively). There were some advances made in trade, with the opening of grain imports and gas exports, and the reduction of nuclear weapons with the SALT I treaty, the first agreement resulting from the Strategic Arms Limitation Talks. But nothing helped the economy.

The worst problem was the absence of the price mechanism. According to Marshall Goldman:

> When the government raised bread prices in 1955, riots broke out and the Soviet authority agreed to hold prices constant. To do this, however, they had to subsidize the collective farms to cover their costs of operations. These subsidies ultimately grew to about 100 billion rubles, at that time over $100 billion a year . . . Russian peasants quickly saw that it was more profitable for them to sell the grain they harvested to the state at the higher subsidized price, rather than feed the grain to their own livestock. They would then buy the heavily subsidized bread at the bakery and feed it to their livestock. Approximately 15 percent of the bread baked each year was wasted in this way.[5]

Stagnation weighed even more heavily on the Soviet consumers. Corruption, bribery, money laundering, and speculation all blossomed in the late 1970s and early 1980s, as the *nomenklatura* (elite members of the Communist Party) sought special privileges for their families. People waited in lines for everything—for train tickets, a piece of meat, a pound of butter. In a book on the oligarchs, David Hoffman describes this as follows:

> The shortages rubbed their emotions raw. Irina had seen the fire in people's eyes when suddenly bags of flour appeared in a store. Soon five hundred people were waiting, writing their place in line—their number—on their palms. The white-smocked counter lady was patient with the first hundred. Then she started snarling. She hated them. People would be begging. Please, give me two kilos of flour. Once cans of condensed milk appeared, hundreds of blue cans, painstakingly arranged in a pattern on the counter. A year later, there was no sausage, only cheese and condensed milk. Then, after another year, no cheese only condensed milk. Then the condensed milk was gone!
>
> The years of marazm [period of senility] turned them all into a vast, informal human network of connections and friends that spread from family to family, from apartment landings to workplaces, from Moscow to the distant provinces, a chain of svyazi, or connections that helped them survive when the system could not provide.[6]

The era of Brezhnev gave way briefly to Yuri Andropov and Konstantin Chernenko, until 1985 when Mikhail Gorbachev acceded to general secretary of the Communist Party.

Glasnost and Perestroika

Only fifty-four when elected, Gorbachev had strong Communist credentials. Yet with a degree in agronomy and a law degree from Moscow State, he was a man of ideas. He held Lenin in high regard, believing that Stalin had hijacked Lenin's idealism. Exhibiting an intellectual commitment to private enterprise at the microlevel, Gorbachev undertook *perestroika* to allow the economic periphery to operate independently of Gosplan. Two important reforms were legislated: the Law on State Enterprises and the Law on Cooperatives. Managers of state enterprises would still have targets but were no longer bound by them. And managers were given more discretion to reallocate funds from one use to another. The Law on Cooperatives gave producers' and sellers' cooperatives autonomy from central control. Wholesale prices were set free, and profits could be converted to cash. Banking reform sprang out of this law, allowing commercial credit beyond central control.

Concurrently with perestroika, Gorbachev encouraged greater intellectual openness, or *glasnost*. Artists and performers were no longer suppressed. Some of the dissidents, most notably Andrei Sakharov, were released from exile. Censorship and religious persecution diminished. This openness, rather than acting as a palliative, became a spur to greater criticism of the Soviet state—both the political and economic system. When Gorbachev began to shrink military expenditures and put an end to the cold war, he effectively eliminated 10–20 percent of the country's GDP. Each effort at partial reform further undermined communism.

Despite his efforts at reform, and his considerable popularity in the West, Gorbachev was extremely unpopular in his own country. His seeming impotence was exaggerated by inaction as Poland, and then Czechoslovakia and Hungary, pulled away from the USSR in 1989 and then the Berlin Wall collapsed. Trying to boost his own legitimacy in 1990, Gorbachev abandoned his title of general secretary and held an election (within the Party Congress) for president of the Soviet Union.

By 1991, issues of nationalism, economic distress, anticommunism, and cultural freedom became paramount. In June of that year, Boris Yeltsin was elected president of the Russian Federation. The climax came on August 19, when Communist hard-liners led by Vice President Gennady Yanaev staged a coup. Gorbachev was placed under house arrest, and thousands of pro-reform protesters poured out into Moscow's streets. When the army and the KGB refused to fire on the crowds, Yeltsin and his supporters emerged victorious. Gorbachev, freed, found his country no longer existed. Fifteen regional presidents signed the Belovezhskaya Accords in December 1991, and Gorbachev resigned on Christmas Day. The Soviet Union ceased to exist.

Russia Under Boris Yeltsin

Yeltsin inherited the presidency of an extraordinary country. Russia, representing about one-seventh of the world's land mass, spans eleven time zones. As one can see from the map in figure 9-2, Russia's topography and climate range from the frozen tundra of Arctic Siberia, to the arid steppes of Mongolia, to the subtropical coast of the Caspian Sea. Most of the population, declining slowly (–0.6 percent annually) from 146 million after 2000, lived and worked west of the Ural Mountains—adjacent to Europe. Its population was literate (99.8 percent), well educated, and relatively healthy, with a life expectancy of 64.8 years.

On the other hand, output had stagnated, and GDP was thought to have dropped some 5 percent during 1991. Inflation—a new phenomenon for Russians—was accelerating rapidly. Trade was positive, although in part due to Soviet-enforced purchasing by Eastern Europe in exchange for Soviet energy. And the exchange rate, set arbitrarily at R0.77 per dollar in 1990, stood at 1.25.

Unlike Gorbachev, Yeltsin sought to destroy the Soviet economy, not save it. The Congress of Deputies gave Yeltsin a year, from November 1991 to December 1992, to make changes by decree—changes in strategy, structure of government, and ownership—without parliamentary approval. Yeltsin was convinced by a group of young reformers to undertake radical reform—so-called shock therapy—similar to the reform program embraced by Poland.

The young reformers included an interesting collection of Russians, advised by westerners. The head of the group was Yegor Gaidar, a young mathematical economist at the Moscow All-Union Institute for Systems Research. He was joined by Anatoly Chubais, an economist from Leningrad, and casual interest from Alfred Kokh, a sharp-tongued young bureaucrat who would head the newly created privatization agency. These three, described by Vice President Aleksandr Rutskoi as "small boys in pink shorts and yellow boots,"[7] received advice from several western economists, including Jeff Sachs and Andrei Shleifer of Harvard University, Anders Aslund from Sweden, Richard Layard from the London School of Economics and Political Science, and Stanley Fischer, the senior economist at the IMF.

All of these economists believed that Russia should leap to the market all at once. Gradual reform, they felt, would be impossible—causing too many distortions slowly and piecemeal—and be suppressed by constant, irrefutable political opposition. Their model was an extreme form of the "Washington consensus" that we saw in the chapter on India. Here, however, the key was privatization, since all the productive assets of Russia were in the government's hands.

FIGURE 9-2

Map of the Soviet Union

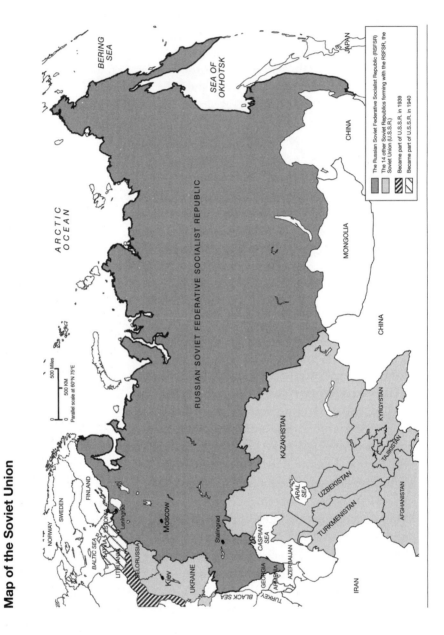

Gaidar's reform strategy was to remove price controls immediately and then privatize as soon as possible. Thus, on January 2, 1992, the government liberated prices on 90 percent of consumer goods and 80 percent of intermediate goods. A few staples—including bread, sugar, and vodka—remained under state control. The government also liberated trade, ending many of its subsidies.

Price liberalization was accompanied by a sharp rise in inflation. With food shortages and the black market ending almost overnight, many ordinary citizens were feeling extreme hardship—their paychecks or pensions could no longer keep up with escalating prices. The consumer price index jumped almost 300 percent, with inflation heading toward 2,500 percent by the end of 1992.

The key to stabilization was the central bank. Monetary policy needed to be tightened by restricting credit, raising interest rates, and slowing the growth of the money supply. However, Victor Gerashchenko, head of the central bank, rejected the Gaidar team's idea of shock therapy. Gerashchenko, who had ties to senior members of the Supreme Soviet, actually expanded money and credit to Russian firms, which quickly led to hyperinflation and collapsing exchange rates that would take three years to ameliorate.

While the economy floundered, the Gaidar team moved ahead quickly with privatization. The young reformers were certain that any private owner would manage assets more efficiently than the state. "Institutions would follow private property," they thought, "rather than the other way around."[8] When those people acquired ownership rights, thought the reformers, they would have the incentives to increase the value of their firms.

Privatization began by distributing nearly 140 million vouchers to the Russian citizenry. Each voucher could be exchanged for stock in a privatized firm, or invested in a voucher fund (like a mutual fund), or sold for cash. The Bolshevik Biscuit Company was the first government asset auctioned off to voucher holders. Over the next three years, one hundred twenty-two thousand businesses—half the state-owned assets—were auctioned off.

Yet the speed of the privatization process had overwhelmed citizens' ability to understand and participate fairly and fully in the process. Many vouchers were sold at deep discounts, accumulated by managers at nominal prices. Most of the voucher funds were scams, which went broke. Anatoly Chubais, responsible for several rounds of privatizations, remarked of the emerging property owners: "They steal and steal and steal. They are stealing absolutely everything, and it is impossible to stop them. But let them steal and take their property. They will then become owners and decent administrators of this property."[9]

This, however, was only the beginning. Most of Russia's prize assets—its crown-jewel companies with hugely rich natural resource properties—were excluded from the process of mass privatization until 1995. By then, the Yeltsin government was facing a crisis. Its budget was in difficulty, because revenues had not kept up with expenditures. The economy was in a deep depression, and rich individuals and state-owned firms avoided taxes in every way possible.

In March 1995, Vladimir Potanin, chairman of Oneksimbank, proposed a fiscal solution to Yeltsin. He suggested that several of the leading banks would lend the government money for one year. As collateral, the banks would bid on blocks of shares in Russia's largest (and richest) firms. Winning bids would be loaned to the government to help fund its budget. When the government repaid the loans in 1996, explained Potanin, the shares would be returned.

The Loans for Shares plan, approved by Yeltsin in August 1995, unfolded in a series of twelve "pledge auctions." The auctions, of course, were rigged. Each auction was dominated by a single bid. Foreigners were excluded, and outside bidders were disqualified, on technical grounds, by Alfred Kokh, a one-time reformer who had become head of the State Property Committee. Among the assets auctioned were Russian oil firms LUKOIL, Sidanko, Yukos, and Sibneft; Norilsk Nickel, the principal metals asset; the Far Eastern Shipping Company; and the Bratsk Timber Complex.

Perhaps the most outrageous of these pledge auctions occurred on November 17, 1995. Oneksimbank, which was also the auctioneer, offered $170.1 million for Norilsk Nickel, with a starting price of $170 million. This company produced a quarter of the world's nickel and a third of its platinum, earning more than $100 million a month. When another bidder (Rossiiski Kredit) prepared to offer $355 million, Alfred Kokh cited a procedural irregularity and excluded the bidder from the auction.

In another auction held three weeks later, Mikhail Khodorkovsky acquired 78 percent of Yukos for $309 million. (By 2002, Yukos was Russia's largest oil company, capitalized at $15 billion. Before his arrest, Khodorkovsky was worth an estimated $8 billion.) The entire set of auctions netted $800 million for the government, in exchange for priceless assets. One year later, of course, the government was still broke, forcing Yeltsin to turn the properties over to their buyers.

The problem with this entire approach was the lack of capitalist institutions. Many of the Russians were either sick of their own failing institutions or relatively unfamiliar with western ones: a legal system that recognized property rights, a regulatory system that controlled monopolies, or a security exchange commission that validated the integrity of financial transactions. And most western economists—although not all of them—apparently were too preoccupied with their conception of markets (as opposed to on-the-ground institutions) to care. Speaking in 1997 to a group of scholars, Alan Greenspan offered his own views of Russia's problem: "Little contemporary thought had been given to the institutional infrastructure required of markets. Black markets by definition are not supported by the rule of law. There are no rights to own and dispose of property protected by the enforcement power of the state. There are no laws of contract or bankruptcy or judicial review and determination, again enforced by the state. The essential infrastructure of the market economy is missing."[10]

The infrastructure of democracy was pretty weak. Since communism had prevailed for seventy-four years, Russians had no experience with democracy and its institutions. In fact, there was not even the memory of democracy, as there was in Poland and some of the other Eastern European countries, with their older professionals and private farmers. Yeltsin, an increasingly sickly president, spent more and more time away from Moscow, recuperating at various *dachas*. And given the weak performance of his government, the hyperinflation, and the pledge auctions, it was hardly surprising that his public approval rating had dropped below 10 percent. This did not bode well for his reelection campaign, in the election scheduled for July 1996.

At the World Economic Forum in Davos, Switzerland, in February 1996, a group of Russia's most powerful businesspeople got together to discuss the coming election. Organized by Anatoly Chubais, these included Boris Berezovsky, Vladimir Gusinsky, Mikhail Khodorkovsky, Vladimir Potanin, and Alexander Smolensky. These were the oligarchs. They controlled the banks, natural resources, heavy industry, telecommunications, and the media. One of them had foolishly bragged that the group controlled 50 percent of Russian assets! They had acquired their assets through a combination of cunning, graft, and corruption. And the oligarchs were worried about Yeltsin's reelection.

Gennady Zyuganov, the head of Russia's Communist Party, also attended the Davos forum. Leading in early polls, Zyuganov gave repeated press conferences and hung out with western business executives. He spoke of a gentler communism that would respect democracy and private property. As he did, it became patently clear to the oligarchs that he would win the summer election and likely renationalize their holdings. After several days of worried conversations, the oligarchs committed themselves, in the "Davos pact," to defeating Zyuganov and working to reelect Yeltsin.

To do this, they would spend millions of dollars—perhaps $200 million (despite a campaign cap of $3 million)—and use the power of the media, which they controlled: newspapers, radio, and the most powerful medium, television. The two most important channels, ORT and NTV, were controlled by Boris Berezovsky and Vladimir Gusinsky, respectively. The third publicly owned channel was easily controlled by the Kremlin. Throughout May, June, and July, the campaign ground up candidate Zyuganov and touted the democratic strengths of Yeltsin. More and more journalists, especially in the leading oligarch-owned papers, supported Yeltsin in their news coverage and editorials.

On July 3, Yeltsin was reelected with 53.8 percent of the vote (40.3 percent went to Zyuganov). The Davos pact had succeeded, and within weeks, Yeltsin would sign over the national assets to the oligarchs and appoint Vladimir Potanin deputy prime minister. During the remainder of the year, the oligarchs consolidated their control of these assets and asserted their power over the state more explicitly. Yeltsin, meanwhile, had quadruple bypass surgery in November, leaving him incapacitated for weeks. Over the few years of his final term, he would appoint five prime ministers, leaving the government in chaos and without any clear developmental strategy.

Although the worst appeared to be over, the Russian economy continued to shrink until 1999. Since 1990, real output had fallen 54 percent. Government spending had also declined significantly, leaving housing, agriculture, health care, and the military in far worse shape than they were under the Soviet Union. Worse yet, capital investment had dropped annually by 17 percent, letting the physical and productive infrastructure deteriorate significantly.

Between 1992 and 1995, hyperinflation had wracked the country. Yeltsin's appointment to head the central bank, Viktor Gerashchenko, had consciously printed money to help fund failing Communist firms. Only in 1996, after Gerashchenko's removal, did the central bank finally begin to control the money supply. Inflation fell that year to 22 percent (having averaged 900 percent annually for four years) and then to 11 percent before the crisis in 1998, which we will look at later in this chapter. The exchange rate had collapsed, requiring remonetization (issuance of new currency, with three decimals removed) in 1993. The government, running huge deficits (and printing money) rapidly added to the national debt. In fact, by 1998, foreign debt had reached $149 billion, or about 88 percent of Russia's GDP. Only trade was positive, given Russia's sales of oil. The surplus stood at $13 billion in 1998.

Amid these disastrous economic and political circumstances, Russia's institutions broke down further. Demonetization exemplifies these problems. When the Soviet Union collapsed in 1991, Russia inherited the Soviet ruble. While Russia's central bank could print new rubles (and did so), other states could issue their own new currency. By 1993, some Russian firms began to rely less on rubles to negotiate transactions. Business-to-business transactions turned increasingly to barter.[11] By 1999, perhaps 50 percent of industrial sales entailed barter. Intermediaries organized the complex supply chains needed to accomplish deliveries.

One of the problems associated with barter was taxation. The government could not easily tax bartered transactions, because it was unable to evaluate prices and profits. Provincial governments began to tax in kind, which even the federal government had to accept eventually. To facilitate commerce, quasi-monies began to appear in the regions. Some governments issued their own money substitutes, while firms and local banks developed promissory notes, called *vekselia*.

Tax collection was a major issue. The government created an armed tax police to cope with the tax authority's lack of data and with massive tax evasion problems. Tax collectors were often beaten, kidnapped, or even killed, and more than forty had their homes burned down.[12]

The regional autonomy posed other problems. When the Soviet Union had collapsed, the Russian Federation that emerged was complex. It consisted of eighty-nine federal units, including twenty-one republics bearing the names of non-Russian ethnic groups; forty-nine *oblasts* and six *krais*, generally populated by ethnic Russians; Moscow and St. Petersburg, which had special status as federal cities; and ten autonomous *okrugs* and one autonomous *oblast*. Boris Yeltsin had told the leaders of these regions to "take as much sovereignty as you can swallow." He wanted to destroy the government. Regional leaders seized on this opportunity to claim a great deal of sovereignty. Many signed treaties with the Kremlin, limiting its control of natural resources, foreign economic policy, and budgets. Chechnya is a blatant example of how this quasi-autonomy would cause problems.

Part of these issues sprang from the breakdown of law and order, the increase of alcoholism, and the rise of the Russian mafia. This process, begun as early as the 1970s, had progressed to the extreme by the mid-1990s. Homicides tripled from 1987 to 1995, leaving Russia the most dangerous state next to South Africa. Instances of hooliganism, drug use, prostitution, and felonies also rose sharply. Alcohol consumption, already significant, jumped to 6.5 liters of pure alcohol per capita (compared to the EU, for example, at 1.64) by 2000. One immediate consequence was the spread of HIV/AIDS, to the point where the U.S. CIA estimated a potential of 8 million cases by 2010. In this environment, security became an attractive business, with more than eleven thousand registered agencies.

The 1998 Financial Crisis

After Gerashchenko was fired from the central bank in November 1994, macroeconomic policy improved noticeably. By slowing the growth of money and raising interest, the bank ended Russia's hyperinflation. However, to finance the federal budget, the government replaced monetary financing with foreign debt. It created a bond market, issuing bonds that paid interest of 30–40 percent. Only a few banks were licensed to operate in this new market. They borrowed dollars, which they exchanged for rubles to buy more bonds. The government eventually opened the domestic bond market to foreign participation. By 1998, nearly 50 percent of the government's domestic debt was held by foreigners.

Several factors led to crisis. Falling oil prices left the government with less revenue and the country with less foreign exchange. The Asian financial crisis, which began in the summer of 1997, made foreign investors skittish, hurting exchange rates. The government had certainly borrowed too heavily at too high a price. But finally, with debt-to-GDP ratio at 88 percent, the foreign purchases of Russian bonds simply did not match capital outflows. The oligarchs, among others, were exporting materials but not repatriating the foreign exchange they earned. Instead, they banked it abroad.

As table 9-1 indicates, this amount virtually matched portfolio borrowing. But the net errors and omissions, which also represent capital flight, added to another $31 billion loss in reserves, which precipitated the crisis. On August 17, 1998, the Russian government defaulted on its domestic debt and imposed a moratorium on foreign debt. During the succeeding week, the

TABLE 9-1

Russia's balance of payments, 1994–1998 (millions of U.S. dollars)

	1994	1995	1996	1997	1998
Current account	**8,850**	**8,025**	**12,448**	**2,545**	**1,040**
Trade balance	10,958	11,323	17,809	11,611	13,250
Exports	76,250	93,481	103,844	103,088	87,255
Imports	−65,292	−82,158	−86,035	−91,476	−74,005
Investment income	−1,802	−3,371	−5,434	−8,706	−11,801
Transfers	−306	73	72	−360	−409
Capital account	**−8,612**	**730**	**−6,774**	**5,480**	**8,193**
Direct investment	538	1,658	1,708	4,036	1,734
Portfolio investment	21	−2,444	4,410	45,807	8,619
Other investment	−11,634	11,173	−13,786	−41,610	−7,032
Errors and omissions	−238	−8,755	−5,674	−8,025	−9,234

Source: Rawi Abdelal, "Russia: The End of a Time of Troubles," Case 9-701-076 (Boston: Harvard Business School, 2001), 20. Used with permission.

ruble dropped 70 percent (from R5.9 to R20.6 per dollar). Numerous bank runs closed most banks to depositors. Inflation again skyrocketed, as much as 40 percent on some consumer goods.

This immense economic setback again staggered the standard of living. By the end of 1998, more Russians were poor than ever before—perhaps 40 million, using the World Bank's definition. Unemployment (or unpaid employment) had reached 11.9 percent, with an additional 10 percent of the workforce on a shortened workweek. Income distribution, at least measured by the Gini index, had worsened; it fell from 0.28 to 0.45 by 2004—worse than any OECD country except Mexico and the United States. Perhaps most significantly, the birthrate had declined so precipitously that population growth had turned negative (–0.6 percent). Russia's population was also decreasing, reaching 144.2 million by 2004 (from 146.2 four years earlier).

Vladimir Putin and the Reconstruction of Russia

Although economic growth had recovered sharply in 1999 due to significantly higher oil prices, the closing of the millennium was not a happy for time for Yeltsin's "family" (advisers), the oligarchs, or the Russian people. Yeltsin, now frequently ill, made fewer public appearances other than to announce changes in prime ministers. He became cogent only occasionally, as when he sharply opposed the U.S. bombing of Belgrade, but then he would slump again. On August 9, 1999, he nominated Vladimir Putin to take the job of prime minister. Pundits, unfamiliar with the one-time KGB agent and director of the Federal Security Bureau, dismissed the candidacy as short-lived.

Politically, Putin came out of nowhere. Yeltsin had identified the forty-five-year-old technocrat, at least according to Yeltsin's memoirs, as early as 1997 when Putin first moved to Moscow. Yeltsin was "amazed by Putin's lightning reflex." He felt that "this young man was ready for absolutely anything in life." Yeltsin, like many western observers, was taken with Putin's eyes: "Putin has very interesting eyes. It seems that they say more than his words."[13]

Before being plucked by Yeltsin to serve as head of the Federal Security Bureau, Putin had served for decades in the KGB, having retired as a not-too-distinguished colonel. He was loyal to friends and did not seem ambitious politically. When Yeltsin asked Putin to serve as prime minister, Putin was stunned.

No one in Moscow knew Putin, at least until the outbreak of the Second Chechen War, when Putin engaged the rebels violently. His popularity skyrocketed! And so, on December 14, Yeltsin broached the subject of the presidency with Putin. On the thirty-first, at noon, Yeltsin apologized to the Russian people and withdrew. Putin became president.

In an essay published two days before assuming the presidency, Putin wrote that "Russia needs strong state power." According to Putin, "we are at a stage where even the most correct economic and social policies can start misfiring because of the weakness of the state and managerial bodies."[14] Two months later, in February 2000, he published his "Open Letter to the Russian Voters." Here, he called for "the supremacy of legality, a dictatorship of the law that is equal to all." He complained of the absence of firm rules that were needed to guarantee order. "The stronger the state," concluded Putin, "the freer the individual."[15]

In May 2000, Putin issued a decree creating seven new federal *okrugs*—super-regions to be headed by presidential appointments. Their purpose was to implement federal law in the regions. Former generals and KGB officers, loyal to Putin, were appointed to these positions. He sponsored legislation for the Russian president to dismiss executive authorities in the regions that disregarded federal law. And in 2001, the regional governors were prohibited from holding seats in the Federation Council.

After winning the election in March 2000, Putin distanced himself from the oligarchs. While some maintained their relations with the Yeltsin "family," others began to taste retribution. First was Vladimir Gusinsky, whose Media-Most headquarters were raided by masked officers of the tax police in May. Eventually, Gusinsky was forced to sell his media empire to Gazprom and then flee the country. Next came Boris Berezovsky, who was investigated for tax fraud. He resigned his seat in the Duma and eventually fled the country. On July 28, Putin met with twenty-one of Russia's oligarchs (not including Gusinsky and Berezovsky) to "redefine the relationship between the state and big business."[16] Vladimir Potanin and Roman Abramovich were also threatened by presidential power; the former quietly retired from political life, while the latter sought the governorship of the Chukotka region, thousands of kilometers from the Kremlin.

But it was Khodorkovsky who posed the greatest threat to Putin. In October 2003, the major shareholder and chief executive officer of Yukos—Russia largest oil conglomerate—was arrested. The Russian stock market dropped 14 percent on the news, although it subsequently recovered. Yukos, the government alleged, owed $5 billion in back taxes. Yukos has since been broken up and its top management replaced; Khodorkovsky was sentenced to eight years in a jail thousands of kilometers east of Moscow. He had made the mistake of engaging in politics, endorsing and supporting Putin's presidential opponents. This fact has led western critics to accuse the Russian president of ignoring human rights and asserting dictatorial power.

In Russia, however, Putin's popularity, according to polls, was higher than ever. The populace resented the oligarchs and was glad to see them defeated.

And while Russia still had 36 billionaires—a disproportionate number for the size of its economy—the president has made it clear that the state can stand alone without the oligarchs' help.

In foreign relations, Putin was off to a good start with President George W. Bush. They met in July 2001, in Ljubljana, Slovenia. Putin, who seemed to have an intuitive grasp of diplomatic relations, realized he needed a positive relationship with the West—in part as a counterweight to Europe and China. Bush, who looked into Putin's eyes "and saw his soul," immediately invited Putin to the ranch in Texas.

Less than a month later, on the morning of September 11 when terrorists destroyed the twin towers of the World Trade Center, Putin unambiguously established Russia as an ally of the West. Without hesitating, he used the presidential hotline to be the first head of state to sympathize with President Bush. "Americans, we are with you!" sealed a lasting relationship with the United States, which even opposition to war in Iraq could not undo.

Oil and the Russian Economy

Putin articulated a goal of doubling GDP by 2010, raising Russia's GDP to Portugal's level. His macroeconomic policy entailed tax cuts to stimulate growth, a balanced budget, and gradually tightening monetary policy to reduce inflation. In mid-2000, after winning the election, Putin pushed through a broad-based tax reform. This reform eliminated turnover taxes, fuel taxes, and sales taxes; it reduced personal income taxes, lowered corporate taxes from 35 percent to 24 percent, and lowered the value-added tax to 18 percent. In 2001, Putin restructured income taxes to a flat tax of 13 percent. In 2003–2004, he simplified taxes for small businesses and agriculture.

The budget, which had long been in deficit, was balanced in 2000 and swung positive in 2001. Since then, the surplus has averaged 1.8 percent of GDP. While oil revenues contributed to this, Putin has pushed hard to minimize noninterest expenditures, including international, sectoral, and social expenditures. Defense, law enforcement, and education were allowed to rise.

A particularly innovative and useful policy was the Oil Stabilization Fund, created in 2003 and modeled on a similar fund in Norway. In January 2004, the remaining funds in Russia's debt repayment fund were transferred to the new oil fund, and more than R300 billion were added in 2004. The purpose of this fund was twofold: isolate excess revenues from the economy to avoid inflation and, in a slowdown, provide extra funds to stimulate growth.

At the central bank, monetary policy was gradually tightened by slowing the growth of broad money. By December 2003, the inflation rate was reduced to 12 percent and was projected to reach 9 percent by the end of 2005.

Putin had recruited new blood to implement his ambitious agenda. He fired Viktor Geraschenko (who Yeltsin had reappointed in 1998) from the central bank, replacing him with Sergei Ignatiev. Ignatiev espoused an immediate banking reform and a more rational monetary policy. Second, Putin named Mikhail Kasyanov, a powerful figure in the field of debt negotiations, to be his prime minister during his first term. Putin named liberal-minded Andrei Illarionov as his chief economic adviser. And finally, German Gref became minister of trade and development. In that capacity he devised the Gref Plan, which highlights a reduction of the bureaucracy, the breakup of monopolies, and greater welfare for those in need.

Putin had also overseen further currency liberalization; new civil, criminal, and commercial codes (Putin was a lawyer); trial by jury; more funding for the judiciary (to curb bribery); and enhanced power for judges. Finally, he had introduced a new land code, which legitimized informal sales of industrial property and provided for the sale of agricultural land (albeit not to foreigners).

With the startling help of high oil prices, Russia thrived under Putin. Between 2000 and 2004, real GDP grew at an annual rate of 6.8 percent—even exceeding the growth of India. Fixed investment had risen to more than 18 percent, while private consumption held constant at 50 percent.

The most stellar performance was international (see table 9-2). Russia's balance of trade, and its current account, soared with the price of oil. While imports remained almost stable in nominal terms, exports rose from $74 billion to $129 billion in the six years after the crisis. While the service deficit grew a bit, interest payments remained about constant—and huge surpluses resulted. While net capital continued to flow out of Russia, representing continuing capital flight and (perhaps) a lack of secure domestic investment opportunities, foreign capital inflows had nonetheless risen sharply. For the first nine months of 2004, $29 billion in loans to Russian business had flowed into the country.

Among these foreign investors was British Petroleum (BP), back again after getting taken for about $500 million in 1999. In 1997, it had bought 10 percent of Sidanko, owned by Vladimir Potanin. In 1999, another Russian oil company, Tyumen Oil Company (TNK), bought the debt of a Sidanko subsidiary, Chernogorneft, and then took control in a bankruptcy auction. Somehow, TNK took control of Sidanko, leaving BP out.

In 2003, however, a wiser BP, determined to play a significant role in Russia's oil development, was back with $6.5 billion to undertake a joint venture with TNK. Russia, after all, has oil reserves of about 50 billion barrels, and something approaching 1,700 trillion cubic feet of gas—nearly a third of the world's reserves. As one BP executive commented, you can't be a global oil

TABLE 9-2

Russia's balance of payments, 2000–2005 (millions of U.S. dollars)

	2000	2002	2004	2005
Goods exports	105,033	107,301	183,452	245,300
Goods imports	−44,862	−60,966	−96,307	−125,000
Net services	−6,665	−9,886	−13,000	−14,600
Net factor income	−6,667	−7,333	59,920	−18,100
Current account	46,839	29,116	59,920	86,600
Capital transfers	10,955	−12,388	−667	−12,200
Financial account	−48,638	−10,227	−50,883	−2,100
Capital and financial account	−37,683	−22,615	−51,550	−14,400
Change in reserves*	−16,010	−11,375	−45,235	−61,461

*Negative sign indicates an accumulation of reserves.
Source: Russian Central Bank.

company if you're not in Russia! For the same reason, Royal Dutch/Shell was closing a deal for $10 billion in 2003 to develop oil and liquefied natural gas off shore of Sakhalin Island in Russia's far east. This investment, now estimated at $20 billion and approaching operation, is the biggest investment ever made by an oil company anywhere and the biggest single foreign investment in Russia. Both projects suggest that western investors have a growing confidence in Russia's management.

So healthy was Russia's economic growth and its international performance since 2000 that foreign debt declined and Russia was eventually able to pay off the IMF and continue servicing its remaining debt. In November 2004, Fitch Ratings, an international rating agency, actually upgraded Russia's sovereign risk to investment grade. Official foreign exchange reserves, which were virtually depleted in 1998, had risen to $107 billion by November 2004, or $127 billion if one includes monetary gold. And the ruble's exchange rate had stabilized since 2002 and actually strengthened against the falling dollar, from 31.3 to 28.9 by the end of 2004.

Russia's Future

Russia still had scores of problems—economic, institutional, social, and geopolitical. But if one asked most Russians today about their perspective on the future, they would certainly be more optimistic than any time in the past two decades. They liked Vladimir Putin (who enjoyed more than a 70 percent approval rating), perhaps because there was no better alternative, and thought he managed effectively.

In this chapter, we saw the failure of instant liberalization—of the big bang in an ethnically complicated, hard-line Communist country. The state lost its autonomy, becoming dependent on oligarchs. It then lost its capacity to accomplish key functions—collect taxes, provide security, and provide money with value. And finally, after the events of 1998, it had lost its legitimacy among the Russian people.[17] Politicians, oligarchs, and economic advisers all contributed. There were many reasons for this success, but the absence of capitalist institutions stands out. It is now clear to most observers that institutions are crucial to economic development.

In the case of Russia, the existing institutions, created over seventy years of Marxist totalitarianism, were utterly ineffective when the nation turned to capitalism and democracy. To reform before rebuilding its institutions proved to be a costly mistake. The Putin government has begun again to build these institutions and in the process is reconsolidating the Kremlin's political power. We see in the Russia story the importance of government—of good government—in building a nation, directing strategy, and managing growth.

In the Russian story, of course, the role of government seems obvious and explicit. That is because its institutions, along with legitimacy, utterly failed in the 1990s. Thus, what Putin and the Russian people now are doing is what every nation must do—only most do it more gradually and less autocratically. But either way, it needs to be done. They must construct a new organizational structure to implement Russia's energy-led development strategy.

I'm more optimistic about Russia, despite continuing failings, than I've been at any time in my adult life. I'd invest there, as I think others are now doing, with the hopes that it emerges as a strong capitalist democracy over the next couple of decades.

PART III

Deficits, Debt, and Stagnation

TEN

European Integration and Italian Competitiveness

FOR MORE THAN FIVE DECADES, Western Europe has been undergoing a process of integration: first tariffs, then exchange rates, then barriers to movement, and finally monetary union. Each of these steps, deemed successful, led to the next—in an atmosphere of enthusiasm for integration that would end internal wars and make Europe globally competitive.

Yet for the last of these five decades, Western Europe has been stagnating in productivity growth, in competitiveness, and in its structural adjustments to globalization. "Structural rigidities," writes the Commission of the European Communities, "may be the origin of sluggish adjustment." The Commission goes on to identify "wage rigidities and imperfect competition . . . the lack of resolve in addressing budgetary consolidation, structural reforms and pension reforms [that] have raised uncertainty and thereby adversely affected consumer confidence and spending."[1]

Since the mid-1990s, Western Europe has grown slowly and its GDP per capita has slipped to two-thirds that of the United States. Unemployment is unacceptably high, and employment relatively low. Despite reform, government regulation still seems excessive. Fiscal deficits exceed Europe's own Stability and Growth Pact. Labor markets are rigid, despite some recent reforms. Higher education lags severely behind the United States, as does the innovation process in general. The population is aging, yet pension systems remain grossly underfunded.

In the midst of these substantial challenges, Europe has embraced the huge new task of integrating ten Eastern European nations that entered the European Union in mid-2004. These countries, recovering from decades of Soviet domination, have far less developed economies, and less sophisticated institutions, than their new partners in the west. The per capita incomes of their citizens (adjusted for purchasing power parity) are less than half those of Western Europe—and the poor ones are less than a third. These huge differences pose competitive problems, unemployment and immigration issues, and asymmetric investment flows.

Italy, one of the four largest nations of Western Europe, suffers from all of these problems. Its economic growth in 2005 was negative. It is running huge budget deficits and a significant current account deficit. Its debt is rising. While employment rates have improved between 2003 and 2005, they remain low even compared with Europe. Unemployment among young adults and women, especially in the south, is exceedingly high. Italy's two-tiered industry structure—a handful of large, uncompetitive firms and thousands of specialized clustered industries—is becoming more and more exposed to foreign competition. Labor unions are unwilling to make significant changes in their inflexible labor markets. And immigrants are pouring in from the east (Albania) and the south (North Africa). Silvio Berlusconi, the prime minister from 2001 to 2006, headed a weakening coalition government that seemed unable to act.

This chapter explores Europe's accomplishments in integration—a degree of integration never before achieved peacefully and the cutting edge of globalization. And to illustrate these developments, it will focus as a case in point on Italy—today one of the richest countries in the world. The chapter will also look at Europe's problems during the past ten years, especially illustrated by Italy. It will conclude by examining the major challenges facing the region—identifying, perhaps, the sorts of institutional and policy changes that are most needed for continued future success.

European Integration

The destruction wrought by World War II convinced many Europeans that the time for unification had come. In 1946, Winston Churchill, speaking in Fulton, Missouri, called for a "United States of Europe." Over the next few years, several efforts to create a political union failed as governments declined to surrender political sovereignty.

Economic integration, however, remained more tractable. In 1951, France, West Germany, Belgium, Luxembourg, the Netherlands, and Italy created the European Coal and Steel Community (ECSC). The ECSC was essentially a customs union for coal and steel. It served to enhance efficiency and profitability in these two industries and fostered cooperation between former adversaries like France and West Germany.

Treaty of Rome

With this positive experience behind them, the six ECSC countries signed the Treaty of Rome in 1957, establishing the European Economic Community. This treaty laid out a timetable for its members to remove all internal tariffs and establish a common external tariff by 1970 (an objective actually reached two years earlier). It also provided for the creation of a common agricultural policy and the removal of some nontariff barriers to the free movement of people, services, and capital. This treaty would "lay the foundations of an even closer union among the people of Europe to preserve and strengthen peace and liberty." The community's membership also increased. Britain, Ireland, and Denmark joined in 1973; Greece in 1981; Spain and Portugal in 1986; and Austria, Finland, and Sweden in 1995. These additions brought the number of member states to fifteen.

Institutions of the European Union

The European Union (EU), as the European Economic Community was renamed in 1992, was composed of four principal institutions: the Commission, the Council of Ministers, the European Parliament, and the Court of Justice. The responsibilities of these institutions have been amended by subsequent regulations. In particular, the Amsterdam Treaty of 1997 increased the power of both the council and the parliament relative to the Commission.

The Commission was the executive or bureaucratic arm of the EU, administered by a president and twenty commissioners. The president was chosen by member countries for a renewable five-year term. The commissioners were appointed by national governments and the president—two from each of the five larger countries, and one each from the smaller ones. The parliament approved the appointment of the president and his entire commission. The different directors were supposed to represent the interests of the EU as a whole, supported by a staff of more than fourteen thousand professionals.

The Commission was given three principal responsibilities. It initiated all the EU's proposals, represented the EU in international trade negotiations, and administered the EU's budget. It was responsible for the management of such EU policies as agricultural subsidies and antitrust enforcement, and for overseeing national policies to ensure they were consistent with EU policy. The Commission investigated violations of EU treaties and could refer them to the Court of Justice.

The Council of Ministers, somewhat akin to the U.S. Senate, served as the EU's principal decision-making body. It could not initiate legislation, but it had the power to approve, amend, or reject Commission proposals. The council consisted of ministers from each national government—not as a permanent body, but convening to deal with specific issues. Thus, agricultural ministers composed the council when it dealt with agricultural policy; trade ministers when it dealt with trade policy. The council presidency was responsible for setting the agenda, and it rotated among member states every six months. Decisions were mostly adopted by a qualified majority (e.g., sixty-two votes out of a total of eighty-seven before the admission of Eastern European states).

The European Parliament—once described as the "democratic deficit"— was composed of 626 members (expanded to 732 in 2004) and was directly elected by voters in each nation. The parliament met in both Brussels and Strasbourg. In 1992, parliament began to share joint decision-making powers with the council on issues such as freedom of movement of workers, free circulation of products, and freedom to set up a business. The parliament had the power, shared with the council, to reject the Commission's budget proposals. It could even turn out the Commission through a vote of no confidence. Although never exercised, the threat of such a vote in 1999 brought down the Commission of Jacques Santer in the wake of a corruption scandal.

Finally, the Court of Justice, with a judge from each country, interpreted EU treaties and directives and sought to apply the community's law in a uniform manner. The Amsterdam Treaty allowed the court to rule on issues affecting people's freedom and security. Court decisions had precedence over national rulings, but in numerous cases, companies and states disregarded the court.[2]

EU regulations and directives began as Commission proposals. The process for approving proposals typically took from two to five years. Proposals were initiated by the Commission and then sent to parliament for study and debate. Review by parliament was followed by approval (or amendment) by the council. After a second reading by the parliament, the proposal became a directive. Member states were then obligated to change ("transpose") their national laws to conform to it.[3]

After operating successfully for a decade without internal tariffs, proponents of a single Europe took another step toward integration with the formation of the European Monetary System (EMS) in 1979. Formally proposed by Chancellor Helmut Schmidt of Germany and President Valéry Giscard d'Estaing of France, the EMS established a system of "fixed but adjustable" exchange rates. It was designed to insulate intra-European trade from the effects of sharp exchange rate fluctuations and to promote greater macro-economic convergence.

On March 1, 1979, eight European states tied their exchange rates together in an exchange rate mechanism. Thereafter, they agreed to maintain their rates within a narrow band, fluctuating up or down 2.25 percent from the initial parity. Foreign exchange reserves and central bank interest rates were used to maintain currencies within the band. Germany, with its strong central bank (Bundesbank) and low inflation, was the anchor.

During the 1980s, the EMS seemed to work well, reducing inflation in France and Italy, and minimizing inflation differentials between the eight member countries. By 1991, the average inflation of the EMS's eight countries had fallen to 3.6 percent, down from a high of 12.2 percent in 1981.

Single Europe Act

With trade and monetary integration working well, Eurocrats pushed harder for more integration. In 1985, the Commission released a white paper outlining a program to complete the integration of European markets by 1993. It proposed 282 targets for integrating and harmonizing rules and regulations that interfered with the free movement of goods, services, and people. Doing so, argued the paper, would eliminate costs and foster efficiency and competitiveness. This "adventure in deregulation," as the *Economist* put it, would create a stronger and more prosperous Europe.[4]

At the time, Europe was coming under increasing competitive pressure from both Japan and the United States. The GDPs of both countries were growing faster than Europe's; they had less inflation and significantly lower unemployment. Multinational firms from America and Japan—GE, Toyota, Canon, Toshiba, Boeing, and Microsoft—seemed to be rising to world dominance, leaving more traditional European firms behind.

Europeans felt that small markets, with inadequate economies of scale, were a large part of the problem. While Japanese and American firms produced for huge markets at a limited number of more efficient plants, Europeans competed for markets of 5 million to 45 million with too many companies operating fragmented, smaller-scale production facilities. Since an integrated Europe would have a slightly larger population than the United States, it was hoped that rationalization could force European business to become competitive.

The Single Europe Act of 1985 amended the original Treaty of Rome to alleviate three obstacles: (1) physical barriers, including intra-EC border stoppages, customs controls, and associated paperwork; (2) technical barriers, which involved meeting divergent national product standards, technical regulations, and conflicting business laws, and opening nationally protected public procurement markets; and (3) fiscal barriers, which mainly dealt with diverse value-added tax rates and excise duties.

Border controls—including tax collection, agricultural checks, veterinary checks, and transportation controls—were to be eliminated. Customs costs alone were estimated to be 30–45 percent more per unit of revenue for smaller firms than larger ones.

Harmonization of more than a hundred thousand different regulations and standards would create an immense savings—in design, production, packaging, and rationalization of plants. These regulations affected health, safety, the environment, and technical standards. EC member countries set their own national standards for industries ranging from food processing to automobiles, from electrical products to telecommunications. Each country ran its own testing facilities and licensing bureaucracy.

The Commission realized that harmonization of so many standards by negotiation could take a thousand years, given entrenched interests within each country. Fortunately, the Court of Justice (in Cassis de Dijon) recognized a new approach to harmonization, based on the principle of "mutual recognition." If a producer met the standard of its own country, its product would be acceptable in the other EC countries, even if the standard did not apply there. Thus, products lawfully produced or marketed in one EC nation, if legal at home, would have access to all other EC markets.

One sees immediately how this worked. Country A sold its product in Country B, although Country A's own standards were less costly than those of Country B. As soon as Country B's consumers began buying Country A's product, Country B's producers would lobby their government to change the standard or regulation to that of Country A. In other words, over time mutual recognition would precipitate deregulation—at least down to some common minimum standard set—by the Commission.

Uncompetitive public procurement was another target of the Single Europe Act. Because of Europe's socialist legacy, public procurement (from government-owned companies) amounted to some 12 percent of the EC's GDP. The 1985 program sought to end national protectionism for all public procurement contracts. In particular, the Commission aimed to open four hitherto closed sectors to competitive bidding—energy, transportation, water supply, and telecommunications. The Commission's proposal, nevertheless, allowed national governments to give preference to products with at least 50 percent European content.

The Commission intended to end the divergence in national indirect tax rates, which encompassed both the value-added tax (VAT) and excise taxes.

Divergent rates, from 1 percent to 38 percent, distorted trade flows and locational decisions. Most countries had two or three different VAT rates. The white paper proposed abolishing the highest tier of VAT rates and then reducing the gap between the remaining two tiers to narrower bands—4 percent to 9 percent for the reduced rate and 14 percent to 20 percent for the standard rate—over several years. The tax would be charged at the point of sale, rather than collected at the border.

The Commission believed, in the mid-1980s, that "the establishment of a common market in services [was] one of the main preconditions for a return to economic prosperity."[5] Services embraced a variety of activities, including finance, telecommunications, and transportation. They were all rapidly growing sectors, albeit heavily regulated.

The Single Europe Act placed a premium on creating a common financial market. The liberalization of capital movements, which had begun several years before the act, was deemed crucial to all other cross-border activities. The right of establishment of cross-border branches and the freedom to provide cross-border services were key. Here too the Commission applied mutual recognition to speed integration along.

Market Integration

It would take far longer—decades longer—to integrate markets than the seven years anticipated by the Single Europe Act. By the end of 1998, the Commission had issued 1,374 directives, with more to come. Member states had made extraordinary efforts to transpose these—succeeding with 99.3 percent in the best case, which was Finland, but even 94.5 percent in the weakest case, which was Portugal. In networked or politically sensitive sectors, like telecommunications or transportation, the process of transposition was slower. In more segmented, simpler businesses like cosmetic products or plant health checks, transposition was more complete.

Diverse cultures appeared to remain the biggest barrier to market integration—by far. As one executive who ran an auto-leasing company observed, "[C]ultural barriers and language barriers were huge . . . Integration . . . is a process of hundreds of years."[6] At the end of the century, his firm still did purchasing, maintenance, contracts, programs, accounting, and taxes locally; only finance was Europe-wide. A Dutch executive also observed that culture overwhelmed much else. "Netherlands," he said, "is closer to the USA culturally than to France. This explained slow progress in retail integration—in food, clothes, professional services, retail banking and so on."[7]

Product Markets

The Single Europe Act's first objective—to facilitate the free movement of people, goods, and services—had been substantially achieved. Border checks of passports and shipping invoices had been virtually eliminated. Most external tariffs had been liberalized, with the exception of some sensitive imports (automobiles, textiles, and agricultural products). Even the voluntary restrictions on Japanese auto imports, negotiated in 1991, eventually expired by 2000.

Standardization of diverse regulations had also made significant progress, although it still has a ways to go. Mutual recognition helped immensely for consumer durables and capital goods but ran into problems with foodstuffs, pesticides, and pharmaceuticals, where domestic regulations extended to safety and price. Here the Commission developed another mechanism, the adoption of "essential requirements." Once these were agreed on, national standards organizations were charged to harmonize standards. On the other hand, newly agreed-on national rules, or "notifications," were being created by the hundreds.

All of this harmonization was intended to force rationalization of inefficient assets, to increase competition, and to drive down costs. Indeed, rationalization had begun, but it was mostly in-country rationalization at first. The number of completed mergers jumped from less than fifteen hundred in 1985 to more than four thousand annually for the rest of the century. It made sense that firms would merge within familiar markets first before extending their reach across, or even beyond, Europe.[8] Intra-European mergers increased more gradually, reaching nearly a thousand by 1998. Only after the end of the century did the number of intra-Europe and inter-Europe mergers take off—as European firms began trying to adjust to globalization—rising to more than $700 billion by 2004.

With deregulation and the intensification of competition, the dispersion of prices should have narrowed. Single markets, like the United States, have small regional differences to account for differences in relative wages—but these are generally less than 10 percent. The OECD estimated that consumer-price dispersion had indeed narrowed, from 21 percent to 16 percent, over the first decade of the Single Europe Act. A sectoral study by the Commission revealed price dispersions between 8.3 percent (in mechanical engineering) and 32.1 percent (in pharmaceuticals).

Automobiles are probably the most important sector of Europe's economy—representing as much as one out of six manufacturing jobs. Figure 10-1 shows prices varying by as much as 36 percent across Europe for some models. Of course, differences in value-added taxes and local competitive condi-

FIGURE 10-1

Percentage difference between the lowest and highest prices of selected automobiles in the European Union in 2004

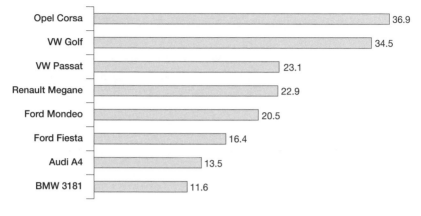

Opel Corsa	36.9
VW Golf	34.5
VW Passat	23.1
Renault Megane	22.9
Ford Mondeo	20.5
Ford Fiesta	16.4
Audi A4	13.5
BMW 3181	11.6

Source: Compiled by author with data from European Commission, 2004.

tions affect these gaps. Yet even for branded consumer goods—like Levi's jeans, Pampers, or a 1.5-liter bottle of Coke—price gaps of 50 percent to 70 percent prevailed.

Thus, integration was happening in product markets but more slowly than anticipated by Eurocrats.

Capital Markets

The Single Europe Act had viewed capital markets, then diffusely regulated and fragmented, as an important barrier to integration and global competitiveness. Thus, one of the EC's principal thrusts had been to lower regulatory barriers in banking, securities, and insurance and to foster a deeper, more modern system of finance in Europe.

Harmonization by the Commission had begun in 1977, with the First Banking Coordination Directive. But a series of directives after 1986 really opened European banking to competition and rationalization. Especially important was the Second Banking Directive of 1988, which "abolished restrictions on movements of capital taking place between persons resident in Member States." In 1989, another directive established the principle of mutual recognition of a single banking license. A few months later, a directive on solvency ratios sought to harmonize credit risk. In the early 1990s, these measures were followed by directives on capital adequacy, deposit guarantees, and liberalization of capital flows.[9]

The impact of deregulation was dramatic. The value of EU bonds, equities, and cross-border bank loans exceeded those of the United States by 1995. Wholesale banking was increasingly integrated. Competition in commercial products benefited most in countries that had relatively less sophisticated financial systems. Prices of loans, mortgages, fees, and deposits were falling as competition intensified.

Retail competition across borders, however, developed much more slowly. There were few cross-border sales of life insurance, for example. But credit card prices differed sharply, and retail banking remained local—or at best, national. As long as the different governments retained separate provisions for bankruptcy, deposit guarantees, and pensions, pan-European markets for retail financial products would develop slowly.

In capital markets, like product markets, the pace of mergers and acquisitions accelerated during the 1990s. The number of mergers jumped from less than two hundred to an average of nearly six hundred—but again, they were mostly national rather than intra-European. Although these would increase in number after the turn of the century, they continued to be resisted by national central banks.[10] One senior banker in Germany opined that it might take fifty years for European banking to achieve the degree of integration experienced in the United States.[11]

Labor Markets

The progress made in product markets and capital markets had not been achieved in labor markets. They remained fragmented and sorely in need of structural reform. In 1996, the total number of migrant workers within the EU amounted to three hundred eleven thousand. Although culture and language were the principal barriers, institutional problems with industrial unions, welfare systems, and pensions remained substantial. While the Commission recognized these difficulties in the 1990s, it was unable to do much about them through 2005.

Low employment rates and persistently high levels of structural unemployment, especially for women and youth, were the critical symptoms. Since the early 1970s, Europe's employment rate had dropped—from 66 percent to 60 percent by 1994—but had recovered to 64 percent by 2004. (The employment rate in the United States, by contrast, peaked at 65 percent in 2000 and currently stands at 63 percent.)[12] Likewise, unemployment for the EU's fifteen member countries (the EU-15) had averaged 10.5 percent during the 1990s and reached a low point of 8.1 percent in 2003. By mid-2005 it had again risen to 10 percent in France and nearly 12 percent in Germany.

Besides culture, the source of these problems could be found in relative productivity differentials, in education and training, in geographic immobility, in minimum wage levels, in benefit levels, and in taxation. To conserve space, a couple of examples must suffice.

Consider the unemployment systems of the EU-15. In 1995, for example, low-wage workers in Belgium received 79 percent of their salary after one month of unemployment. In the sixtieth month, they received 86 percent. In Sweden, unemployed workers could receive 109 percent of their salary in the sixtieth month! True, there were countries like Portugal and Italy that eventually cut off benefits, but even those were incredibly generous during the first year or two.[13] If one adds to this support the near-universal availability of free higher education and health care, it is little wonder that youth unemployment rates surpassed 20 percent in several countries and averaged 16 percent in 2003.

Work rules and firing restrictions were also inflexible in Europe, thanks to decades of successful union activism. Layoffs were all but impossible in some countries, like Italy. And where doable, they required months of negotiations and years of compensation settlement. In 2002, the average annual hours worked in the Netherlands was near 1,300. In Germany, it was 1,450, and in France 1,560. This compared to 1,810 in the United States and 1,820 in Japan.[14] The difference, on average, was 400 hours, or ten weeks (if one actually worked 40 hours per week). It is scarcely surprising that GDPs per capita in Europe had fallen to less than two-thirds of those of the United States and Japan.

During the 1990s, hundreds of labor reforms were enacted by the different EU members. Yet just over half of these 414 reforms moved policy in opposite directions—that is, they increased the rewards for participating in the labor force or increased the generosity of unemployment benefits. These reforms, which frequently undid the effects of one another over a few years, had little discernable effect in total.[15]

Monetary Union

Leaders of all EC member nations gathered in the small Dutch town of Maastricht in December 1991 to discuss proposals for creation of a monetary union. With the successful removal of trade barriers, the linking of exchange rates, and progress toward an integrated market, many European leaders felt it time to take the next step toward unification. They drafted the Treaty of Maastricht, providing added powers for the European Parliament, increased regional funds for the less developed EU members, and a framework for a common foreign policy. But the centerpiece was a timetable for achieving monetary union, by January 1997, or if that proved infeasible, January 1999.

The treaty designated five criteria for convergence:

1. A currency was to remain within a normal fluctuation band (originally 2.25 percent but later changed to 15 percent) in 1995 around parity.

2. Inflation was to be lowered to within 1.5 percent of the average of the three countries with the lowest inflation rates.

3. Long-term interest rates were to be reduced to within 2 percent of the average of the three countries with the lowest inflation rates.

4. National budget deficits were not to exceed 3 percent of GDP.

5. Public debt was to be reduced to 60 percent of GDP.

Once monetary union took effect, the exchange rates of member nations would be irrevocably fixed and a new European currency (the euro) would be substituted over a three-year period. The European Central Bank (ECB) in Frankfurt, controlled by the central bank governors of member countries, would set European monetary policy. Independent of national authorities, the ECB's principal task was the maintenance of prices over the medium term at 2 percent or less—the Harmonized Index of Consumer Prices. "We're given one tool and one objective," observed an ECB economist, "and told to get on with it and that we shouldn't veer from it . . . The countries should know what we will do because that is our goal." He added sardonically, "We're serious about maintaining price stability. There are a lot of very serious people here."[16]

Convergence turned out to be more difficult than anticipated. When Germany reunified in 1990–1991, the West began rebuilding the East with something like $120 billion per year. These expenditures not only added to Germany's deficits but drove up interest rates and, thus, the deutsche mark. When other currencies could not maintain their parities (without also driving up interest rates and thus precipitating recessions), the exchange rate mechanism broke down. It was only restored in 1995, with a new parity band of 15 percent.

But political leadership in the principal European countries was sufficiently committed to monetary union that they slashed budgets and tightened monetary policies—even Italy, where the deficit stood at 9.7 percent in 1992 and interest rates exceeded 12 percent. By 1998, fourteen countries had lowered inflation and interest rates, and reduced government deficits to less than 3 percent. The Commission even adopted the Stability and Growth

Pact in 1998, setting deficit targets for member countries to decline toward zero within five years. Government debt, however, remained a problem for eight of the countries—as high as 119 percent of GDP for Italy. Thus, the Commission modified this criterion, allowing a declining debt to be good enough.

On May 2, 1998, eleven of the EU countries decided to tie the historic knot and lock their currencies together. Greece, which hadn't yet attained the criteria, would join two years later. And three other countries—Denmark, Sweden, and the United Kingdom—chose not to join for political reasons. Monetary union took effect January 2, 1999; by July 2002, there was only the euro.

Structural Adjustment in Italy

In 2003, Italy was the fourth-largest European country by population (57 million) and GDP (€1,379 billion), although it was just the twelfth-largest in GDP per capita ($25,592; see figure 10-2). And it was the oldest Western European civilization, dating from at least the eighth century BC, with the founding of Rome. However, Italy's economy had grown only 1.7 percent annually since Maastricht and had been virtually stagnant since 2002. Prime Minister Silvio Berlusconi was struggling to enact structural reforms but had accomplished little in four years given his fragile coalition government.[17]

Country Background

Italy occupies a central position in the northern Mediterranean, allowing it easy access to Europe, northern Africa, and the Middle East. Northern Italy shares a border with France, Switzerland, Austria, and Slovenia. Italy is home to the Mediterranean islands of Sardinia and Sicily, as well as two independent states: Vatican City and the Republic of San Marino.

After conquering much of Western Europe and North Africa, Rome became the dominant power in the region until the fifth century AD. After a series of foreign invasions, political unity was lost and Italy became an often-changing succession of small states and principalities. During the medieval period, the Catholic Church became the administrative power in central Italy. A series of powerful Italian trading states arose in the fourteenth and fifteenth centuries—Florence, Milan, Venice, and Genoa—which seized control of textiles and spice trade in the Mediterranean region.

With the fall of Napoléon, Giuseppe Mazzini and Giuseppe Garibaldi led a revolution against Italy's Austrian rulers, establishing Italy as a constitutional monarchy in 1861. Yet despite this facade of unification, Italy remained

FIGURE 10-2

GDP per capita in European Union member states, 2003

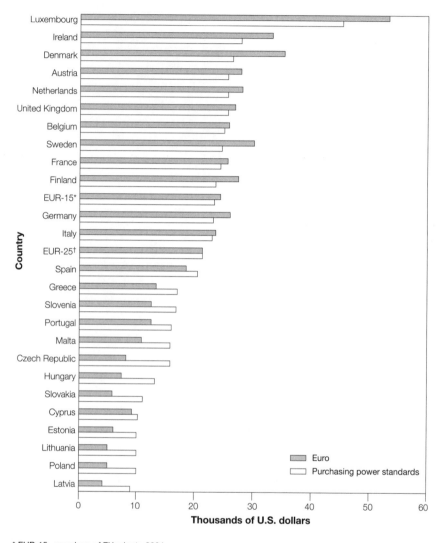

* EUR-15—members of EU prior to 2004
† EUR-25—includes 10 new members

Source: The EU Economy: 2004 Review, Commission of the European Commmunities Directorate General Economic and Financial Affairs: Brussels, October 26, 2004.

deeply fragmented. Class distinctions, especially in the south, continued to divide Italy. After siding with victorious Allies in World War I, Italy deteriorated into a fascist state with the rise of Benito Mussolini. Mussolini signed the Concordant of 1929, a compromise agreement that both the Catholic Church and the state should be "independent and sovereign."

After siding with Hitler, Italy was invaded by the Allies in 1943 and eventually signed an armistice in September. In June 1946, Italians voted by popular referendum to replace their outdated monarchy with a democratic republic. On January 1, 1948, Italians approved a new constitution, representing a compromise between Catholic and Communist ambitions. The constitution established a bicameral parliament, an executive branch to be headed by a prime minister, a judicial system based on existing civil law, and a president elected for seven years.

Modern Italy is divided between two main socioeconomic regions: the north and the south. The north was the industrial heart of the country. This region boasts of low unemployment rates and a well-built infrastructure. Its economy is composed of a few large corporations and thousands of small to medium family-owned manufacturing companies. The south, known as the Mezzogiorno, suffers from a higher crime rate, high unemployment, and a poor infrastructure. The state maintains a considerable presence in the south, where it invested in large government-owned businesses.

The Italian population is relatively homogeneous. About 98 percent are Italian; 99 percent are Roman Catholic. Most people speak Italian, the official language. Italians have very strong family ties. Many children do not leave home until their late twenties or early thirties. Married couples often move within one kilometer of their parents' homes. Bound by their roots, most Italians are unwilling to relocate even when offered higher-paying jobs. "Many people don't want to move because of regional differences," explained one analyst. "They fear leaving the safety of their local region. It is a cultural thing."[18]

Population Growth

By 2001, Italy had a population of 57.5 million. Despite a high population density, Italy had the lowest birthrate in Europe. Its population was virtually constant through 2005, and some expected it would begin declining shortly. Italy's rapidly aging population was a related problem. As life expectancy improved and birthrates fell, Italy's population was aging . . . quickly. Istat, the national statistical institute, predicted that by 2010, the population age fifty-seven and above would be larger than that between twenty and fifty-six.

The government already spent 15 percent of GDP on state-funded pensions. Rising pensions, combined with health care, threatened to bankrupt the government over the next few years.

Income Distribution

Income inequality in Italy is surprisingly flat for a developed, industrial country. Part of the reason is the large segment of population that participates in the underground economy, generally avoiding taxation. The other reason is high and progressive taxation, which serves to redistribute incomes through social spending. Italy's Gini index, somewhere between 0.28 and 0.35, is relatively low.

Organized Crime

One of Italy's distinctive social institutions is organized crime. The major rings of organized crime are located in the south: the Mafia in Sicily, the Camorra in Campania, and the 'Ndrangheta in Calabria. These family-run gangs, which take advantage of the south's high unemployment rates, participate in smuggling, gambling, and most significantly, illegal drugs. The Mafia's use of violence to enforce its control has significantly discouraged legitimate investment in the south. Although Mussolini had nearly eradicated the Mafia, it regained control of political and legal systems after World War II. The government began to enforce anti-Mafia measures in the early 1990s; those efforts have faded more recently as weak political coalitions have focused on economic integration.

The Rise and Fall of the Christian Democrats

Despite massive destruction of its infrastructure, Italy rebounded from World War II and moved quickly through reconstruction. The 1950s gave birth to the first "Italian miracle," an industrial boom that brought prosperity, especially to the northern and central regions. With capital funds generally unavailable to support large-scale enterprise, a structure of family-owned businesses became the mainstay of the Italian economy. Entrepreneurs established small companies that focused on textiles, machinery, and food processing. These businesses took advantage of Italy's proximity to the water and exported goods to the world.

The state established the Cassa per il Mezzogiorno (Funds for the Development of the South) to bridge the economic gap between north and south. Eventually, the government built "cathedrals in the desert"—large plants in steel, coal, petrochemicals, and utilities. Pressures for developmental spending in the south would continue right through 2005, when Berlusconi's government fell and was reestablished in part due to southern unemployment and spending issues.

The Christian Democrat Party (DC) rose to power after gaining a parliamentary majority in 1945. The Church, promoting the belief that wealth should be equally spread, supported this coalition. This Catholic attitude influenced the politics of the DC during its fifty-year dominance of Italian government. And as the cold war unfolded in Europe, the DC also gained the support of the United States. In Italy, the Communist Party had emerged as the most powerful Communist bloc in the west. Fearing that the Communists would gain control of Italy, the United States poured money into the DC's coffers and threatened to withdraw its support if the Communists were to enter government.

The 1980s witnessed yet another industrial and economic revival led by small and medium-sized businesses. Productivity growth and foreign direct investment revitalized Italy's export-driven economy. This second "economic miracle" enthused the Italian polity for European integration when it signed the Single Europe Act.

And just three years later, the Berlin Wall collapsed, rocking the foundations of Italy's political system. That system had been built on fear of the Soviet Union. Yet now, democracy and capitalism had triumphed. Once the threat to democracy was removed, the need to sustain an anti-Communist government slipped away. Thus, the dominance of the DC crumbled as people realized that "automatic collusion in the corrupt practices of the DC and its coalition partners" was no longer required.[19]

At about the same time, corruption investigations, known as Tangentopoli, brought the demise of the DC. Operation Mani Pulite (Clean Hands) uncovered a web of corruption between political leaders, local authorities, and major corporations. Italian magistrates shined light on an institutionalized system of bribes through which profits from state-owned enterprises had flowed directly into the hands of political officials. These scandals led to the death of the First Republic, a fifty-year span of centrist dominance by the DC. Over the next ten years, Italy experienced a succession of ten coalition governments, shifting from the business-right of Berlusconi's Forza Italia to the Communist left of Massimo D'Alema's Ulivo coalition.

In the process, Italy more or less fixed its macroeconomy. Under the leadership of Giuliani Amato, a nonpolitical *techni* government enacted an austere budget, increased taxes, initiated pension reform, and launched an aggressive program of privatization. The lira was devalued by 30 percent, leading to a boom in Italy's exports. Governments headed by Ciampi (1993),

Berlusconi (1994), Dini (1995), and Prodi (1996–1998) extended these reforms, eventually making Italy eligible for monetary union.

The Dual Economy

Italy's microeconomy, however, was less well off. The dual economy was dominated by two tiers of private companies. The first tier consisted of a few large family-owned companies. Using holding companies and cross-shareholdings, families like Agnelli controlled Fiat, Italy's largest conglomerate that produced cars, tractors, steel, machine tools, and airplane engines; Pirelli, a tire company that manufactured industrial rubber products and telecom cables; and Olivetti, a computer and telecommunications business. Other conglomerates were run by the Benetton, Romiti, Marzotto, Del Vecchio, Ferrero, and Gardini families. And for more than fifty years, the powerful Mediobanca, a private merchant bank, had financed this integrated web—"a narrow cartel of northern entrepreneurs."[20]

The second tier of Italy's dual economy was made up of clusters of family-owned small and medium-sized companies. These *distretti*, or "industrial districts," have been described as "geographic concentrations of interconnected firms, specialized suppliers, service providers, firms in related industries, and associated institutions . . . [that] all contribute to a system that produces the goods that are characteristic of the district."[21] For example, the leather footwear industry in Verona spawned a cluster of interrelated business (i.e., tanneries, footwear machinery, leather clothing, athletic footwear, etc.) whose proximity facilitated the sharing of knowledge and resources. Other clusters included ceramic tiles in Sassuolo, silk in Como, textiles in Prato, factory automation equipment in Turin, and packaging machinery in Bologna.

Several characteristics seemed essential to the development of a strong cluster: geographic concentration, close family ties, domestic rivalry, specialization, and cooperation and knowledge transfer between firms and suppliers. Professor Michael Porter has explained that in Italy, "constant competitive advantage was present, due to sophisticated and demanding local buyers, strong and unique distribution channels and intense rivalry among local firms . . . [T]he real uniqueness of Italy, however, was the out-of-school learning process in particular industries."[22]

One such cluster examined by this author was the packaging machinery group, near Bologna. This group included twenty medium-sized firms with fewer than a hundred employees, and about a hundred smaller firms. Industria Macchine Automatiche (IMA), for example, made 70 percent of the tea-bag machines used worldwide. "Our network of over 200 suppliers is extremely important for the transfer of information," said an IMA director. "Our suppliers usually work with three or more different companies, and we learn about new techniques from them."[23] Figure 10-3 illustrates the different elements that composed this cluster.

These firms generally used local banks or family savings to reinvest and avoided mergers or acquisitions in order to maintain family control. They kept the workforce less than twenty employees whenever possible to avoid unionization rules. And while the quality of their products remained high, with extremely strong brand reputation, their costs and thus prices were also relatively high. One cannot help but wonder how long this static strategy will prosper. As more and more Asian countries—especially China—improve their manufacturing capabilities, their significantly lower costs will eventually matter. And as their productivity grows, Italy's stagnant growth leads to rising unit labor costs, undermining competitiveness.

FIGURE 10-3

Bologna packaging machinery district: An industry cluster

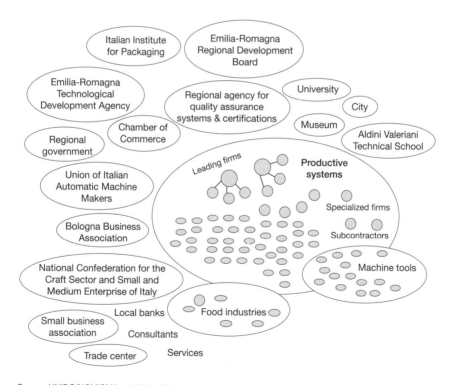

Source: UNIDO/NOMISMA and United Nations Industrial Development Organization, "The Italian SME Experience and Its Transferability to Developing Countries," August 1996.

Europe's Slowdown

Before considering Italy's competitive problems, we need to return to the slow growth environment of Europe. After achieving monetary union in 1999, Europe at first benefited from a falling exchange rate. This helped stimulate annual GDP growth of 2.5 percent and 3.5 percent, but beginning in September 2001, the euro strengthened dramatically. Exports slowed, and European growth fell to 0.5 percent by 2003. While there was some recovery in 2004 (1.1 percent growth), several countries were stagnant midway through 2005—Italy, in particular, was in recession. Unemployment, meanwhile, had risen sharply, especially in Europe's heartland of France and Germany.

These problems were not new. Five years earlier, European leaders meeting in Lisbon had identified the causes of stagnation and sought to mitigate them. They cited repeated macroeconomic shocks and fewer hours worked, lack of investment in new technologies, inadequate entrepreneurship, excessive regulation, inflexible labor markets, and a less-than-modern "social model."[24]

A more recent study by the Commission tried to explain how these factors undermined productivity growth (see figure 10-4). For more than two decades, productivity grew faster in Europe than in the United States. Thus, GDP per capita and competitiveness nearly caught up. But then, in 1995–1996, America's productivity growth surpassed the slowing rate of Europe—and continued to do so for the next decade. This problem, moreover, was severe in four of Europe's largest states—Germany, France, Spain, and Italy.

While noting the slowdown of aggregate demand and the acceleration of employment growth, the Commission concluded that the core problem was structural in nature—an outdated industrial structure and inflexible labor markets.

"The key question is to what extent Europe's problems reflect an inflexible and outdated industrial structure which has failed to fully exploit the direct and indirect productivity benefits from new, leading edge, technologies such as ICT [information and communications technology]."[25] To sustain this viewpoint, the Commission cites the lack of innovative ICT firms (such as Intel, Cisco, and Microsoft), as well as the slow adoption of ICT technologies by European wholesale and retail sectors.

The report expanded this analysis to look at the overall innovative infrastructure. This includes education, R&D expenditures by firms, and venture capital opportunities. Not only did it find education lacking at the collegiate level, but it showed more R&D in the ICT sectors in the United States. The report concluded that inflexible industry structure unresponsive to the pressures of globalization was the principal culprit. Moreover, it pointed to worrying

FIGURE 10-4

Productivity in Europe and compared to the United States, 1965–2002

Labor productivity per hour growth trends in Europe

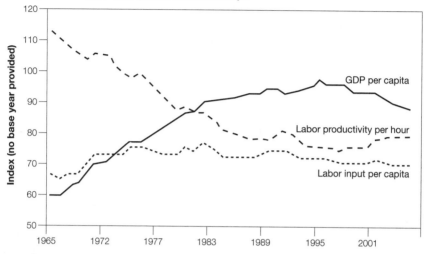

Productivity trends, EUR-15 relative to United States

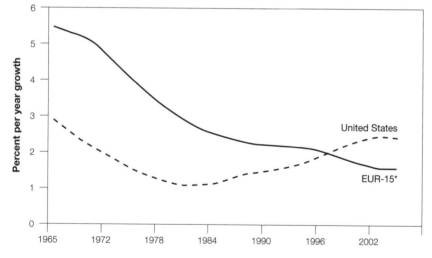

*EUR-15—members of EU prior to 2004

Source: The EU Economy: 2004 Review, Commission of the European Commmunities Directorate General Economic and Financial Affairs: Brussels, October 26, 2004.

evidence that the United States was extending its dominance in new high-technology sectors, such as pharmaceuticals, biotechnology, and computer-related services.

With regard to labor, the Lisbon Agreement called for modernization of social protection systems to ensure that work pays. Many studies show that unemployment is positively associated with generous unemployment benefits, a high tax wedge, and high union coverage. Other research suggests that unemployment can be protracted by institutions that restrict efficient labor market flows.

Monetary and Fiscal Policy

At the macroeconomic level, Europe seemed a bit hamstrung. Since the European Central Bank was solely committed to inflation control, it had held interest rates constant at 2 percent for twenty-seven months (through September 2005). Slow growth mattered not. This was exceedingly frustrating for countries like Italy—in recession and desperate to grow. In fact, in mid-2005, the political party Lega Nord, a coalition partner of Forza Italia, was collecting signatures to precipitate a referendum of whether Italy should abandon the euro.

Issues of fiscal policy were not much better. After failing to enforce provision of its Stability and Growth Pact, the EU had redefined its terms in March 2005. With four countries (including Germany and France) exceeding the 3 percent deficit limit, and Italy (2.9 percent) on the verge of reaching it, the Commission had failed to take punitive action. Instead, it revised the Stability and Growth Pact modestly, so that fiscal deficits of member countries could not exceed 3 percent in 2007 without fines being levied. Meanwhile, slow growth was making it difficult for the likes of Germany and Italy to lower their deficits.

Europe's Ten New Members

In May 2004, ten Eastern European nations entered the European Union (but not monetary union). Comprising 250,000 square miles, 80 million citizens, and $444 billion in GDP, the entrants included Poland, Hungary, the Czech Republic, Slovakia, Slovenia, Estonia, Latvia, and Lithuania, plus Cyprus and Malta. This enlargement, the largest in history, would surely bring profound changes to Europe. Furthermore, Romania and Bulgaria hoped to join in 2007, and Turkey, with a population of 70 million, sometime after that.

For both Western and Eastern Europeans, there would be a number of benefits. Entry had permanently removed the eight Eastern European countries from Russia's political (and military) sphere of influence. These less affluent Europeans would work for lower wages, thus making Europe more competitive. They would also export food, helping lower Europe's cost of living. Foreign direct investment, which was already flowing, would accelerate as European business sought more efficient locations.

For the east, benefits would flow from EU aid (a headline figure of $41 billion, which turns out to be more like $10.6 billion, over the next four years), from lower barriers to trade and investment, from the exchange of knowledge and technology, from greater transparency, and from the adoption of eighty thousand pages of EU rules—the *acquis communautaire*—that would strengthen institutions, environmental practices, and human rights in the east.[26]

On the other hand, there would certainly be costs—especially for the west. Although the accession agreement had delayed, for several years, free movements of people, it was thought that upwards of four hundred thousand might eventually migrate to the west each year. Unemployment was even higher in the east, and wages far lower. This, together with favorable tax rates (compared to the west) made Eastern European member countries more competitive locations for manufacturing jobs. Agricultural protection would also have to give way to imports from the east, and agricultural subsidies would have to be shared. For the east, adopting the *acquis communautaire* would be a very expensive proposition. So the west would have to supply considerable regional aid to the east, where incomes are far lower than in Western Europe. This, in turn, posed a difficult issue for the EU, as a handful of countries traditionally contributed, while the southern countries (and Ireland) had been the beneficiaries. As recently as June 2005, changing the amount of the budget and its direction of flow had stymied negotiations between member governments.

Italy in 2005

Europe's problems were shared by Italy in spades.

By 2001, Italians voters were disillusioned by the left-of-center administrations of Massimo D'Alema and Giuliano Amato. For the second time, they elected Silvio Berlusconi's center-right Casa delle Libertà coalition. Winning a majority in both houses, Berlusconi's coalition had defeated the Olive Tree coalition with the prospect of ruling for an entire term of five years.

In a hundred-day package, Berlusconi proposed immediate structural changes to Italy's administrative tax, judiciary, education, and labor laws. In a matter of months, Parliament had approved more than fifty reforms, including:

- Elimination of seven hundred administrative rules

- Pardon for underground-economy companies, allowing them to enter the official sector by paying taxes and insurance contributions at reduced rates

- Reintroduction of the Tremonti Law, offering lower corporate tax rates for companies that reinvested profits

- Amnesty for repatriated offshore accounts

- Increase of minimum pensions for those over seventy years old

- Introduction of fixed-term employment contracts

"No other government in the entire history of the republic has produced as many measures in its first six months in power," said Berlusconi.[27] Yet critics argued these were small measures; Berlusconi's controversial proposals for fiscal and labor reform were less successful. He had to postpone tax cuts to keep the budget from breaching the Stability and Growth Pact, and labor unions were opposed to suspension of Article 18 of the Workers' Charter. This law gave workers who were employed in companies with fifteen or more employees the right to be reinstated if fired without just cause.

On July 5, 2002, Berlusconi finally overcame this opposition by getting two of the three labor federations to sign a watered-down pact to suspend Article 18 for three years. And the same day, his coalition cabinet adopted his *Economic and Financial Planning Document for 2003–2007*. This budget included some tax relief, unemployment benefits, and a significant public-works program to improve the infrastructure in the south.

But with European growth losing momentum and the United States slow to recover from recession, nothing much seemed to go right for Italy. The economy stagnated, growing less than 1 percent in 2003–2004, and turning negative in the first two quarters of 2005. The decline of tax revenues, together with continued spending, pushed up the government deficit toward the restricted 3 percent.

Unemployment, however, was the good news. Berlusconi's reforms had made temporary employment and contract employment feasible. Not only had unemployment dropped from 9.5 percent to 8 percent, but employment had actually risen by more than 1 million.

Italy's other problem, besides slow growth, had to do with its competitiveness. With inflation averaging 2.5 percent, wages rose 3.3 percent annually in 2003–2004. But productivity (with stagnant output and increased employment) slowed, growing just 0.3 percent per year. Thus, Italy's unit labor costs were rising quickly—3.6 percent in 2003 and 2.4 percent in 2004. This growth, substantially higher than Italy's competitors' (much less the United States and Japan), left the country less and less competitive; yet it could not adjust through exchange rate devaluation, because there was no longer a lira.

Thus, Italy's current account surplus, which was substantially positive from 1993 to 1999, turned negative in 2000 and continued to run a negative balance of $17 billion in 2004. While trade in goods was still positive, it was no longer $30 billion to $50 billion annually, but rather $9.7 billion in 2003 and $8 billion in 2004.[28] The growth of exports in textiles and clothing, leather goods, wood products, and furniture was negative, reflecting stagnant markets and increased competition.

Prime Minister Berlusconi continued to struggle. His complicated coalition, Casa delle Libertà, was pulling the government in different directions. The populist, anti-immigrant Lega Nord supported greater regional devolution (with the ultimate goal of northern secession). Its leader, Umberto Bossi, espoused a xenophobic, populist line. The Union of Democratic Christians, representing the less wealthy central and southern Italy, focused more on economic growth and the deteriorating fiscal balance. The National Alliance was a right-wing party with a fascist heritage. And there was Berlusconi's own reform-oriented Forza Italia.

Controlling these diverse political interests and pushing forward his legislative agenda has been a difficult task for Berlusconi. Indeed, this has been made more difficult by Berlusconi's controversial past. The wealthiest man in Italy, Berlusconi has been repeatedly indicted on corruption charges and criticized for conflicts of interest. In 2004, a Milanese court cleared Berlusconi of allegedly bribing a judge in 1985 to block the sale of a state food conglomerate to a rival. A second indictment was dropped when the court invoked the statute of limitations. The conflict-of-interest charges came from Berlusconi's continued control of two Italian television stations while he presided over the government.

In March 2005, the cabinet approved a new legislative package to reform the bankruptcy law, create fiscal incentives for small and medium-sized business, and to cut red tape for start-ups. Yet critics complained that the measure did little for inefficient state enterprise, for heavy-handed regulation of professionals, or for providing family-owned businesses better access to credit.

But even this was too much. Casa delle Libertà, which was routed in regional elections in April 2005, finally collapsed. With the economy in recession, frictions between coalition members became overwhelming. While Berlusconi managed to form a new government, it had too little political support to accomplish much of anything. In mid-2006, after stagnating under a single government for the longest period in postwar history, Italian voters turned left once again. They elected a coalition headed by Romano Prodi, just back from heading the European Commission. Perhaps, they hoped, any new government could somehow pull Italy out of the funk into which it had sunk.

European Integration and Italian Competitiveness

So Europe and Italy, as a part of it, have serious issues ahead. The government of the European Union needs to decide how economic and political integration are to proceed. The four-hundred-page constitution, which failed in French and Dutch referenda in 2005, symbolizes this set of problems. A budget spread across twenty-five disparate countries, with centralized monetary policy and local fiscal policies, agricultural subsidies, and immigration pressures all rank high among these issues.

The EU is emerging, haltingly, as a supergovernment for the twenty-five European nations. As such, it has had a strategy of gradual economic and political integration—emulating the United States. But as we have seen in this chapter, building the institutions to integrate this strategy continues to be confounded by semiautonomous national politics. Unaffordable social policies, inadequate educational systems, and a lack of entrepreneurship are among the problems that undermine growth. This is unfortunate, as European nations are increasingly being pressed competitively—not just by Japan and the United States, but by China, India, and a half dozen developing countries.

We can see some of these competitive problems up close, in the case of Italy. Productivity growth remained a central issue—tied to macroeconomic shocks, wage rigidities, excessive regulations, a dated industrial structure, and a welfare state that puts excessive pressure on fiscal budgets. The Italian government is the only force that can accomplish the needed structural reforms. Berlusconi realized that, for sure, but was unable to build the political coalition necessary to accomplish such reforms. Perhaps Prodi can do better.

So here we see clearly the strategic objectives—becoming more productive and more competitive in a globalizing marketplace. And the policies are also clear, at least for the EU—rationalize labor, liberalize regulation, control fiscal deficits (and debt), and become more entrepreneurial. But these targets seem to clash with interests vested throughout most member states. In Italy, it is easier for organized labor to hold on to its current perquisites; for bureaucrats to retain their comfortable jobs; for people retiring in their mid-fifties to retain their generous pensions; and for small businesses merely to cope with the growing threat of Asian competition.

While economic growth can only be accomplished by individuals and business, government must create the suitable macroeconomic environment and define the microeconomic rules of the game that are competitive. Government policy in the past helped make Europe rich. But globalization and global competition have overtaken past policy. Adjustment is overdue.

—〰〰—

ELEVEN

Japan

BEYOND THE BUBBLE

"RESTORING THE PRIMARY fiscal balance," observed Heizo Takenaka in June 2005, was "the most important task facing the Koizumi government." Japan's economic czar also worried about deflation, pensions and medical care, declining savings, postal privatization, and deregulation. But all these issues came together in continuing fiscal deficits, which, if not alleviated, would soon become "unsustainable."[1]

How could the "miracle economy"—Japan of the 1950s and 1960s—have arrived at so difficult a juncture? At $4.6 trillion, its economy was the second largest on earth. With a real GDP per capita of $43,000, its standard of living was among the very highest. Unemployment was low, at least by European standards, and its cars, consumer electronics, and machinery were sold all over the world, delivering a trade surplus of $140 billion. Life expectancy stood at eighty-two—about the highest in the world. Yet "it [was] becoming clear," said Prime Minister Junichiro Koizumi, "that the system that worked in the past may not necessarily be suited to twenty-first century society."[2]

In this chapter we will explore the reasons for Japan's stagnation; the problems of deficits, debt, and demography; and the difficulty of structural adjustment for another advanced country.

Fruits of the Miracle

From 1971 to 1991, Japan's economy grew at about 4.4 percent per year. This was indeed a healthy growth rate, but hardly miracle growth. The pressures of globalization had begun to impinge on Japan's success.

Nixon Shock

On August 15, 1971, when President Richard Nixon took the United States off the gold exchange standard and imposed a 10 percent import surcharge, Japan's miracle ended abruptly. Its currency, previously pegged to the dollar at ¥360, jumped to ¥308 per dollar, producing a sharp drop in net exports. The Japanese economy slowed by half, growing 4.4 percent annually for the next two decades.[3] (See figure 11-1.)

Within a year, President Nixon visited China. The Japanese were again caught totally unawares by this sudden realignment of world powers and were thoroughly embarrassed by their lack of foreknowledge. The entire affair reinforced Japanese sensitivity to their limited political connections in Washington and their overdependence on the United States.

Oil Shocks

Late in 1973, the first oil shock hit the world as OPEC enforced an oil embargo and quadrupled prices. Japan, which relied almost exclusively on imported oil, was forced to pay significantly more. Inflation skyrocketed in 1974, imports rose by 40 percent, and growth vanished. After a year, however, trade came back into balance as Japan benefited from far lower import costs (in yen) of raw materials for steel, ships, and textiles. Again at the end of the 1970s, the Iranian Revolution forced oil prices to double, engaging an-

FIGURE 11-1

Japan's GDP growth rate, 1954–2005

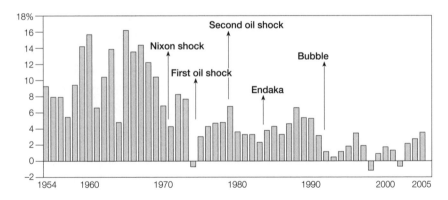

Source: Compiled by author with data from International Monetary Fund, *International Financial Statistics,* various years.

other round of inflation, a slump in the balance of trade, and intense conservation.[4] And because Japan was also reaching technological parity with the rest of the industrialized world, its advantageous productivity growth was slowing.

Nevertheless, during the early 1980s, Japanese exports in a few industries began to swamp American production. The depreciation of the yen due to the second oil shock reopened the gap between the yen-dollar exchange rate and the yen cost of manufactured exports. As Japanese cars and car parts, motorcycles, consumer electronics, and machinery gained U.S. market share, the United States threatened Japan with "reciprocity" legislation. And the government used its existing trade laws to bring temporary and "voluntary" limitations on the import onslaught, while U.S. industry hopefully adjusted.

With the onset of Reaganomics in 1981–1982, however, the value of the dollar climbed 63 percent. Over the next few years, the yen depreciated from about ¥200 to ¥270 per dollar, and by 1985, Japan's trade surplus had risen to $56 billion. This generated huge profits for Japanese exporters and allowed them to expand their operations, now through direct investment into the United States. In September 1985, the G-5 finance ministers (from the governments of Japan, the United States, England, France, and Germany) met at the Plaza Hotel in New York and concluded that the dollar was overvalued. Within weeks, the dollar began to fall, and the yen rose, eventually reaching ¥125 per dollar by 1988. This initiated the period of *endaka*, as it was called in Japan—or "high yen."

Endaka

Now the pressure was really on Japan, as the dollar prices of its exports rose sharply. If Japanese firms were to continue to grow (and prevent a balance of payments crisis), they would have to cut costs, lower prices, and eventually reinvest in more modern plants and equipment. This they did with a vengeance! Once again they benefited from the massive drop (in yen) in the prices of their raw materials imports—especially oil, the price of which had collapsed. And the Bank of Japan lowered interest rates to 2.5 percent, helping stimulate investment that jumped to 32 percent of GDP by 1990—an unprecedented level of investment for a developed country. Net exports, meanwhile, approached $100 billion—despite the strong yen.

As these surpluses soared, Japanese invested in their stock market, in foreign equities, in real estate, and in foreign debt. Savings were immense, accumulating to nearly $10 trillion—more than double the GDP—and there appeared to be no end to investment possibilities. Land prices in Tokyo and Osaka more than tripled, and the Nikkei stock market index rose from eleven thousand to thirty-nine thousand points. Japanese banks and investment funds bought U.S. Treasury bills, and Japanese businesses bought nearly $140 billion of U.S. equities and real estate, including Columbia Pictures, Pebble Beach Golf Club, and New York's Rockefeller Center. Japanese manufacturers built plants in the United States, Europe, and Southeast Asia to gain market access, mitigate protectionism, and lower labor costs, which were too high at home. *Fortune* magazine began reporting the names of several Japanese billionaires.

The Bursting Bubble

Eventually, endaka caught up with Japan. Under the pressure of asset speculation and rising inflation (from 0.1 percent in 1987 to 3.3 percent by 1991), a new governor of the Bank of Japan moved to raise interest rates and cool off the economy. Between 1989 and 1991, the discount rate was raised repeatedly and returned to 6 percent. Because Japan's economy was highly leveraged (on bank loans), it stopped growing abruptly and plunged into recession by 1992. Economic growth had barely recovered to 3.3 percent by 1996 when it again fell into recession. Stagnation persisted, until a brief upturn in 2004.

When growth slowed, the asset bubble burst. Grossly inflated land prices began falling, eventually stabilizing in 2004 at 15 percent of their prior level. The stock market dropped below eight thousand in 2003 before finally stabilizing. Entrepreneurial investors and leveraged firms found it increasingly difficult to service their debt. As loan defaults and bankruptcies rose sharply, Japan's banking system came under increasing pressure.

Institutional Concerns

There was no simple explanation for Japan's continuing stagnation. Since the Japanese had long been motivated to catch up with the United States, the parity they had achieved in 1989 perhaps left the country without a strategic goal. And to the extent that globalization had induced westernization, some Japanese pointed to traditional institutions as the key to their problem. After all, the miracle had been built on a framework of distinctive institutions—group-oriented financial institutions, labor markets that rewarded permanent employment, a bureaucracy-dominated political system, informal corporate governance, and some unique social arrangements. While these institutions worked well in the era of Bretton Woods, now they didn't seem to fit as well with the imperatives of globalization.

Capital Markets

When the bubble burst, Japan had a half dozen of the world's largest banks—Mitsubishi, Dai-Ichi Kangyo, Fuji, Sanwa, Sumitomo, and Sakura each had more than $400 billion in assets. For years, Japanese banks were all but guaranteed by the Bank of Japan. They had loaned easily to Japanese firms, assuming that economic growth would service their debt. Their balance sheets were loaded with equity holdings, and loan classification and risk assessment were skills yet to be discovered.

Japan's banks were historically weak in part because Japan's capital markets were protected, relatively uncompetitive, and poorly regulated. Japanese law had allowed interlocking relationships between banks and the businesses to which they lent. Japanese banks could own up to 10 percent of the outstanding shares in other businesses and could lend up to 20 percent of their capital to a single borrower (versus 10 percent in the United States). There were no restrictions, moreover, on the use of real estate as collateral (although banks could not hold it on their balance sheets).[5]

By 1993, as real estate loans defaulted, as businesses dependent on a rapidly growing economy (e.g., construction) failed, and as loans to Southeast Asian countries went bad, these banks were forced to downgrade more and more loans to "substandard" and "doubtful." Loan-loss charges jumped to ¥11 trillion ($137 billion) by 1995. The cumulative total of nonperforming loans would eventually exceed $1 trillion—about one-quarter of the Japanese GDP.

Under these circumstances, bank lending turned negative in 1997 and continued to decline through 2005. The banks, of course, were desperately trying to improve their balance sheets—especially to comply with new international standards. At the same time, there was no demand for loans in Japan. The endaka-era investment had sharply increased capacity, and then recession had killed demand. Moreover, excess capacity seemed to exist across Southeast Asia, so that even Japan's export sector had stagnated.

In November 1997, the Japanese government finally allowed a regional bank—Hokkaido Takushoku—to collapse. A few weeks later, Yamaichi Securities—with $260 billion in off-the-books debt—declared bankruptcy. Bad loans now became a public scandal. As Japanese banks were forced to shrink, they eventually began to merge. Seventeen of the biggest names in Japanese banking reorganized in six huge banking groups: Chuo Mitsui Trust, Resona (Daiwa and Asahi banks), Mitsubishi Tokyo Financial Group, UFJ Holdings, Sumitomo Mitsui Banking, and the world's largest (with $1.3 trillion in assets)—Mizuho Holdings.

Labor Markets

Job security had always been paramount for the Japanese. Most people would choose a lower-paying permanent employment position in a prestigious company rather than work for a higher-paying start-up company that did not guarantee job security. These more secure positions generally were offered by medium- and large-sized firms that accounted for one-third of all private sector positions. For many years, this business practice was admired—companies garnered tremendous employee loyalty, and their substantial growth required increasing numbers of employees. Japan enjoyed the lowest unemployment rate among its industrial counterparts.

Japanese corporations promoted from within, following a seniority system. Tax advantages encouraged this policy; the longer employees worked for a company, the less tax was imposed on their retirement allowance. Wage disparity was markedly low, and most firms had few senior executives under the age of fifty-five. Labor costs rose steadily with productivity growth.

Thus, many Japanese were shocked in the late 1990s when major firms such as Yamaichi Securities declared bankruptcy, forcing their employees to find alternative positions. Most firms, however, maintained large payrolls through the slow-growth period; few firms issued layoffs. Companies instituted hiring freezes and offered some early retirement packages, reducing payrolls through attrition. But many tolerated hundreds of "window watchers"—employees with nothing to do, merely waiting out the remaining years to retirement. As stagnation continued, the number of corporate bankruptcies rose, reaching twenty-five hundred monthly in 2001.

Bureaucratic Power

Japan was a representative democracy. There was a parliament (the Diet), which consisted of a 500-member House of Representatives and a 252-member House of Councilors. In the House of Representatives, elections occurred at least every four years. Members of the House of Councilors were elected to six-year terms. The Diet elected a prime minister, whose primary executive duty was to select a cabinet to oversee the bureaucracy.

The Diet had traditionally been controlled by factions of the Liberal Democratic Party (LDP)—groups of powerful senior politicians within the party. Kakuei Tanaka, who was prime minister for almost two years, was perhaps the best example. In 1974, Tanaka was forced to resign due to financial improprieties. Thereafter, he continued to build a faction of more than a hundred Diet members and acted as kingmaker in Japanese politics for yet another decade. After Tanaka's death, no one stepped forward to replace him, and Japanese politics stagnated. Problems simply festered until the LDP splintered in 1992, losing power for some eighteen months.

Besides the legislature there was the bureaucracy, which most people believed held the real power in Japanese politics. The bureaucracy consisted of twenty-one ministries by the time the bubble burst. The head of each ministry, a member of the Diet, sat in the cabinet. All cabinet decisions had to be unanimous; effectively, each minister had veto power over cabinet activity. Yet the true decision makers for each ministry were the vice ministers, who began competing to head their ministry from the time they entered, usually just out of college. If the prime minister wanted to address policy, he would need the entire cabinet's support, whose members in turn required the support of their vice ministers. The desire for consensus was popular in Japan, as people felt that achieving *wa*, or "harmony," was worth almost any cost.

One of the two key ministries was the ministry of finance (MOF), which held power in all areas of the financial world. MOF had managed government fiscal policy and tariffs. In conjunction with the Bank of Japan, MOF was the linchpin for much financing of big business. Large city banks effectively needed MOF consent for their lending policies. And because the ministry had command over the tax code, maintaining tax advantages for its policies further secured its control.

MOF had also held influence over monetary and securities policy. Although the head of the Bank of Japan (BOJ) was officially appointed by the prime minister and cabinet, MOF officials were involved in the selection process, and a MOF representative could attend BOJ policy meetings. Ministry officials also managed restrictions throughout the capital markets, including limiting the scope of foreign exchange.

MOF, in other words, was in Japan's economic driver's seat. And yet, its responsibility for supervising the banks' reserve capital led to scandals. Some ministry officials notified banks before inspections, allowing problem loans to be concealed. Even more serious were allegations that MOF had helped some banks and securities firms hide losses to prevent failure. In March 1998, these scandals forced Finance Minister Hiroshi Mitsuzuka to resign and led to arrests in both the ministry and several major banks.

The other key ministry that had powered the miracle was the Ministry of International Trade and Industry (MITI). After the occupation, MITI had used its control over trade and investment to pick and support a handful of industries to lead Japan's export-oriented growth. Its success continued into the mid-1980s, as MITI set its sights on the semiconductor and computer industries.

But while MITI still had considerable influence in the business community, much of its original power had dissipated. Japan had removed formal barriers to foreign direct investment and reduced tariffs to among the lowest in the OECD. As MITI gradually shifted its focus away from heavy industries and toward the service sector and telecommunications, it ran squarely into other ministries with significant political constituencies. In the later 1990s, the Industry Structure Council of the prime minister would urge MITI to focus on more structural measures, such as deregulation and the acceleration of intellectual-capital formation.

Corporate Governance

Intertwined with this network of institutions was Japan's business sector. Government officials often retired to a life of business when their governmental responsibilities ended, usually around age fifty. This process was called *amakudari* (descent from heaven), and bureaucrats could move from company to company as distinguished advisers, receiving large paychecks each step of the way. Playing a critical role in the business sector were the *keiretsu*, descended from the *zaibatsu*—the prewar industrial combines dominated by old industrial families, dissolved by the occupation. Instead of being centered around a family, the keiretsu were centered around large city banks, which reemerged in the late 1950s.

Initially, the main bank in each keiretsu played a crucial role in financing the businesses within the enterprise group. Businesses borrowed three or four times their net worth. With thin earnings and high-interest coverage ratios, they essentially acceded management control to the group's main bank. The main bank then overborrowed from the Bank of Japan. Because the central bank held the ultimate responsibility for the system, it also had the ultimate control over lending decisions of dependent banks. By the 1980s, many of the larger companies had grown independent enough to generate funding on their own.

This debt-financing system permitted Japanese business to focus on long-term issues, as opposed to the shorter-term concerns of western-style shareholders. Taking the long view allowed Japanese businesses to acquire market share, which could eventually be mined for profit. Tax incentives encouraged borrowing over equity funding.

Business groups with a strong main bank were known as "horizontal keiretsu." Six large horizontal keiretsu dominated Japanese business: Mitsubishi, Mitsui, Sumitomo, Fuyo, DKB, and Sanwa. As shown in table 11-1, the Mitsubishi group, the largest of these horizontal keiretsu with nearly $400 billion in sales by the mid-1990s, included about thirty companies in businesses as diverse as heavy industries, electricity, aluminum, paper production, beer, and automobiles. While the business group had played a critical role in creating partnerships between companies in the past, leaders explained the relationship was less important in the 1990s. Under equal conditions, members would choose to deal with other group members, but given a better deal with an outside company, the outsider would likely be favored.[6]

A smaller group of vertical keiretsu had also emerged. These groups typically included a large manufacturer with its suppliers and distributors as subsidiaries. A prominent example of the vertical business group was Toyota. These groups were called "vertical" because they were managed in a rough pyramid structure, with the parent company maintaining a long-term relationship with the subsidiaries. A third type of keiretsu was the "satellite" group, in which a core company formed subsidiaries to perform after-market functions or to engage in new ventures. Hitachi and Nippon Telegraph and Telephone were examples.

Cross-holding of shares was another distinctive feature of Japanese corporate governance. Much of the limited equity of Japanese firms was held by other members of the same group—especially the banks. The amount of cross-holding had generally increased, despite the Anti-Monopoly Act of 1977, reaching a high of 52 percent by the early 1990s. Although it had shrunk to 36 percent in 1999–2000, it continued to accommodate an environment of low equity earnings. In other words, corporations felt little pressure from shareholders or the market. Company priorities placed value on labor-market issues and long-term market share. Thus, while Mitsubishi had forty-six board members, all but two were insiders; the two outsiders were the chairman of Mitsubishi Heavy Industries and the president of Mitsubishi Electric.

Social Issues

Like any country, Japan had a number of social issues that periodically preoccupied the polity. Among these were youth unemployment, the role of women in society, the effectiveness and appropriateness of the education system, and aging.

According to the 2000 census, Japan's total population was 126.93 million. Based on existing birthrates, expected fertility, and mortality rates, this number would likely peak in 2006 at 127.74 million, as shown in figure 11-2. Thereafter, it will begin a secular decline, dropping gradually at first but eventually reaching 100.6 million by 2050.[7]

Japan's baby boom generation generally includes those born from 1947 to 1949. In 2004, this group comprised 6.8 million people—larger than all groups before or since. These boomers will begin retiring in 2007, when they reach the age of sixty. But because of a sharp drop in Japan's fertility

TABLE 11-1

Distribution of companies in horizontal business groups

	Mitsubishi	Mitsui	Sumitomo	Fuyo	DKB	Sanwa
Financial services	Mitsubishi Bank Mitsubishi Trust & Banking Meiji Mutual Life Tokio Marine & Fire	Mitsui Taiyo Kobe Bank Mitsui Trust & Banking Mitsui Mutual Life Taisho Marine & Fire	Sumitomo Bank Sumitomo Trust & Banking Sumitomo Life Sumitomo Marine & Fire	Fuji Bank Yasuda Trust & Banking Yasuda Mutual Life Yasuda Fire & Marine	Dai-Ichi Kangyo Bank Asahi Mutual Life Taisei Fire & Marine Fukoku Mutual Life Nissan Fire & Marine Kankaku Securities Orient	Sanwa Bank Toyo Trust & Banking Nippon Life Orix
Computers, electronics, and electrical equipment	Mitsubishi Electric	Toshiba	NEC	Oki Electric Industry Yokogawa Electric Hitachi*	Fujitsu Fuji Electric Yaskawa Electric Manufacturing Nippon Columbia Hitachi*	Iwatsu Electric Sharp Nitto Denko Kyocera Hitachi*
Cars	Mitsubishi Motors	Toyota Motors*		Nissan Motor	Isuzu Motors	Daihatsu Motor
Trading and retailing	Mitsubishi	Mitsui Mitsukoshi	Sumitomo	Marubeni	C. Hoh Nissho Iwai* Kanematsu Kawasho Seibu Department Stores	Nissho Iwai* Nichimen Iwatani International Takoshimaya
Food and beverages	Kirin Brewery	Nippon Flour Mills		Nisshin Flour Milling Sapporo Breweries Nichirei		Itaham Foods Suntory
Construction	Mitsubishi Construction	Mitsui Construction Sonki Engineering	Sumitomo Construction	Taisei	Shimizu	Toyo Construction Obayashi Sekisui House Zenitaka
Metals	Mitsubishi Steel Manufacturing Mitsubishi Materials Mitsubishi Aluminum Mitsubishi Cable Industries	Japan Steel Works Mitsui Mining & Smelting	Sumitomo Metal Industries Sumitomo Metal Mining Sumitomo Electric Industries Sumitomo Light Metal Industries	NKK	Kawasaki Steel Kobe Steel* Japan Metals & Chemicals Nippon Light Metal Furukawa Furukawa Electric	Kobe Steel* Nakayama Steel Works Hitachi Metals Nisshin Steel Hitachi Cable

Real estate	Mitsubishi Estate	Mitsui Real Estate Development	Sumitomo Realty & Development	Tokyo Taternono	Tokyo Dome	
Oil and coal	Mitsubishi Oil			Tonen	Showa Shell Sekiyu	Cosmo Oil
Rubber and glass	Asahi Glass		Nippon Sheet Glass		Yokohama Rubber	Toyo Tire & Rubber
Chemicals	Mitsubishi Kasei Mitsubishi Petrochemical Mitsubishi Gas Chemical Mitsubishi Plastics Industries Mitsubishi Kasei Polytec	Mitsui Toatsu Chemicals Mitsui Petrochemical Industries	Sumitomo Chemical Sumitomo Bakelite	Showa Denko Nippon Oil & Fats Kureha Chemical Industry	Kyowa Hakka Kogyo Denki Kagaku Kogyo Nippon Zeon Asahi Denka Kogyo Sankyo Shiseido Lion	Ube Industries Tokuyama Soda Hitachi Chemical Sekitsui Chemical Kansai Paint Tanabe Seiyaku Fujisawa Pharmaceuticals
Fibers and textiles	Mitsubishi Rayon	Toray Industries		Nisshinbo Industries Toho Rayon	Asahi Chemical Industry	Unitika Teijin
Pulp and paper	Mitsubishi Paper Mills	Oji Paper		Sanyo-Kokusaku Pulp	Honshu Paper	
Mining and forestry		Mitsui Mining Hokkaido Colliery & Steamship	Sumitomo Forestry Sumitomo Coal Mining			
Industrial equipment	Mitsubishi Heavy Industries Mitsubishi Kakoki	Mitsui Engineering & Shipbuilding	Sumitomo Heavy Industries	Kubota Nippon Seiko	Niigata Engineering Iseki Ebara Kawasaki Heavy Industries Ishikawajima-Harima Heavy Industries	NTN Hitachi Zosen Shin Meiwa Industry
Cameras and optics	Nikon			Canon	Asahi Optical	Hoya
Cement		Onoda Cement	Sumitomo Cement	Nihon Cement	Chichibu Cement	Osaka Cement
Shipping and transportation	Nippon Yusen Mitsubishi Warehouse & Transportation	Mitsui OSK Lines Mitsui Warehouse	Sumitomo Warehouse	Showa Line Keihin Electric Express Railway Tobu Railway	Kawasaki Kisen Shibusawa Warehouse* Nippon Express*	Navix Line Hankyu Nippon Express*

*Companies affiliated with more than one group.

Source: Dodwell Marketing Consultants, in Fortune, July 15, 1991, 81. Copyright © 1991 Time Inc. All rights reserved. Used with permission.

FIGURE 11-2

Population trends in Japan by age group, 1950–2100

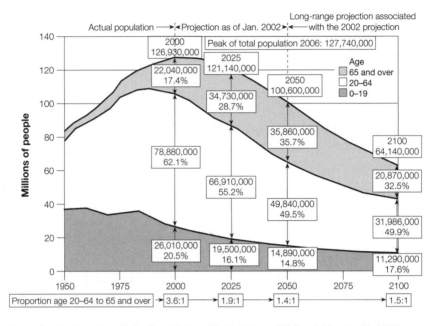

Source: Compiled by author with data from Ministry of Health, Labor and Welfare, in Masaharu Usuki NLI Research Institute, "Points of Discussion," May 30, 2005, 9.

rate, these workers will not easily be replaced. The fertility rate began dropping just after the baby boom, from 3.7 in 1950 to a surprisingly low 1.28 by 2004. Japanese women have been marrying later and later, and generally producing only one child, in their early thirties. Since the replacement rate in Japan is 2.08, this effectively means a decline in the population, in the absence of significant immigration, is inevitable.

At the same time, improvements in health care and rapidly increasing incomes had increased life expectancy to a record high level—seventy-eight years for males, eighty-five years for females. The confluence of these two trends, as figure 11-2 indicates, produced a bubble of elderly people—some 22 million by the year 2000. This number will continue to grow rapidly through 2025, when it reaches 34.7 million.

One implication of these numbers is that Japan's labor force was shrinking—and had been shrinking since 1999. On the one hand, this trend helped hold down unemployment rates at a time when Japanese business was rationalizing. The decline in Japan's working-age population, from 68 percent in 2000, will reach 60 percent in 2020 and just 53 percent by 2050. As this trend deepens, many Japanese worry about maintaining the sort of skilled workforce that Japan needs for advanced manufacturing and services. And because of the structural adjustment that Japanese firms have recently engaged in, the number of permanent employees has dropped sharply (especially males), with more job openings in temporary employment and part-time employment.

Thus, the proportion of working-age to elderly Japanese will drop by nearly half, from 3.6 to 1 in 2000, to 1.9 to 1 in 2025. This trend already had startling implications for savings and social security funding, and thus for pensions and medical care for the elderly.

Stagnation

The government's response to stagnation appeared aggressive—but had little effect, at least on the macroeconomy. Having spent more than a decade trying to reduce fiscal deficits in the 1980s, the Diet reversed course in 1992 and returned to fiscal stimulus. Between 1992 and 2000, the Diet approved the ten stimulus packages illustrated in figure 11-3, cutting taxes cumulatively by 3.3 percent of GDP and increasing spending by about 2.9 percent of GDP. Total government revenues, which stood at 33 percent of GDP in 1991, had fallen to 28 percent by 2004; expenditures, however, had risen

FIGURE 11-3

Japan's economic stimulus packages, 1992–2000

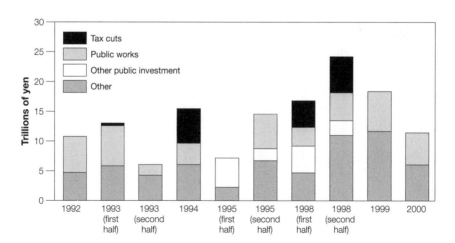

Source: Sanjay Kalra, "Fiscal Policy: An Evaluation of Its Effectiveness," in *Japan's Lost Decade: Policies for Economic Revival*, eds. Tim Callen and Jonathan Ostry (Washington, DC: International Monetary Fund, 2003), 168. Used with permission.

from 30 percent to 35 percent. The budget, as a consequence, plummeted from a deficit of 1 percent to a deficit of 8.3 percent in 1999.[8]

Despite massive spending on infrastructure, and significant tax cuts, these policies provided little stimulus. It seemed that Japanese, worried about the need for government to reduce deficits *in the future*, simply spent less and saved more. Paul Krugman has called this peculiar effect "Ricardian equivalence."[9] Keynesian stimulus, which we'll learn more about in the next chapter, simply did not take hold.

On the monetary front, the Bank of Japan quickly lowered interest rates in an effort to stimulate investment. From a discount rate of 6 percent in 1991, the BOJ hastily cut rates to 0.5 percent by 1995, where they remained constant for the next six years. However, there was simply no demand for money; Japan was in a "liquidity trap." Banks were reducing loans, trying desperately to improve their balance sheets. And businesses, faced with prolonged domestic recession, had excess capacity and accumulating free cash, and did not need to borrow. Moreover, the combination of excess capacity, falling asset prices, and stagnant consumer demand (at about 55 percent of GDP) precipitated deflation. The GDP deflator turned negative in 1994 and the consumer price index followed in 1998, deepening to about 1.0 percent by 2001. (See figure 11-4.)

Free, Fair, and Global

After briefly losing power in 1993, the LDP regained control by allying with the Social Democrats in 1994. After two years of languor, Ryutaro Hashimoto, a prominent LDP politician and minister of MITI, ascended to

FIGURE 11-4

Japan's consumer price index, 1981–2005

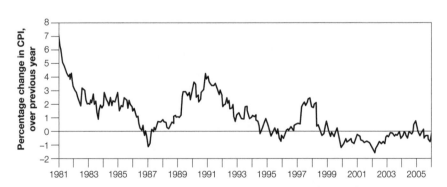

Source: Compiled by author with data from Japan's Ministry for Internal Affairs and Communication (http://www.stat.go.jp/english/data/cpi/index.htm).

prime minister. Hashimoto then surprised the country when he proposed radical reforms to the traditional Japanese system. In November 1996, he announced a grand plan to restructure administration, deregulation, education, the financial system, social security, and fiscal policy. The centerpiece of this package was the "big bang," an effort to substantially deregulate Japanese financial markets. If all went according to plan, Japan's new capital market would be "free," completely following market principles; "fair," totally transparent and reliable; and "global," used by the entire world.

Hashimoto sought to reduce the ministries' power to control policy and to enhance the power of the prime minister. His Action Plan for Economic Structure Reform listed fifteen sectors that the government would encourage and dozens of regulations—in logistics, energy, telecommunications, and retail—where he called for control. In education, the Hashimoto government sought reforms to cultivate creativity and humanity. Autonomous learning (instead of rote memorization), computer training, and improved teacher quality were to be pursued. To fix social security, the Ministry of Health and Welfare elaborated five possible options, ranging from increasing premiums 34 percent or cutting benefits 40 percent. Voters were asked to consider these choices for the next couple of years.[10]

Hashimoto's plan for fiscal reform set a goal of reducing the budget deficit to 3 percent by fiscal year 2003. No area was to be spared from budget cuts. Long-term spending, particularly for public works, would be curtailed over ten years. And the national burden (the ratio of taxes, social welfare premiums, and the fiscal deficit to national income) would be reduced to 50 percent. In June 1997, the cabinet announced a package of reduced public-works spending, a reduction in defense spending, and a pending increase in the sales tax, from 3 percent to 5 percent. While the economy boomed during the months before the tax hike, it tanked in 1998—ignominiously finishing off Hashimoto's term in office.

Hashimoto's Legacy

Although his term ended abruptly, Hashimoto, as head of the LDP's largest faction, continued to play a key role in implementing many of the structural reforms of his 1996 agenda. Several reforms were enacted during the administration of Keizo Obuchi (July 1998–April 2000) and Yorshiro Mori (April 2000–April 2001).

In financial services, the Foreign Exchange and Foreign Trade Control Law completely dismantled controls over foreign exchange. Japan's remaining controls over the capital account, including limitations on citizens investing abroad, were eliminated. Bank supervision, moreover, was taken away from the Ministry of Finance and vested in the independent Financial Service Agency—an organization with regulatory teeth.

In January 2001, the number of ministries was consolidated from twenty-one to eleven (with a maximum of three additional state ministries), and the prime minister's office and the cabinet secretary were strengthened. The prime minister received the authority to initiate policy, and his cabinet office got final control over fiscal policy, through the consolidating power of a newly formed Cabinet Council on Economic and Fiscal Policy.

And finally, the Diet passed its first pension reform bill in March 2000. Retirement ages were gradually raised to sixty-five, and benefits were cut for new retirees by 5 percent over time. Earnings-related pension payments were indexed to the consumer price index (CPI), rather than disposable income.

Junichiro Koizumi: Intensive Adjustment Period

Junichiro Koizumi succeeded to power in the spring of 2001 with a sweeping victory (298 out of 486 votes) in the Liberal Democratic Party. His closest political opponent, Ryutaro Hashimoto, won only 155 votes. Koizumi, an unusually colorful candidate, succeeded in raising the prime minister's popularity from 9 percent to 78 percent in less than one month.

Koizumi came to office on an explicitly reformist, four-part economic platform: (1) to privatize the post office, including its huge pool of savings deposits; (2) to force the banks to write off bad debt in two to three years; (3) to accelerate the implementation of structural reforms, even at the cost of economic contraction; and (4) to cap the issuance of Japanese government bonds (JGBs) at ¥30 trillion ($244 billion). "We want to establish a new economic and social system that's appropriate for the twenty-first century," said Koizumi. He called his plan the New Century Restoration.[11]

This ambitious agenda would be difficult to implement. Given the continuing stagnation of the economy, a more restrictive fiscal policy and the acceleration of structural reforms threatened recession. And while forcing the banks to write off bad loans was long overdue, private estimates of nonperforming loans (NPLs) were as high as ¥100 trillion, well above the government's estimates of ¥33 trillion. And deregulating the post office, with the world's largest pool of savings ($2.5 trillion), was certainly a long-term objective that would entail intense political wrangling and multiple years to phase in.

Bank of Japan's Return to Quantitative Easing

Just a month before Koizumi's election, in March 2001, the Bank of Japan announced it would return to a zero interest rate policy, called "quantitative easing." Deflation was deepening. The BOJ would target the current account balances of banks. The *current account balance* (unrelated to trade) was the reserve that private banks held with the Bank of Japan. By increasing its purchases of JGBs, the BOJ could pump liquidity into the economy (although it could not force private banks to use it). The bank also lowered the discount rate to 0.25 percent and, four months later, lowered it further, to 0.1 percent.

With reserve requirements for private banks at about ¥6 trillion, the BOJ began acquiring bonds. Member banks, with declining loan demand, added to their current account balances, gradually at first and then more rapidly, in the spring of 2003. By early 2004, the BOJ had settled on purchase levels necessary to maintain the current account between ¥30 trillion and ¥35 trillion—just over $300 billion. Short-term interest rates fell to 0.0005 percent. Even the ten-year bond rate had fallen to 1.2 percent. Still, bank lending continued to shrink throughout 2005. Deflation moderated, and the consumer price index finally reached zero by the end of the year. In March 2006, the BOJ ended its five-year effort at quantitative easing.

Banks and Bank Lending

The Koizumi government took a three-pronged approach to improving performance of the banks: accelerating the disposal of nonperforming loans (NPLs), strengthening loan classification and provisioning practices, and reducing exposure to the price risk of assets held as equities.

The Financial Services Agency called on the banks to dispose of existing NPLs within two years, bringing down the ratio of NPLs to assets from 8.7 percent to 4.4 percent by March 2005. This initiative was made more difficult by the recession of 2002, pushing loan losses back up to ¥13.3 trillion. Nonetheless, the big banks exceeded the government's goal, lowering the ratio to 2.9 percent by May 2005. Smaller banks and credit unions, however, lagged behind.

With these reforms mostly accomplished and with bank profitability returned to the black (barely), the government imposed a final reform in April 2005. Deposit insurance on ¥10 million was limited to one account per adult, and the long-standing government guarantee on bank deposits was abolished.

Pension Reform

Although the Koizumi government was not initially focused on the pension and medical-care systems, it quickly realized that fiscal reform—indeed fiscal sustainability—was not possible without further reforming social security. In the absence of reform, the rapid increase in the number of retired people would force the monthly premium rate for the national pension to rise to ¥29,000 by the early 2020s. Worse still, the premium for employees' pension insurance would need to rise to 25.9 percent of net income. Moreover, medical care, of which 70 percent was paid by government (90 percent for elderly people), would rise even faster with the aging of the population. If not reformed, it would likely reach ¥59 trillion by 2025, or about 14 percent of net income. (See figure 11-5.)

After two years of deliberation, the Diet approved pension reform in 2004. While far from perfect, and no doubt needing further revision sometime in the next decade, any legislated improvement was a significant accomplishment. The reform package dealt with premium levels, benefits, and government subsidies.

FIGURE 11-5

Trends and projections in Japan's social security expenditures

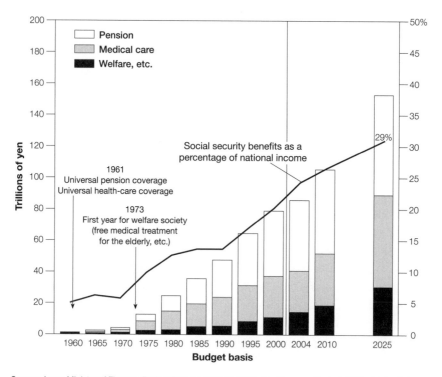

Source: Japan Ministry of Finance, Budget Bureau, *Understanding the Japanese Budget 2004*, chapter 4, 1.

Premium rates for the pension would rise from 2004 until 2017. For the national pension—a flat rate contribution that all working citizens make—an annual increase of ¥280 per month would increase monthly contributions from ¥13,300 to ¥16,900. Much more important, however, was the hike in the employees' pension. This system, for which 38 million private sector and public sector employees were eligible, was financed by premiums, shared equally by employee and employer. The reform would raise the combined contribution rate by 0.354 percent annually, from 13.58 percent in 2004 to 18.30 percent by 2017.

Benefit levels, meanwhile, would drop gradually through a complicated adjustment tied to the CPI. While nominal pensions would rise in line with the CPI, the benefit rate, as a portion of net income, would decline from the current 59.3 percent to 50.2 percent by 2023.

To support this proposed premium rate, the eligibility age for retirement had already been lifted in 2000 from sixty to sixty-five years old—phased in gradually through the year 2025. Yet to keep the revised benefit rate on schedule, the government subsidies for the basic pension would still have to rise. The government, which currently contributed one-third of the benefit, would increase its share to one-half by 2009. This, of course, would only make fiscal reform more difficult.[12]

Fiscal Reform

Perhaps the most difficult task facing the Koizumi administration was fiscal reform. Not only were the budget deficits already substantial, but the effects of aging would put greater pressure on spending, irrespective of the 2004 pension reform or the hoped-for reform of medical care, later in 2005–2006. Added to these challenges were the government's interest payments on debt, which had fallen from ¥10.8 trillion to ¥8.9 trillion over the past seven years, thanks to declining interest rates. If rates were to rise even a couple of percentage points over the next few years, the government's burden would grow sharply.

The Japanese government's fiscal deficits had averaged 5.7 percent annually since 1993. The primary deficit (fiscal balance excluding interest costs), which Japan had come to target, stood at 4.5 percent in 2004. "We have a serious deficit problem," acknowledged Hiroshi Yoshikawa, a member of the Cabinet Council on Economic and Fiscal Policy.[13]

In January 2005, the cabinet issued its "Medium-Term Economic and Fiscal Perspective," based on the budget for 2005. The Diet approved it in March. This budget, for the fourth year, had cut public investment and limited or cut education and defense. Implementation of the final third of the "three-part reform" package would eliminate another ¥404 billion from subsidies to local governments.

By holding spending constant (and raising taxes), the government hoped to reduce the primary deficit to 4.1 percent toward eventual balance in 2012. The primary deficit amounted to ¥20 trillion. The government needed to cut this by nearly ¥3 trillion annually to meet its target. Thus, if nominal GDP growth of 1 percent generated revenues of about ¥1 trillion annually, that would leave ¥2 trillion to be raised from taxes (or ¥3 trillion if expenditures rose 1 percent annually). This target optimistically assumed persistently low interest rates. (See figure 11-6.)

Even with this schedule, government would have to issue a lot more bonds. In fiscal year 2005, the government would issue ¥34.4 trillion to support 41.8 percent of expenditures. Gross public debt, currently at 163 percent of GDP, would certainly rise to 175 percent or 180 percent. Worse still, if one considered the need to refinance off-the-book debt of the Fiscal Investment and Loans Program, then debt might climb as high as 200 percent.[14]

All of these forecasts included some level of tax increases. No one believed that fiscal sustainability was possible without raising income taxes and value-added taxes. While opinions varied, most observers of government policy anticipated a higher value-added tax. Responsibility for tax policy lay with the Tax System Council, of which Hiromitsu Ishi was chairman. The

FIGURE 11-6

Japan's real and estimated growth rate and primary balance, 2002–2012

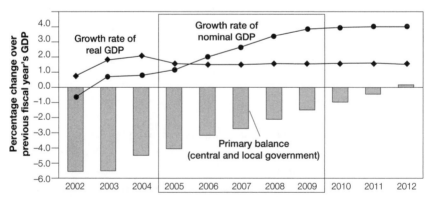

Note: These estimates were carried out by the cabinet office and presented to the Council on Economic and Fiscal Policy for discussion on the structural reform and medium-term economic and fiscal perspectives for fiscal year 2004.

Source: Ministry of Finance, Seminar on the Japanese Economy and Japanese Government Bonds, January 2005, 32.

council would not make its final recommendations until September 2006, after the end of Koizumi's term. It was constrained by Koizumi's election promise to not raise value-added taxes.

Ishi figured that approximately one-third of the primary deficits could be reduced with expenditure cuts. This left two-thirds for tax increases. Raising either income or corporate taxes would be difficult, as Japan's maximum marginal rates were already quite high. However, because of a host of exemptions, only half of high-level incomes was taxable. Thus, the council's short-term strategy was to broaden the base, getting rid of deductions for spouses, students, elderly persons, and "parasite singles" (over-thirties people living with their parents). Together, such cuts might generate an additional ¥1 trillion to ¥2 trillion in revenue. But since social security and medical care would increase government spending substantially, Ishi agreed that a significant hike in value-added taxes (VAT) would likely be necessary.[15]

The size of the hike in the VAT was widely disputed. This important *zaikai* (financial circle group) with fourteen hundred members was recommending a gradual rise in the VAT from 5 percent to 19 percent (approximately 12 percent covering pension requirements, 5 percent for increased medical care, and 2 percent for nursing). Thus, the Keizai Doyukai (Japan Association of Corporate Executives) had begun lobbying on behalf of significantly higher VAT taxes.[16]

Privatization of Postal Services

"We'll be privatizing Japan Post in 2007," Heizo Takenaka said in early June, just after his election to the upper house of parliament. Takenaka was Koizumi's minister of economic and fiscal policy and minister for privatization of postal services. Koizumi had aggressively pushed privatization as his signature policy, even before he ascended to prime minister.

Japan Post will take up to ten years from 2007 to be broken up and then privatized. Currently, the postal service operates about 60 percent more branch offices than the combined network operated by the nation's banks. Japan Post, which manages about ¥208 trillion of savings and ¥124 trillion of insurance, holds about ¥110 trillion in government bonds. The combination of savings, insurance, and delivery services is "too big," a monopoly that undermines competition, said Kakutaro Kitashiro, chairman of IBM Japan and president of the Keizai Doyukai. The public, said Takenaka, wanted the postal service to improve its service, extend operating hours, and cut costs. The plan was to break it into four parts—mail delivery, post office management (of twenty-five thousand offices), a bank, and an insurance company. Government would retain a controlling share in the mail delivery and post office management units. The bank and the insurance units would be spun off through IPOs. On July 5, 2005, the Diet approved the plan, despite opposition from four hundred thousand postal workers. By the end of the summer, postal privatization was law.

Current Account Surplus

When Takenaka was not worrying about postal privatization, social security reform, and the deficits, he worried about the consequences of Japan's huge current account surplus and its likely effect on exchange rates.

In trade, Japan had continued to enjoy incredible success. Its trade balance now exceeded $139 billion, the largest portion of which was with the United States. And after nearly four decades of surplus, Japan's cumulative foreign investments now generated a net inflow of $90 billion in interest and dividends. Thus, the country ran even larger surpluses in its current account ($171 billion in 2004). Its reserve assets thus exceeded $800 billion.

Japan, therefore, had become the largest purchaser of U.S. debt, despite incredibly low interest rates. This was necessary, of course, to finance the United States' huge trade deficits on which Japan depended for its economic growth. Thus, the Japanese continued to buy the debt, despite the risk that the dollar would devalue sharply, reducing the yen value of their foreign exchange reserves.

Japan Looking Forward

One can't help but wonder what will happen to the Japanese economy over the next few years. On the one hand, it appears to many observers that Japan is back. Its growth is positive, investment is positive, prices are no longer falling, and its trade surplus is huge.

Yet despite these positive signs, Japan's currency remains weak, at ¥112 per dollar. In fact, when I discussed this recently with the chair of ITOCHU, he bet me that the yen would remain below ¥100 per dollar at least through June 2007. Either the BOJ would intervene to keep the currency weak and trade strong, or people feared for the long-term future of the country. If the yen were to appreciate significantly, however, Japan would lose 10–20 percent of the value of its exchange reserves in dollars. More than ten years ago, we should recall, the yen stood at 78!

The worry here is government debt. If the government cannot significantly reduce its deficits to below the GDP growth rate, then debt to GDP will grow—possibly reaching 200 percent. And if interest rates rise even a bit (from the current 1.2 percent), then debt service will grow—from its already unbelievable base of 39 percent of government revenues. With an aging population putting more and more pressure on the budget, and saving less and less, one could imagine that fairly soon Japanese savings will not be sufficient to support domestic debt service, domestic investment, *and* the debt issues of the United States.

Since 1992, Japan has struggled more politically and economically to rebuild its institutions. All of the systems and institutions that so effectively delivered miracle growth had ossified. They no longer suited a fully globalized world. Japan needed to modernize—not the manufacture of technology but its own organizational structure.

Modernizing institutions and running the macroeconomy are two of government's most important responsibilities. While agonizingly slow, Japan has surely made progress. But the job is still not complete. Its government will need a firm hand on all of the areas we've discussed if Japan is to remain an important player in Asia—and an economic partner of the United States.

TWELVE

Managing the American Dream

ONCE THE UNITED STATES began to recover in 1938 from its worst depression ever, the wisdom of Keynesian economics gradually became conventional. During these years, the United States widened its lead as the world's preeminent economic and political power.

Yet no sooner was Keynesian demand management accepted as a national policy tool in the late 1960s than it began to fail. Inflation increased even as the economy slowed. When President Nixon did what economists recommended, the situation only got worse. And to deal with the country's deteriorating competitive position globally, he rejected fixed exchange rates—again following the best economic wisdom. By the late 1970s, the U.S. economy was deteriorating in every imaginable way—slow growth, lagging productivity, high inflation, trade and fiscal deficits. The United States was importing more and more petroleum and watching key industries in automotives, electronics, and machinery lose ground to foreign competitors. The exchange rate of the dollar slumped.

In November 1980, a Republican president was elected to office, promising a revolutionary new way of thinking. Ronald Reagan implemented supply-side economics—to restore American economic power. While inflation dropped sharply and the Soviet Union collapsed, the Reagan revolution failed. It delivered slow growth, huge budget and trade deficits, and perhaps most seriously, worsening income inequality. Reagan's successor only exacerbated things.

The correction began in 1993, when the Clinton administration committed itself to deficit reduction. With the benefit of free trade and a technological revolution in computing and communications, the U.S. domestic economy turned around and grew at its fastest rate in decades. In 1998, the budget deficit disappeared.

But as most indicators of economic performance were improving, George W. Bush was elected president in November 2000. With an elaborate ideological agenda led by a return to tax cuts, the Bush administration restored economic growth but with huge fiscal deficits, trade and current account deficits, a decline of savings and investment, and a worsening of income distribution. The terrorist attacks of 9/11, and the administration's response, only made these problems worse.

By 2006, the government's huge fiscal deficits were rising, the current account deficit exceeded $800 billion, oil prices had reached $72 a barrel, and climate change (in the form of Hurricane Katrina) was bearing down on America. Somehow, U.S. development policy had gotten off track.

The Golden Years, 1946–1971

In 1933, Franklin Roosevelt was only one of millions who did not understand what had happened to the United States—why its economy had shrunk by 34 percent in four years and forced 8.5 million people out of work. Banks had failed, industries from airlines to railroads were bankrupt, and thousands of American farmers had lost their farms to foreclosure.

Yet the United States was an incredibly prosperous country; its land was fruitful. From its founding in the 1600s, the country's area grew even faster than its population through the mid-1800s—eventually reaching 3.717 million square miles, of which 19 percent was arable. Until the 1860s, Americans could acquire land either for free or for modest payments of survey fees. This wide distribution of land was perhaps unique in world history and certainly helped account for the peculiarly democratic system of governance that Americans adopted.

All this land, moreover, was bountiful. Fertile black soil allowed the early development of profitable commodities—cotton in the South, and wheat, corn, and soybeans in the Midwest. And beneath the land were further riches—abundant supplies of oil, coal and natural gas, copper, iron, bauxite, gold, and most other metals needed for industrialization.[1]

So alluring was this frontier of abundance that it attracted immigrants from around the world. By the mid-1900s, America's rapidly growing population had reached 121 million—fewer than half of which were both white and children of native-born parents. There were more Irish (4.3 million) than in Ireland, and more Poles in Chicago than any Polish city save for Warsaw. Three-quarters of New York's population were immigrants or children of immigrants.[2] And there were 13 million African Americans who still suffered the legacy of slavery.

This rich context—together with a rapidly growing population, early state-funded investments in infrastructure, and a superb system of public education—gave rise to two industrial revolutions: the first transferred from Great Britain in the 1840s and 1850s, and the second an American development in the 1880s and 1890s. This second industrial revolution, as Alfred Chandler has explained, was based on "three-pronged investments" in production, distribution, and management. Led by the capital-intensive sectors of petroleum and steel, new industries with immense-scale economies appeared in packaging, tobacco, meat processing, glass, and rubber. After the turn of the century, these expanded to automobiles, power, locomotives and railcars, paper, aluminum, nonferrous metals, and chemicals.[3] By the 1930s, half the companies that would make the *Fortune* 500 in the 1990s had already been founded.

Yet despite the immense productive power, something in the early 1930s had utterly failed. Franklin Roosevelt knew he had to fix the banks, which he did in the first two weeks of 1933 of his presidency. And he knew he had to provide sustenance for people in desperation. But beyond that, he was pretty unclear about what to do next.

At the microeconomic level, Roosevelt led Congress to enact a series of regulatory controls over failing or troubled industries. In addition to railroads, the United States moved to regulate agriculture, banking and securities, airlines and trucking, communications, oil, natural gas, and electric utilities. Together, this was more than a third of GDP and the operational infrastructure of the American economy. Prices, services, and competition itself were to be regulated to avoid the excesses on which the Depression was partially blamed.[4]

But no amount of regulation would fix the macroeconomy—the collapse of aggregate demand. Demand for goods and services had simply floundered by 1933 and was far below aggregate supply. This concept of aggregate demand was a new idea in the 1930s, and one that few Americans appreciated. In the spring of 1933, President Roosevelt received a letter from John Maynard Keynes, the British economist who developed this perspective. Keynes explained to Roosevelt that lowering interest rates would not help jump-start the economy. The country was in a liquidity trap, where businesses did not need to invest and banks were uncomfortable making loans.

The way to stimulate aggregate demand, argued Keynes, was for government to spend money in excess of its revenues, a lot of money. Government should run a massive deficit, borrowing people's unused savings, and spending the money on agriculture, infrastructure, welfare, and defense. The recipients of these expenditures would, in turn, spend more money on meals, clothes, housing, and automobiles. The resulting "multiplier" of expenditures would stimulate aggregate demand and eventually restore the economy to its previous rate of growth.[5]

Roosevelt was not persuaded by Keynes enough to depart so radically from the conventional wisdom of trying to run balanced budgets. His fiscal deficits remained modest for the next several years, and the U.S. economy did not recover. Only in 1936, when the deficit reached $3.6 billion, did economic growth turn positive. But when the deficit was again reduced, growth slumped, only recovering in 1941, when mobilization for war drove the government's deficit above $5 billion.

The fiscal lessons of World War II led Congress to legislate the Employment Act of 1946. Remembering the Great Depression, many Americans feared the rise of unemployment after demobilization. The Murray-Wagner Full Employment Bill would have calculated the full-employment gross national product (GNP) and, if the actual GNP were less, provided deficit stimulus to fill the gap. But the business community adamantly opposed this notion. It supported an alternative, the Whittington-Taft Employment Act, which did not include the notion of a full-employment GNP. Instead, Congress identified government's responsibility to "foster and promote free competitive enterprise" and, in so doing, promote maximum employment.[6]

Both Truman and Eisenhower preferred the conventional wisdom of trying to balance the budget and putting up with unemployment as the result of a natural business cycle. But President John Kennedy was different. Kennedy had taken economics at Harvard and was surrounded by both Keynesians and non-Keynesians. Kennedy's idea for dealing with the slow-growing economy was to use a tax cut to stimulate growth. Walter Heller, chairman of the Council of Economic Advisors, and David Bell, director of the budget, were the chief advocates of this approach. They anticipated an output gap of $30 billion to $40 billion, which could be alleviated by a tax cut of about $19 billion over two years. Other Keynesian advocates included John Kenneth Galbraith, then ambassador to India, and Leon Keyserling, former chairman of the council, who preferred spending increases rather than tax cuts.

Opposing the idea of any intentional deficit were Treasury Secretary Douglas Dillon and Commerce Secretary Luther Hodges. Arguments against tax cuts were that they would stimulate consumption at a cost to investment. In the *Saturday Evening Post*, former president Eisenhower attacked the tax cut as "spending for spending's sake." He argued that a deficit was simply robbing the next generation, who would service the debt, so that the current generation could consume.

The administration debated this question for a couple of years. But with the economy slowing, and the president looking for some way to appeal to business, Kennedy finally decided to do it. In January 1963, he advocated tax cuts both to spur consumption and business investment, but only when needed for economic stimulus. The cut actually came three months after Kennedy's death—in the Revenue Act of 1964. Real GDP growth jumped to 6.4 percent annually in 1965–1966. And while the inflation rate accelerated from 1.6 percent in 1964 to 2.8 percent annually by 1966, unemployment fell from 5.2 percent to 3.8 percent.[7] Keynes, I think, would be satisfied.

Indeed, 1966 was probably the United States' economic high point since the Korean War. During the late Johnson years, government spending on the war in Vietnam and the programs of the Great Society were already pushing fiscal deficits to record peacetime levels of $25 billion by 1968. With inflation up to 4.2 percent, the prime lending rate reached 5 percent for the first time since 1929. And then, even when growth slowed in 1969, inflation continued to rise, hitting 5.5 percent in 1970. "Stagflation" had begun.

Richard M. Nixon, a Republican with a Democratic Congress, faced some difficult economic and social choices, inherited from his predecessor. The Vietnam War had less and less support from the American people. Too many Americans were dying, too much money was being spent, and the point of American involvement in Southeast Asia was increasingly unclear. At home, growth was slowing while inflation worsened. Apparently, expectations of more inflation had begun to fuel inflation itself.

In international commerce, the United States' trade surplus had shrunk to less than $1 billion, and its current account balance was reduced to $399 million. The country's dependence on foreign oil continued to worsen, driving up energy prices. While the dollar, since 1944, had been fixed at $35 per ounce of gold, all other currencies were tied to the dollar at relatively fixed rates. A substantial "dollar overhang" had now built up among foreign central banks, as their economies accumulated more and more U.S. dollars.

So to stop inflation, Nixon submitted a budget with a surplus of $3.4 billion. "We must cut expenditures while maintaining revenues. This will not be easy," said the president. "Dealing with fundamentals never is." Not only did he cut expenditures broadly, but he extended a tax surcharge (due to expire) and excise taxes on telephone charges and automobiles. "This ordering of our economic house—distasteful as it is in many respects," he said, "will do much to slow down the rise in the cost of living, help our seriously weakened position in international trade, and restore the sound basis for our on-going prosperity."[8]

But Nixon's fundamental economics failed to stop inflation. Sharply rising wages (7 percent) were driving up prices by more than 6 percent annually by spring of 1970. Economic growth turned negative as high interest rates cut off investment. Unemployment rose to 4.9 percent in 1970, hitting 6 percent in 1971.

To make matters worse, some of the United States' allies began exchanging their surplus dollars for gold. As a consequence, the country's gold cover—the ratio of reserves to dollar liabilities—had fallen to three to one by the spring of 1971. At the time, President Nixon asked Peter Peterson, his special assistant for the Office of International Economic Affairs, to prepare a review and analysis of the changing world economy.

In April, Peterson presented his findings. American allies—Germany, France, Britain, and Japan—had recovered and were fast catching up with the United States, but without adjusting their tariffs and other trading protections. They continued to use capital from the United States to invest and markets in the United States to grow. Their exchange rates, moreover, were generally fixed to the dollar at rates set in the late 1940s. As economies recovered quickly in Japan and Europe, their currencies appreciated in value but not in price. Peterson concluded that "benign neglect" of this asymmetrical trading system could not last much longer. The United States would eventually run out of gold. Thus, major adjustments were needed, at home and abroad.[9]

By late spring of 1971, the administration had grown increasingly worried. Inflation was not receding, and outflows of gold were increasing. It was obvious that the only way to stop these outflows was to devalue the dollar—that is, to go off the gold exchange standard. Treasury Secretary John Connally, moreover, was not averse ideologically to doing so or, for that matter, to imposing wage and price controls on the domestic economy.

On August 13, the president called a meeting at Camp David. Sixteen people—all of the president's economic advisers, politicos H. R. Haldeman and John Erlichman, and speechwriter William Safire—were invited. Safire later recalled that on the helicopter to Camp David, he asked Herb Stein what was up. "This could be the most important weekend in the history of economics since March 4, 1933," Stein intoned. Trying to recall what had happened that day, Safire queried, "We're closing the banks?" "Hardly," Stein chuckled. "But I would not be surprised if the President were to close the gold window."[10]

And that is what Nixon did. At eight o'clock on Sunday night, the president preempted *Bonanza* to announce his new economic policy. First, he proposed the Job Development Act of 1971 to encourage investment and repealed the excise tax on automobiles. To avoid a deficit, he cut spending by $4.7 billion. Second, he announced a wage-price freeze for ninety days. And third, he suspended the convertibility of the dollar and imposed a 10 percent surcharge on imports.

Stagflation, Deficits, and Inequality, 1971–1993

The effects of the "Nixon shock," as the Japanese called it, were immediate. The next day, the dollar tumbled in value while the yen and the deutsche mark appreciated sharply. And the import surcharge was akin to an additional 10 percent devaluation. The effects of devaluation would not be felt for another eighteen months—the so-called J-curve effect. But by 1973, with exports growing even faster than imports, the U.S. trade balance swung positive, and the current account even more so. Economic growth picked back up to 5.8 percent, while unemployment slowed to 4.9 percent. Although central bankers meeting at the Smithsonian tried to fix rates again in the late fall (gold at $38 per ounce), that system lasted for little more than a year before it broke down completely. In mid-1973, all of the major currencies moved to floating rates.

As the Nixon administration got swamped by Watergate, the United States was in a difficult spot. Although economic growth and the trade balance were positive, most other indicators were not. The government was running a sizable deficit for the fourth year in a row. The costs of Johnson's Great Society, plus a variety of new regulations created during the Nixon years, were considerable. Inflation was rising again by 5.6 percent in 1973, despite wage and price controls that were repeatedly extended and modified three times before eventual decontrol.

But worse was to come. As spare capacity for petroleum production in the United States dissipated, OPEC had begun raising prices. In October 1973, when Nixon decided to rearm the Israelis in their Yom Kippur War, Saudi Arabia used oil as a weapon, imposing a boycott on exports to America. By November, prices had risen from $2.40 to $11.65 per barrel.

This first oil shock would have a dramatic effect on world economic growth in general, and the United States in particular. Recession engulfed the American economy, while inflation pushed upward to 12 percent. To make matters worse, the federal government responded by extending price controls to the oil sector—holding down oil prices, thus fueling consumption. These price controls would remain in effect until 1981, when Ronald Reagan assumed office.

For the remainder of the 1970s, economic performance in the United States worsened. Fiscal deficits increased sharply, exceeding $50 billion in 1975. Inflation, which seemed to ease in 1975, was back at 10 percent by 1978. The dollar was again depreciating against such strong currencies as the yen and the deutsche mark. And unemployment, less than 4 percent during the last four years of the 1960s, now rose above 6 percent for most of the 1970s.

But perhaps worst of all was productivity growth, which had long carried the American economy to new heights. Now it slowed abruptly, to just 0.5 percent annually. It actually turned negative in 1979 and 1980, as shown in figure 12-1. With wages growing at 9 percent annually, unit labor costs outstripped all of the United States' competitors. As a consequence, the trade balance turned negative in 1976 and then jumped to –$30 billion annually for the rest of the decade. Japanese cars and German machinery were now overwhelming American business.

Faced with all of these difficulties, American voters turned to Jimmy Carter, the down-home, Democratic governor of Georgia, for solace as president of the United States. Yet as smart and as moralistic as he was, Carter could do little to alleviate America's economic problems.

To deal with energy shortages and high prices, Carter introduced the National Energy Plan in April 1977. This complicated plan, with more than a hundred legislative proposals, was designed to encourage conservation, convert power plants to coal, stimulate nonconventional energy sources, fix the pricing of natural gas, and price oil more equitably. Eighteen months later, after the most complicated legislative battle in history, Congress finally passed the National Energy Act.[11] But its provisions for gradual price decontrol were not enough. The Iranian Revolution, in October 1978, reduced

FIGURE 12-1

Declining competitiveness of the United States, 1968–1980

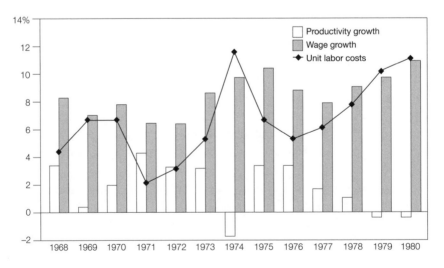

Source: Compiled from *Economic Report to the President* (Washington, DC: U.S. Government Printing Office, 1999).

global oil supplies by more than 2 million barrels daily. World prices jumped this time to $36 per barrel by February 1981. The United States became engulfed in the second oil crisis.

President Carter had more luck with deregulation. The National Energy Act provided for the gradual deregulation of interstate natural gas prices and the unbundling of monopoly regulation of electric utilities. And Carter's decision not to renew oil price controls in the Energy Policy and Conservation Act would have eventually deregulated oil prices, too. But Carter's views that economic regulation was not working went deeper than the energy crisis. He supported airline deregulation in 1978—actually abolishing the Civil Aeronautics Board and leaving prices and routes to the market. In 1980, Carter approved the Staggers Act, deregulating railroads, and the Motor Carrier Act, deregulating trucking. In March 1980, he signed into law the Monetary Control Act, forcing the Federal Reserve to deregulate interest rates. A few months later, his Federal Communications Commission issued Computer Inquiry II—a ruling to deregulate telecommunications prices.[12]

But President Carter's macroeconomic record was considerably less successful. Deficit spending by the government worsened, and the president seemed unable to deal with inflation. As the trade deficit widened, the dollar depreciated, making imports more expensive, thus adding to inflation. The President and his Council of Economic Advisors thought it important to maintain a strong dollar. Early in 1978, the Federal Reserve began defending the dollar, selling gold and using swap arrangements with other central banks. The Fed repeatedly raised interest rates, in July and September, but to no avail. The dollar kept depreciating. High interest rates, however, helped choke off investment, eventually inducing recession.[13]

In November 1980, as Jimmy Carter ran for reelection, the U.S. economy was growing at –0.6 percent. Consumption was stagnant, and as market interest rates passed 13 percent, investment fell 6 percent. The housing market, moreover, had collapsed with negative growth of 17.6 percent in real terms. Productivity growth was negative, and both inflation and unemployment were rising. The government was running a fiscal deficit of $59 billion, and the trade balance was –$25 billion. The Soviet Union had just invaded Afghanistan, and oil prices were going through the roof. Jimmy Carter was finished.

In November 1980, the governor of California and one-time movie actor Ronald Reagan was elected to the presidency of the United States with 51 percent of the popular vote. Reagan was the forefront of a new wave of Republican conservatives—Republicans who had concluded that too much government was the cause of America's economic problems, and too little defense was accommodating the military aggression of the Soviet Union. For the first time since 1954, a Republican president would enjoy a Republican majority in the U.S. Senate (and a large minority in the House). This, together with widespread public support for change, would allow President Reagan and the new Republican values he represented to achieve a revolution.

Before the inauguration, two Republican congressmen—Jack Kemp from New York and David Stockman from Michigan—were elevated to chair of the House Republican Conference and director of the Office of Management and Budget, respectively. Analyzing the difficult economic circumstances facing the new president, they prepared recommendations entitled, "Avoiding a GOP Economic Dunkirk."

In it they warned the president-elect of a "hair-trigger market psychology poised to respond strongly to early economic policy signals." They feared that "a double-dip recession in early 1981 is now at least a 50 percent possibility." Quick-fix remedies for various wounded sectors of the economy threatened to damage the budget even more as the GNP slowed. The deficits that people anticipated would likely "produce an intense polarization between supply-side tax cutters [like Kemp himself] and the more fiscally orthodox [Stockman]." The supply-siders to whom Kemp and Stockman referred were a new group of economists (led by Arthur Laffer from the University of Southern California) who believed that tax cuts could so stimulate the economy (and thus tax revenues) that resulting deficits could be avoided.

Kemp and Stockman urged president-elect Reagan to declare an economic emergency to get Congress immediately focused on a stabilization plan. They recommended five principles:

1. A static "waste-cutting approach" would not work. Fiscal stabilization could only be achieved through an improvement in the economy.

2. A large tax cut was needed to stimulate the economy.

3. This tax cut should be accompanied by a "major regulatory ventilation" to boost business confidence.

4. To reduce the "high, permanent inflation expectations," the government must cut the explosive growth of long-term government deficits.

5. Monetary stability needed to be achieved.[14]

On February 19, 1981, Reagan presented "New Beginning: A Program for Economic Recovery" to a joint session of Congress. His plan had four parts. First, he proposed cutting spending by $49.1 billion in fiscal year 1982. He would cut waste, regulation, and revenue sharing with the states, but not "the social safety net of programs" that the poor depended on, nor social security, nor spending on defense; the defense spending, in fact, was scheduled to rise by $7 billion more than President Carter had already planned. Second, Reagan would cut taxes—a 30 percent across-the-board cut of the income tax rate, and an accelerated depletion and investment tax credit for business. Third, he would reduce regulation—appointing Vice President George H. W. Bush to head a task force. And fourth, Reagan would urge the Federal Reserve to adopt a monetary policy that "does not allow money growth to increase consistently faster than the growth of goods and services."[15]

The Reagan administration forecast that if Congress adopted this plan in total, real GNP growth would jump immediately to 4.3 percent in 1982. Inflation would fall to 8.3 percent, and unemployment to 7.2 percent. The extra GNP growth of $300 billion would generate enough tax revenues to balance the budget by 1984!

Of course, there were some assumptions. Reagan and his advisers thought a reduction of government spending could reduce the deficit, regardless of cutting taxes by $700 billion. Again, the idea was that more economic growth could generate so much revenue that it would equal the taxes lost. They also believed that a reduction of future spending would reduce inflation expectations, and that would reduce nominal interest rates, as well as inflation itself. They hoped that Americans would save some of their increased disposable income and that more savings would also help lower interest rates. Moreover, the balanced-budget target, it was later revealed, contained what one senator called a "magic asterisk"—that Congress would cut $80 billion more later that same fiscal year. Needless to say, Congress never did.

The business tax cuts were key. The administration assumed that business would invest domestically, despite the growing slowdown of the economy; despite business's increasing interest in investing abroad; and especially, despite the fact that free cash flow was invested in short-term U.S. Treasury bills paying 20 percent—more than most equity investments could make. On the regulatory changes, the administration assumed that government regulation was mostly to blame for slow productivity growth and that Congress could turn that around quickly.

But the most important assumptions involved monetary policy. Reagan's people hoped on hope that a tighter monetary policy would lead to *falling* interest rates, rather than higher ones, *in the short term*. This would happen through expectations. But if a tougher monetary policy caused high interest rates to persist, then for sure investment would decline and the economy would fall sharply. Moreover, for the tough monetary policy to work on prices alone, it could not affect real GNP growth or the velocity of money—just prices.

Finally, these actions—less regulation, less inflation, and more investment—were supposed to improve exports and weaken imports. But there the key assumption was that the value of the U.S. dollar would not rise.

All of these assumptions needed to work—interactively and right away. But of course, almost none did. High interest rates persisted. Businesspeople waited to see whether real interest rates would fall and whether the government would balance the budget. Americans spent their increased income and didn't save. And the dollar went through the roof—up 63 percent over the next five years.

Congress put through the tax cut, with a 25 percent reduction in income taxes, in less than sixty days. At the Fed, Paul Volcker slowed the growth of the money supply sharply. The budget was passed in fall of 1982, cutting the path of increasing spending by about $39 billion.

So with high interest rates persisting, growth slowed sharply, and the economy plunged into the worst recession since the Great Depression. Unemployment rose to more than 10.6 million in 1982 and remained at that level through 1983. And as the dollar rose, U.S. exports contracted sharply (while imports got even cheaper), and the trade deficit turned even more negative—reaching –$159 billion by 1987. The only good news was the inflation rate; it dropped sharply from 10.4 percent to 5.2 percent by 1982, and on down to 3.1 percent by 1987. Ronald Reagan, it appeared, had broken the back of inflation expectations.

The Laffer curve, meanwhile, was slow to take hold. As figure 12-2 shows, the U.S. deficit worsened abruptly—hitting $184 billion by 1984.

FIGURE 12-2

U.S. fiscal balance, 1929–1992

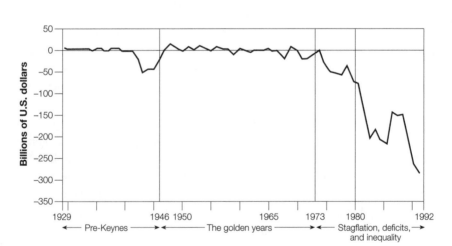

Source: Compiled from *Economic Report to the President* (Washington, DC: U.S. Government Printing Office, 1985, 1994).

Government expenditures went up, not down, from 22 percent to 25 percent of GDP during Reagan's first three years. Social entitlements and defense spending accounted for all of the increase. Yet revenues, not surprisingly, dropped from 20 percent to 17.5 percent during the same period. By 1992, the deficit had reached $290 billion.

Yet President Reagan was deemed a hero by most Republicans, both for busting unions (breaking the air traffic controllers' strike) and leaning hard on the Soviet Union. By increasing defense spending significantly—from $157 billion to $303 billion by 1989—the United States put more pressure on the USSR than that country could possibly bear.

Even giving Reagan credit for these accomplishments—lower inflation and a bankrupt Soviet Union—we still need to turn to two other important economic consequences of the Reagan revolution: the decline of savings and income equality.

National savings—the total of business savings (retained earnings), personal (or household) savings, and government savings (e.g., a surplus)—is important because it funds investment. If national savings is below investment, then money must be borrowed from foreigners (a capital account surplus), and the country must run a current account deficit. Especially if the government is running a fiscal deficit, which is dissavings, it is exceedingly important that households save enough to fund investment.

In 1981, personal savings was $244 billion or about 11 percent of disposable income. In 1987, that number was the same ($241 billion), but GNP had grown significantly. Thus, the savings rate had fallen to 6 percent. During the administration of George H. W. Bush, personal savings grew to $366 billion, but the savings rate fell a bit further. With retained earnings at $143 billion, this was not enough to fund private investment of $865 billion. The rest had to come from Americans selling assets to foreigners. Although President Reagan had created an incentive to save $2,000 per taxpayer, it simply wasn't enough. Yet that would be it, by way of incentives, until at least 2005.

Poverty and income distribution were not unrelated. Because of the United States' relatively free-market version of capitalism, income distribution was already worse than in most other developed countries. For decades, however, that had seemed a reasonable consequence of the American Dream. However, the Reagan tax cut, of 25 percent, was more regressive. It helped the rich far more than the poor. High unemployment and the restructuring of old industry jobs—in steel, automobiles, machinery, and electronics—led to lower average wages for a great many Americans.

As a consequence, the number of people in poverty rose by 10 million in the early 1980s, and the poverty rate rose by 3 percent. Poverty is currently defined by the U.S. Census Bureau as a family of four living on about

$16,500 a year. But even more significantly, the distribution of income worsened—and has continued to worsen ever since. From figure 12-3, one sees that the share of income of the top one-fifth of the population has risen by about 7 percent, to 50.1 percent in 2004. Each of the other fifths has lost a percentage point or two. Likewise, we see that the Gini index had risen from 0.39 in 1981 to 0.46. (Latin American and African countries rank at about 0.50 or so, Europeans at about 0.30 or so, and Japan at about 0.25.)

In the late Reagan years, performance of the U.S. economy did begin to improve. Strong economic growth eventually generated more revenues, while spending after 1986 was brought back under control. Thus, deficits shrank to $150 billion before starting to rise again. With sharply lower inflation and solid productivity growth (2 percent annually), unit labor costs slowed to 1–2 percent annually.

In the international economy, U.S. manufacturing firms learned their lessons the hard way. After shuttering plants across the nation and laying off millions of workers, they reinvested in new technology, new equipment, and new plants. And in October 1985, after the G-5 finance ministers agreed that the dollar had risen too far, it began to fall. Over the next ten years, the dollar depreciated about 53 percent in trade-weighted terms. Finally, the United States began competing. Its exports rose sharply—in integrated cir-

FIGURE 12-3

Share of aggregate income by quintiles in the United States and the Gini Index, 1967–2004

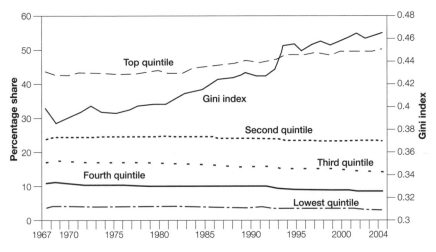

Source: Compiled from U.S. Census Bureau, *Income, Poverty and Health Insurance Coverage in the United States*, August 2005, 40.

cuits, computers, and communications equipment—while the growth of imports slowed. The U.S. trade deficit receded to $76 billion by 1991, while the current account balance actually turned positive.

Vice President George H. W. Bush, who easily succeeded to the presidency in 1989, faced a number of more difficult challenges. It was Bush who had to raise taxes in 1990 to stanch Reagan's deficits. It was Bush who had to deal with air pollution, approving the concept of tradable permits in the 1990 Clean Air Act. And it was Bush who had to engage Saddam Hussein, on behalf of Kuwait and Saudi Arabia, in the Gulf War. Although realizing a swift victory, the United States perhaps erred by not finishing the job of attacking Baghdad and getting rid of Saddam Hussein.

The expense of this war, together with a slowing economy, pushed the federal deficit to the record height of $290 billion. With recession looming and unemployment rising in an election year, Bush was in trouble. Although his approval rating stood at 90 percent just after Desert Storm, another year would increasingly cast a spotlight on the economic failures of the previous twelve years.

Bush's second problem was his principal opponent—a not-well-known young governor from a backwater state—Bill Clinton of Arkansas. Clinton, a smart Rhodes Scholar from Yale, fought a tireless campaign. Like the Energizer bunny in the TV ads, "he just kept on going and going and going."[16] Clinton followed Jim Carville's advice that the central issue was "the economy, stupid." Republicans, avoiding blame for those problems, adopted a strategy of "anything but the economy," mostly stressing doubts about Bill Clinton's character.[17]

The third and distinctive aspect of the 1992 election was the presence of a third-party candidate—Ross Perot, the billionaire founder of EDS, a data-processing firm. Perot ran on a two-pronged platform—he opposed the United States' entry into the North American Free Trade Agreement (NAFTA), and he opposed the fiscal deficit. Perot used television effectively, lecturing with flipcharts on the severity of deficits and where he would make budget cuts. He forced Clinton to take a position supporting NAFTA in the waning months of the campaign. Unions objected but had nowhere else to go.

When the votes were counted in November 1992, Clinton was elected the forty-second president, and second youngest after Kennedy, by a plurality of 42.9 percent. George H. W. Bush received only 37.4 percent of the vote; the rest went to Ross Perot. This election, as Walter Dean Burnham has put it, represented "a repudiation, but not a radical realignment," of the Reagan revolution.[18]

Correction: The New Economy, 1993–2000

The economic team Clinton put together in December 1992 included Robert Rubin, the head of Goldman Sachs, as chairman of the National Economic Council; Lloyd Bentsen, a senator from Texas, as treasury secretary; Leon Panetta, a congressman, to head the Office of Management and Budget; Alice Rivlin, former director of the Congressional Budget Office, as Panetta's assistant; and Laura Tyson, an economist from Berkeley, to chair the Council of Economic Advisors. This group was to prepare an economic plan and present it to the president-elect in early January.

At the meeting in Little Rock on January 7, the group spent the first hour laying out details of the worsening deficit. They showed that the accumulating deficits of the previous twelve years had pushed gross federal debt to $4 trillion (up from $994 billion), or 63 percent of GDP. Annual interest charges on this debt were already $202 billion. And given the United States' low savings, this burden would only push up interest rates and strangle investment. Clinton's campaign promise to cut middle-class taxes quickly went out the window. "I get it," said Bill. Deficit reduction was a threshold issue. "I know it won't be easy," continued Clinton, "but I was elected to deal with the economy and this is what we need to do to get the economy back on track."[19] Pleased, but nervous, his advisers collectively took a deep breath.

Five weeks later, President Clinton proposed "A Vision of Change for America" to a joint session of Congress. He was flatly critical of his predecessors:

> *Twelve years of neglect have left America's economy suffering from stagnant growth and declining incomes. They have left the average American family worried about its future, working harder, and getting less in return. The specter of rapidly rising health care costs threatens every family and business. They have left a mountain of debt and a Federal Government that must borrow to pay more than a fifth of its current bills. Perhaps most sadly, they have left the great majority of our people no longer dreaming the American dream. Our children's generation may be the first to do worse than their parents.*
>
> *Such is the sorry legacy of 12 years of short-sightedness, mis-management, and protection of the privileged. All of this must be changed.*[20]

To do this, the Clinton administration introduced a budget that would reduce spending by $375 billion over five years and increase revenues by $328 billion. He asked Congress to reduce defense spending and entitlements, where most of the budget resided. For revenues, he sought to increase taxes on the rich and to impose a significant tax on energy. Table 12-1 summarizes the proposed budget. The Democratic revenue proposal was, not surprisingly, progressive. The top income tax bracket of 36 percent was to be raised to 39 percent. For people with incomes over $140,000, the cap on medical insurance for Medicare was removed; for people with incomes over $240,000, a 10 percent surcharge would raise their tax rate to 41.5 percent.

And finally, Clinton would adopt Vice President Al Gore's environmental agenda—concern for global warming—by imposing a significant tax on energy (British thermal units, or BTUs, which release carbon dioxide when burned).

This revolutionary budget proposal was obviously hard for Republicans to swallow. Doing so would amount to implicit recognition of the Reagan revolution's failure. In the summer, both Republicans and Democrats from energy-producing states killed the BTU tax, substituting instead a gasoline tax (of $0.04 per gallon), which would generate a mere $4 billion annually. But a few months later, after interminable debate, the Congress did finally enact the Deficit Reduction Act of 1993. It cut spending by $203 billion and increased tax revenues by $217 billion—a political compromise that would reduce the deficit by two-thirds of what the president had requested.

Optimistic expectations, in part stimulated by this legislation, spurred the "dot-com bubble"—a boom in new Internet, biotechnology, and telecommunications investments. Growing at 9.6 percent per year, investment in

TABLE 12-1

Clinton's proposed budget plan, 1993–1998 (billions of U.S. dollars)

	1993	1994	1995	1996	1997	1998	1994–1998
Baseline fiscal deficit	319	301	293	297	346	390	1,630
Spending changes							
Defense		−7	−12	−20	−37	−36	−112
Other discretionary		−4	−10	−15	−20	−23	−73
Entitlements		−9	−18	−30	−41	−47	−144
Debt service		−0.4	−3	−7	−14	−22	−46
Total spending cuts	1	−20	−43	−73	−112	−128	−375
Revenue increases	3	46	51	66	83	82	328
Personal income tax	3	37	36	44	55	54	254
Corporate tax	0.4	8	5	5	6	6	25
BTU tax		1	10	17	22	22	49
Stimulus and investment	15	27	39	47	55	62	231
Total deficit reduction	**13**	**−39**	**−54**	**−92**	**−140**	**−148**	**−473**

Source: Economic Report of the President (Washington, DC: U.S. Government Printing Office, 1995, 1999).

equipment and software led real GDP growth of 3.7 percent annually—the longest sustained recovery in U.S. history. Productivity during this period grew 1.9 percent annually—the highest rate in decades.

Combined with this stimulus from investment was low inflation, a lower growth in unit labor costs, and finally, a 1995 turnaround in real wages. (See figure 12-4.) Once again, Americans began getting richer. No only that, but the fiscal deficit fell more rapidly than even Clinton advisers had hoped. By late fall of 1998, for the first time in twenty-eight years, the deficit turned to a surplus. By 2000, the surplus had reached $236 billion—the largest surplus ever recorded. (See figure 12-5.) The treasury, for the first time in decades, began redeeming debt—albeit a very small amount.

But all was not well. Americans were overconsuming. During Clinton's two terms, a trend of rising consumption worsened. Consumption as a portion of GDP rose further, from 67.3 percent to 68.6 percent (it would eventually hit 70.7 percent by the end of 2004). Most of this increase (plus the increase in investment) was balanced by a decline in government spending, from 21.2 percent to 17.5 percent and leverage was also going up. With mortgage rates falling sharply, consumers were taking on more and more debt—from 66 percent to more than 100 percent of their disposable income.

As a consequence, personal savings were falling—even more sharply than during the 1980s. Between 1992 and 2000, they fell by almost half, from $366

FIGURE 12-4

Real average weekly wages in the United States, 1955–2005

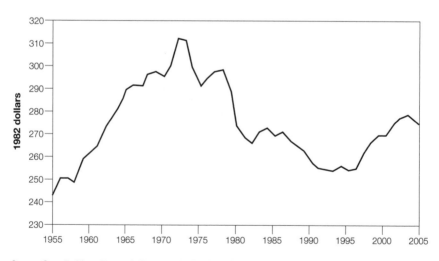

Source: Compiled from Economic Report to the President (Washington, DC: U.S. Government Printing Office, 2006).

FIGURE 12-5

United States fiscal balance, 1992–2006

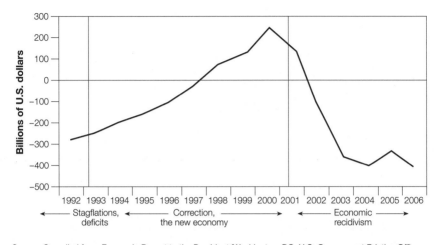

Source: Compiled from *Economic Report to the President* (Washington, DC: U.S. Government Printing Office, 2006).

billion to $168 billion. With interest rates low and consumer confidence at record highs, Americans did not worry about savings. They spent on housing, cars, electronics, and vacations. And much of what they spent, they spent abroad. Thus, the trade deficit, at –$97 billion in 1992, rose to a record of –$452 billion by 2000; and the current account, to –$414 billion. It mattered not that the dollar had depreciated through 1995. Americans, with higher incomes, spent and spent and spent.

Good economic performance was not the only accomplishment of the Clinton era. In 1993, Clinton pushed NAFTA through Congress, and it took effect in 1994. He bailed out Mexico from its second debt crisis in 1994; approved the Uruguay round of GATT negotiations in 1995; helped precipitate the cease fire in Northern Ireland and the Good Friday peace agreement in 1998; and authorized Gore to sign the Kyoto Accord in 1999. Despite these achievements, he left office under the cloud of a sex scandal—and having lied about it under oath.

Economic Recidivism: The Era of George W. Bush

In a very close election, which some Americans still feel was a victory for Al Gore, George W. Bush was elected the forty-fourth president of the United States. His Republican backing included most of the South and a surprisingly strong turnout by the "religious right." Bush took office under a mantra of "compassionate conservatism." He called for a revitalization of public schools, reinvigoration of civil society by faith-based initiatives, refunding social security and modernizing Medicare, supporting free trade, retiring $1 trillion in national debt, and delivering "tax relief to everyone who pays income taxes" to "give our economy a timely second wind."[21] Not surprisingly, there was no sign of the problems to come.

The centerpiece of Bush's legislative initiative was a tax cut of $1.6 trillion over the next ten years. Taxes were cut for all income groups, with the rich benefiting the most. Their tax burden would drop from 41 percent to 36 percent. Expecting a cumulative surplus of $5.6 trillion over the next ten years, Bush's advisers believed they could make deep cuts in taxes and still run surpluses averaging $260 billion annually through 2011. On June 7, 2001, Bush signed the Economic Growth and Tax Relief Reconciliation Act (EGTRRA) into law.

We will never know the precise economic effects of EGTRRA, because they were swamped by the heinous terrorist attacks on the World Trade Center and the Pentagon, on September 11, 2001. Besides killing nearly three thousand Americans, the attacks pushed the U.S. economy into a brief recession. And it caused a paradigm shift within the Bush administration, from a focus on "democratization" to a more aggressive preoccupation with international terrorism.

The recession, of course, lowered tax revenues even beyond the effects of the tax cut. Combined with increased spending for homeland security and the invasion of Afghanistan, the budget surplus dropped sharply to $128 billion in fiscal year 2001, and then to $158 billion by 2002. GDP growth slumped to 0.8 percent—technically not a recession.

However, in the spring of 2003, President Bush decided to invade Iraq, on the grounds of eliminating Saddam Hussein's "weapons of mass destruction" and bringing democracy to the Middle East. After a stunning air bombardment and a two-month military incursion, Iraq fell quickly, and Saddam was captured. But instead of peace, a terrorist insurgency soon developed, attracting al-Qaeda volunteers from across the Middle East. Throughout 2004 it worsened steadily, threatening to become a civil war by the spring of 2006.

The cost of these two wars—of maintaining one hundred forty-two thousand troops in Iraq and of strengthening homeland security—was $432 billion by 2006, not counting annual defense appropriations that exceeded $468 billion.[22] Far more importantly, twenty-five hundred Americans and an estimated thirty thousand Iraqis had already been killed.

Not withstanding these significant spending obligations, the Bush administration continued to pursue aggressively its ideological commitment to tax cuts. In 2002, Congress cut taxes by $100 billion; in 2003, by $360 billion; and in 2004, by another $156 billion. In 2006, the administration still hoped to make the 2001 EGTRRA permanent after 2010, at a cost in lost revenues estimated at $1.228 trillion.

Despite these tax cuts and the war in Iraq, Republicans did not reduce domestic spending—not on roads and dams nor on social entitlements. In fact, discretionary spending actually rose, with the passage of agricultural subsidies and a huge pork-laden infrastructural bill of $286 billion. With defense at a record high of $466 billion, and entitlements continuing to grow uncontrollably, Bush proposed a 2005 budget of $2.48 trillion—a government budget bigger than the GDPs of all but two countries.

With a halting, so-called jobless recovery in 2002–2003, the deficit had widened sharply, to –$412 billion by 2004. Only when the recovery gained strength did the deficit begin to fall, toward an estimated –$317 for fiscal year 2005. The tax cuts had a significant impact on the American economy. The administration estimated total tax relief of $159 billion in 2003, rising to a peak of $272 billion in 2004. Real economic growth jumped to 7 percent in the third quarter of 2003, producing yearly average growth of 3 percent. In 2004, GDP expanded even faster, at 4.4 percent. George W. Bush easily won reelection.

The American economy also benefited significantly from the monetary policy imposed by Alan Greenspan at the Federal Reserve. Pretty certain that inflation expectations were dead, the Fed began lowering the discount rate in June 2000, as soon as growth began to slow. As figure 12-6 illustrates,

FIGURE 12-6

Effective federal funds rate in the United States, 1996–2006

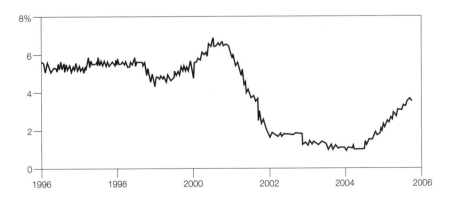

Source: Board of Governors of the Federal Reserve System, Federal Reserve Bank of St. Louis, 2005, research.stlouisfed.org.

the rate was eventually lowered to 1 percent by 2004. The impact of these low rates was to stimulate investment—particularly residential investment—to grow at 13 percent.

One huge benefit of this investment stimulus, and all the investment of the 1990s, was that productivity grew at an unprecedented rate. The growth of manufacturing productivity in particular exceeded 4 percent annually after 1997 and actually surpassed 6 percent in 2002. American business had laid off more than 2.6 million workers in the 2001–2002 recession but could produce even more without rehiring them once demand recovered. As a consequence of high productivity, growth of unit labor costs turned negative in 2002–2003 and scarcely grew in 2004. This was wonderful for U.S. competitiveness.

Two big problems were associated with this growth. First, Americans spent more and saved less. And as the dollar strengthened, the trade balance deteriorated to record levels.

Personal savings, as previously noted, had already deteriorated, to 2 percent by the time Bush took office. But as American consumers continued to spend, it fell to a record low of –1.1 percent by July 2005. (See figure 12-7.) That's right—*negative*. In May 2006, it was still negative! This meant that any difference between retained earnings (e.g., business savings) and private investment, plus all the fiscal deficit, had to be funded by foreign savings. And that meant huge trade and current account deficits.

FIGURE 12-7

Personal saving in the United States as a percentage of disposable personal income, 1980–2006

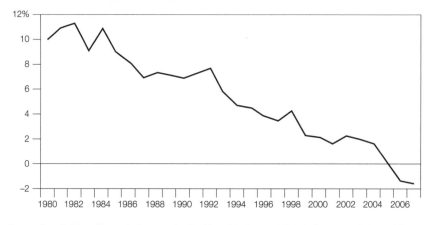

Source: Compiled from *Economic Report to the President* (Washington, DC: U.S. Government Printing Office, 2006).

The trade deficit ballooned from $427 billion in 2001 to an estimated $791 billion in 2005, as depicted in figure 12-8. The current account deficit worsened further, to $792 billion. Higher imports were driven by consumer demand and record-high prices for petroleum. The United States ran sizable deficits with every major region—Japan, China, Europe, and Mexico and Canada. Capital goods and industrial supplies composed most of the country's exports, while consumer goods, capital goods, automobiles, and petroleum were the largest exports. While services ran a surplus of about $50 billion, income was a wash and unilateral transfers were –$81 billion.

The value of the dollar dipped sharply after 2002, losing 27 percent of its value on a trade-weighted basis. However, most of this loss was against the euro, which appreciated from $0.85 to $1.28, before slumping a bit to $1.25. But against the yen and the yuan, the dollar had not depreciated. The Bush administration, while maintaining a strong-dollar policy on the surface, had sent Treasury Secretary John Snow to Beijing and Tokyo to elicit some appreciation. In both cases, he was told no. During the course of 2005, the Japanese yen had actually weakened to ¥113 per dollar, and the yuan remained fixed until August at 8.3, when the Chinese allowed it to appreciate by a mere 2.1 percent, to 8.1.

To finance its immense and growing deficits, the United States had to sell real assets and financial assets—stocks, bonds, and government securities. The consequences of doing so, as figure 12-9 indicates, raised America's net

FIGURE 12-8

U.S. balance of trade and current account, 1969–2005

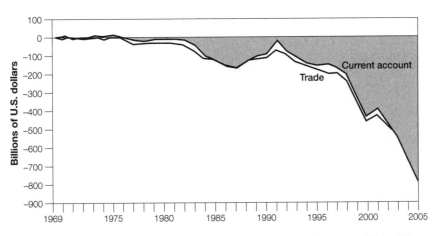

Source: Compiled from Economic Report to the President (Washington, DC: U.S. Government Printing Office, 2006).

foreign debt sharply. Of course, the United States still had plenty of assets to sell—Yellowstone, GE, Harvard, and so on. But at some point, Americans might want to think about reducing consumption and saving more while they still have some assets left.

In the late fall of 2005, the United States faced choices—important choices. Its budget deficit was unsustainable, even more so in the wake of hurricanes Katrina and Rita. In September 2005, the Senate had authorized another $50 billion for military operations in Afghanistan and Iraq during fiscal year 2006. The country's trade and current account deficits were even less sustainable. Savings were zero as the housing bubble threatened to burst. America was dependent on foreign sources for 64 percent of its oil consumption, which together with China's demand, had pushed prices to $72 per barrel by July 2006. And increasingly, the United States could count few foreign populations among its friends and allies.

So Is Government Important?

For any open-minded reader, this brief history of macroeconomic policy in America must have demonstrated that good government is vital. Although the United States has enjoyed considerable economic growth since 1983, much of that growth is attributed to huge deficit spending, due to massive

FIGURE 12-9

U.S. net international investment position at year end

Direct investment positions are valued at current cost

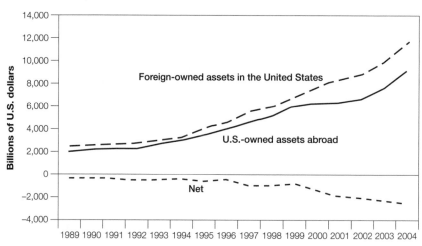

Source: Compiled from Department of Commerce, Bureau of Economic Analysis.

tax cuts. And it is financed by foreign savings. As America's household savings have dipped below zero, the country has financed its consumption by selling assets. True, American business has invested heavily to reap great productivity. And true, American entrepreneurship still leads the world in innovation. And true, America continues to support great institutions in education, health, law, and finance. Yet Americans' average real wages are below the levels achieved in the 1960s and 1970s.

Perhaps most worrisome of all is the current account deficit—$792 billion in 2005. This means that Americans spent $792 billion more on foreign goods and services than they sold to foreigners. As a result, they needed to borrow $792 billion from foreigners to finance the difference between national savings and national investment. Thus, the United States' net foreign debt exceeded $3 trillion.

While the behavior of firms and individuals is responsible for this in a microeconomic sense, the government has surely affected it. Government fiscal deficits alone account for more than half this amount. The U.S. government's policies on health care, education, and trade—and its *lack* of policies on savings and exchange rates—all affect the current account.

The United States needs good government. It needs good policies on national security, on health and welfare, and especially on energy and the environment. But above all, it needs macroeconomic management that will provide a base for the country's next decade of growth. In the next and final chapter, we'll consider scenarios for future policy of correction and adjustment, or collapse.

Conclusion

TRAJECTORIES OF GLOBALIZATION

BECAUSE OF GLOBALIZATION, countries now compete to develop. This is clear from our look at ten countries that comprise three-fourths of the world economy. They compete for export markets and foreign investments. They compete in education, productivity, and defense. Success in this competitive environment breeds growth and wealth. Before World War II, autonomous growth was more common and more feasible. But now, with the global integration of markets, competition between nations has become ubiquitous. And in this global competition, government is key.

Governments not only conduct essential fiscal and monetary policy, but they create and foster all the crucial institutions that facilitate growth. Trade policy, savings incentives, a financial environment conducive to investment, corporate governance, equitable income distribution, and the absence of crime and corruption are just a few of the institutional conditions created and sustained by national government. Taken together, these economic policies amount to national strategy, and these institutions create the necessary organizational structure. It is the pursuit of national strategy by the organization of the state that either makes countries great or strands them in underdevelopment.

In chapter 1, I described four elements of successful economic development: (1) national strategy, (2) economic structure, (3) resource development, and (4) efficient use of resources. Strategy, either explicit or implicit, includes both macroeconomic and microeconomic components. The organizational structure is a set of institutions (both narrowly and broadly defined) that a national polity has to create to implement its strategy. The strategy

271

and structure together have to develop resources—natural, human, techno-logical, and capital—and choose ways of ensuring their efficient use.

From the ten countries we've examined, we can see a very wide range of choices, some of which have been incredibly successful in the past—for example, those of Singapore, Japan, China, and the United States. Some—like the choices made by Mexico, South Africa, India, and Italy (as a representative of Europe)—have experienced a mix of success and failure over time. And a couple—like Russia and Saudi Arabia—generally failed until 2000 or so when resource wealth and institutional reform together succeeded.

The Crucial Role of Government

While drawing conclusions is risky, because the contexts vary so widely, there are ten policy generalizations that I think it's safe to pose. But we should remember, too, that how these various policy strands fit together strategically is crucial to their effectiveness.

The place to start is basic property rights. These are essential. If a country cannot guarantee private property, its protection, and the right to exchange it, development of a working market economy will at best be slow. Consider China before 1983 or Russia during the 1990s. The absence of secure property rights, a constitutional legal system, and enforceable contracts made market development impossible. Markets work, and contribute to growth, only within a secure legal framework, which the state provides.

After secure property rights, sound macroeconomic policies are vital. First, there's the necessity of fiscal probity. In the ten cases we've examined, and in most other economic histories that I know of, fiscal deficits cannot continue indefinitely without severely weakening the country. In Mexico, India, and Russia, we saw deficits precipitate debt crises; in China, the banking system failed; and in Italy, Japan, and the United States, we saw how debt induces huge interest obligations that begin to threaten sustainability.

For sure, there are episodes of stagnation or economic crisis in which deficit spending by government makes sense. Enough deficit spending can stimulate consumption and/or investment until economic growth becomes self-sustaining. (Look at the growth of the United States since 2002.) But too often, deficits become entitlements and are allowed to grow excessively. And of course, they need to be funded. If monetized, they cause inflation. If not, they cause interest rates to rise, crowd out private domestic investment, and accumulate foreign debt. In the long run, spending beyond one's means is as unwise for countries as it is for households.

A third important corollary to this is that savings and investment are crucial to economic growth. Countries that save more and invest more grow.

We see this with Japan, Singapore, and China. And we see the obverse in Mexico and South Africa. Countries that do not invest in human and physical capital cannot compete for long. Mexico, India, South Africa, and Saudi Arabia maintain low levels of private investment—about half the levels of Singapore and China. Sooner or later, these relatively paltry commitments to the future will leave their countries uncompetitive.

Having some sort of policy, institution, incentives, or cultural bias that encourages savings is key. Singapore's Central Provident Fund is a model that the United States and South Africa should adopt. Of course, it is possible to attract foreign savings to fund investment. That is just what the United States has done for the past two decades. But in the long run, domestic savings is obviously preferable to foreign savings—for several reasons. Debt service is denominated in domestic currency and relatively less connected to exchange rates. And one does not have to sell domestic assets to foreigners to obtain the savings, thus depleting the wealth on which future generations must rely. This is a major problem facing the United States today.

Consumption meets present needs; savings meet future needs. In any society, there needs to be a balance between these two. In 2006 in the United States, Mexico, and South Africa, that balance is not being sustained. The costs of excess consumption are hidden for the moment but will eventually reveal themselves. Before then, those countries need to adjust—they need to find an impetus to save—if they are to remain competitive with countries that do.

Fourth, we've seen that strong (but not necessarily independent) central banks are necessary for noninflationary growth. This is evident in Singapore, Japan, the United States, and Europe—and more recently, with Mexico, India, and South Africa. Central banks need to provide adequate liquidity for growth but must not provide excessive liquidity, or prices will rise. Today, especially in the global economy, inflation is disastrous. It drives up interest rates and eventually weakens the currency. That is why more and more central banks have moved toward inflation targeting or at least putting a strong focus on inflation.

Sound microeconomic policies are also important. For all of these countries, we see that liberalization *sometimes* is necessary to facilitate growth. (By "liberalization," I mean the removal of barriers to trade and foreign investment, an exchange rate policy that follows the market, and eventually, privatization of potentially competitive assets.) For sure, restrictions can (and did) work for a time. We saw this with Japan, China, and even Italy. But in every case, as the country matured and as the global economy developed, microeconomic restrictions caused growing distortions and needed to give way. That is happening in China, India, and Russia today. And it needs to happen soon in Saudi Arabia and throughout Western Europe as well.

Sixth is labor market flexibility. The United States has a relatively unfettered labor market—with almost no restrictions on hiring and firing, a low minimum wage, and severely meager (e.g., six months) unemployment insurance. This is one of America's greatest strengths. Likewise, China and Singapore have flexible labor—the former because of few labor protections, and the latter because of government-weakened unions. But in Mexico, South Africa, India, and Europe, we see elaborate work rules and labor market rigidities that hamper productivity, prevent firms from structurally adjusting, and drive up unit labor costs. Especially in Italy, where productivity is otherwise high, inefficient labor markets require huge governmental expenditures and make structural adjustment difficult. Likewise in Japan, we saw that cultural and social dictates have had the same effect for nearly two decades.

A seventh observation pertains to resource endowments—in Mexico, Saudi Arabia, Russia, and South Africa, they are difficult to manage. In each case, we've seen how revenue from resources fuels unwise government spending and invariably contributes to corruption. The presence of such valuable assets, moreover, tends to support an overvalued currency. As government spending fuels inflation and prices rise, the country's nonresource exports become less competitive—the so-called Dutch disease. Managing such wealth effectively requires a sound set of institutional controls to keep the rents from distorting all other elements of the economy. Russia, with its new oil stabilization fund, is trying to emulate Norway in alleviating these problems.

Two sets of social issues—corruption and income inequality—also stand out from all our cases. Most countries with high levels of corruption—Mexico, India, and Russia—are slow to develop. Countries with relatively lower levels of corruption—Singapore, the United States, and Japan—have developed more. One could conclude that development leads to less corruption, but I think the relationship is at least reciprocal—less corruption leads to development. China appears to be the exception. That country has high levels of corruption but has nonetheless developed quickly. Still, China would no doubt be better off—socially and economically—had it less corruption.

Inequitable income distribution also seems to hold back economic progress, and it certainly weakens social structure. Mexico (representing Latin America), South Africa (representing Africa), and Russia (representing Eastern Europe) have severely imbalanced distributions of income. Japan, Italy, Singapore, and until recently, the United States had flatter income distributions. I think these relationships are not coincidental. Lousy income distribution not only causes social frictions but, by leaving a large segment of the population without purchasing power, undermines the potential for growth. Colonial legacies, racial differences, and problems with rural infrastructure and education all seem to cause poverty and hurt income distribution; so does corruption and the absence of progressive taxation.

Finally, it is worth reemphasizing the huge asymmetry that has unfolded in the global economy's current account balances. Almost all regions have current account surpluses (or perhaps small deficits). Some, like Japan's, are huge! But the United States has nearly four-fifths of the deficits. This condition will likely worsen in 2006. The problem has short-term and long-term implications. In the short term, it means that the United States hosts most of the world's consumption of traded goods and services. Any slowdown in the U.S. economy will adversely leverage exporting countries—especially China, Germany, and Japan. Conversely, to continue its growth, the United States must borrow massively from the rest of the world's savers—selling its assets and incurring more and more debt in the long run.

This asymmetry, while unfairly burdening America's children, cannot continue indefinitely. Indeed, I personally think that global patience is nearly exhausted. Sooner or later, either exchange rates will adjust or some creditor countries will lose their nerve. When that happens, a severe global adjustment will unfold—undermining the standard of living in the United States and causing severe unemployment and deep recessions elsewhere in the world.

In all of these ten areas of policy and performance, we see the role of governmental institutions—both good and bad—as crucial. That is the point of this book. When political parties allow excessive deficits, the political institutions are failing. When courts allow organized crime or rampant corruption, again, institutions are failing. But when government agencies encourage savings or contain inflation or reinvest resource rents, then government institutions are working. When pensions are funded, health care effectively managed, and poor people educated, government is creating the institutions necessary to engender sustainable economic growth.

Trajectories and Scenarios

Business managers need to understand global markets and government policies to (1) know their competition, (2) evaluate international expansion opportunities, (3) consider the risks and benefits of foreign direct investment, and (4) anticipate the consequences of exchange rate fluctuations on trade, investment, and interest rates. They need to consider these issues, I believe, in light of the developmental trajectories unfolding in the global economy.

But also, for the sake of their country's well-being, business managers and other informed citizens need to *make* their political leadership build strong institutions and adopt effective policies. After all, regardless of what each country has achieved to date, the competitive future is indeterminate.

Trajectories are perhaps most useful for thinking about the near-term future. That is, if one really knows where a country has recently been and where it is today, one can draw some logical inferences about where it is heading. Take the United States. We know the government deficit will persist for years, even if the administration takes immediate action to reduce it. We know that the U.S. trading position—a deficit of nearly $800 billion—can't be reversed in the next few years. Even if exchange rates adjusted abruptly, or if American savings were to increase, it would take years—between five and ten—to repair our own production capacity and to increase our export positions.

In the meantime, we know that an absence of savings means we must sell assets to foreigners, to fund our domestic investments, for years to come. For certain, U.S. net debt will increase $2 trillion to $3 trillion in the next few years. This should tell us something about the value of the dollar and the likely direction of real interest rates.

Barring some sort of political or environmental crisis, we can likewise project forward the growth trajectories of China and India. They will continue to grow at a rapid pace for the next several years. This should tell us something about foreign direct investment, about trading positions in goods and services, and about eventual rises in wages. In the meantime, however, these trajectories should make Mexicans, South Africans, and even Europeans rather nervous, because Asian market shares are certain to grow.

So let's think a bit about the near-term future using scenarios that spring from the trajectories we've so carefully developed. We should start with Singapore, the most developed state in Southeast Asia. Here we saw how hard work, incredibly efficient institutions, and great leadership have made Singapore rich. But today, and for the foreseeable future, Singapore is being increasingly pressed by China and India on the low end, and more competitively by Korea, Taiwan, the United States, and Europe on the high end. Either its strategy of low taxes and networked clusters, particularly biotechnology, will work—or it won't. If it works, we can expect Singapore to become a services powerhouse in Southeast Asia, quickly catching up with the income levels of Europe. But if not, what would happen to Singapore's growth as it loses lower-end jobs and investment to China?

Developing scenarios for China is a more striking exercise. When we think about China's part of this high-growth trajectory, we can frame two developmental paths for its immediate future. China has been growing at more than 8 percent annually and running larger and larger surpluses on its current account. A positive trajectory would have China adjusting gradually to the terms of the World Trade Organization (WTO). If Hu Jintao encourages consumption, allows the renminbi to appreciate, and gradually liberalizes the polity, his trading relations (and thus foreign relations) will doubtlessly improve. If he more aggressively helps the banks write off bad debt, creates a reasonable system of governance, and further privatizes the state-owned sectors, then China can continue to grow fast for at least another decade.

But if China continues on its present path, growing exports too rapidly without liberalizing trade, then trouble will certainly be coming. The Bank of China must spend $100 billion buying U.S. bonds each year, thus stimulating and inflating its domestic economy (prices and assets) too rapidly. If Hu fails to reform the banks or the state-owned sector, and retains too tight a grip on power, then pressures will build within the country. Rapid growth of energy and food imports, funded by a cheap renminbi and manufacturing exports to the United States, will cause imbalances and force the United States to impose barriers to trade. At that point, Chinese workers might rebel.

When the Party Congress met in March 2006, there was clear recognition of these issues. Premier Hu Jintao identified domestic income distribution, efficient use of energy resources, and the environment as key concerns for the next five years. He urged greater consumption and greater productivity, rather than excessive savings and investment. Yet on political reform, he had nothing to offer. A delegation of U.S. senators visited toward the end of the congress to press for exchange rate appreciation. They returned to the United States somewhat more optimistic, willing to wait a bit longer before seeking the imposition of tariffs.

It is something of a toss-up, I believe, which of these paths China will pursue. I suppose the odds favor continued growth and gradual reform. But the government needs to take seriously the imbalances its growth has engendered—domestically, in income, banking, energy, and the environment, and externally, in terms of its overwhelming surpluses, especially with the United States.

For firms, these scenarios make a huge difference. In the positive scenario, continuing investment opportunities abound. A company like GE, moreover, could anticipate huge expansion of its China businesses—power, infrastructure, jet turbines, plastics, and medical systems—all of which China will need as it continues to grow. Banks and other sophisticated service firms could also look forward to more involvement in China as WTO provisions get implemented and as intellectual property rights get enforced.

On the other hand, by keeping wages low and the yuan weak, the negative scenario would continue to threaten smaller manufacturing firms, furniture companies, and anyone in the United States still trying to make things. And it would wreak havoc on Mexico, Malaysia, Turkey, and South Africa as they try to compete in the same wage-intensive markets.

India, which slipped far behind China two decades ago, has further to go with challenges of a different sort. A fragmented democracy with ethnic and religious heterogeneity, India needs to keep opening up. Its biggest threat politically is the friction between Hindus and Muslims—and with Pakistan. Its economic problems center on the fiscal deficit, income inequality, a lack of infrastructure, and the lack of foreign direct investment.

Here, imagine one scenario where India liberalizes substantially, reduces its deficit, and privatizes state-owned enterprise. Doing so might push growth to 9 percent annually, helping develop the infrastructure while further alleviating poverty. With lower unemployment, domestic ethnic and religious frictions might fade, helping negotiate peace with Pakistan. High growth and better tax collection would reduce deficits over the next few years, allowing the debt-to-GDP ratio to decline from its current level of 86 percent. This, in turn, would reduce crowding out, lower real interest rates, and help investment. Such a positive strategy would encourage massive foreign direct investment as western firms build infrastructure and position themselves in higher-value-added downstream markets.

But another scenario is also possible. A coalition government (of congress and Communists) might be unable to accomplish reform and could allow fiscal deficits to escalate. Energy pressures could severely exacerbate the current account deficit, intensifying preoccupation with *swadeshi*. Domestic and international frictions could then fester, undermining foreign direct investment (FDI), the improvement of infrastructure, and eventually India's overall development. This would hurt foreign firms already in India and make FDI far too risky.

Turning from high-growth Asia to Latin America's recovery from debt crisis, we can think about likely scenarios for Mexico during the next five years. Mexico surely needs to consider competition with China, Malaysia, and even Singapore in the near future. Like South Africa, Mexico seems "stuck in the middle," to use Michael Porter's phrase referring to corporate strategies. With the benefit of NAFTA and foreign direct investment, the country has created a huge export sector that employs more than a million Mexicans. But its *maquilas* are increasingly challenged by China, Malaysia, and Turkey, and perhaps by India in services outsourcing. Thus, on the low end of the value-added chain, Mexico's wages and standard of living are too high to compete. Yet on the high end of the value-added spectrum, Mexico lacks adequate supply chains, the education, and the technological experience to compete with the likes of Singapore, Korea, and Taiwan.

So the question is, how will Mexicans continue to grow their exports to be competitive? What changes can they make in their current strategies to grow productivity and add value? How, with a strong anti-inflation program, can they keep their currency from rising to a point where they lose competitiveness—especially if China chooses not to let the renminbi appreciate? Mexicans' energy resources offer some promise, but only if government reform allows PEMEX (or foreign power companies) to significantly reinvest.

In the election of 2006, Mexico's fledgling democracy, and its macroeconomic stability, is under challenge from the disaffected left. If elected president, would López Obrador, candidate of the Revolutionary Democratic Party, be more like Brazil's Luiz Inácio Lula da Silva, talking revolution but practicing sound policy, or like Venezuela's Hugo Chávez, damagingly populist? Or would the Partido Accion Nacional's Felipe Calderón be able to pass legislation to strengthen the country's competitiveness? And how do foreign firms doing business in Mexico, or thinking about investing, assess these choices? What wage rates, interest rates, and exchange rates can they anticipate?

We used Russia to examine the disintegration of communism in Eastern Europe and the process of structural adjustment and recovery. For sure, Russia has had a harder time than Poland, the Czech Republic, or Hungary. While trying to liberalize both its economy and polity in 1993, Russia failed utterly. Not until 2000, with the election of a stronger, more statist president (and a rise in oil prices), did we see any hope for real adjustment. Here, we saw the importance of institutions—formal institutions like banking and courts, as well as less concrete institutions like property rights. The liberalization of Russia initially failed, in large measure for want of basic institutions of democracy and capitalism.

For Russia, one can imagine a future in which crime, corruption, and political instability persist as Putin fails to achieve reform. Inflation rises, separatist issues in southern Russia persist, and FDI remains minimal. Democracy would fade and relations with the United States would deteriorate. Eventually democracy would fail, and state power would return to Communist or dictatorial hands. This would be a blow to energy users in Europe and to potential foreign investors everywhere.

On the other hand, Putin has subdued the oligarchs and begun to restore legitimacy to Russia's institutions. If oil prices were to remain high and the surplus on the current account huge, Russia could begin attracting FDI and might have sufficient funds to reform social and economic institutions. Thus far, I have had an unusual degree of sympathy for Vladimir Putin and support of his heavy-handed use of power. True, he seems to be limiting freedoms and using the state arbitrarily. But the task he faces is immense. If he can rebuild the state without aggrandizing the office of president permanently, he may go down in Russia's history as the great rebuilder of the state.

For any foreign investor, making a bet on Russia at this point is certainly a bet. If it continues to grow and reform gradually, then Royal Dutch/Shell and British Petroleum will look pretty smart for having put billions of dollars at risk. Others—in consumer products, natural resources, technology, and financial services—need to consider these scenarios carefully, lest they come to the party too late . . . or too early.

To appreciate the African renaissance, we looked carefully at South Africa—the continent's most important country economically. After uniquely ending apartheid, South Africa struggled against huge social odds to gets its macroeconomy under control and begin a new strategy of export-led growth. It remains to be seen whether the new industry charters—in mining, finance, and retailing—will work and whether unemployment will begin to fall. In the second quarter of 2005, GDP growth had reached 4.8 percent—the highest level in more than two decades. If Thabo Mbeki and his people can deal with AIDS and crime and ensure a more balanced income distribution, then perhaps South Africa will make it.

Despite its various social issues, I remain optimistic about South Africa. There's an entrepreneurial spirit afoot and plenty of opportunities. It would, of course, be better if privatization would make some progress. But still, portfolio investments and direct investments, where possible, stand a pretty good chance of healthy earnings.

One of the most difficult trajectories to pin down, perhaps, is Islamic resurgence; Saudi Arabia is the home of Islam and the world's most important oil producer. Here, more clearly than anywhere, we could see the problems of "Dutch disease," and the clash between modernization and westernization. With oil prices at record heights, King Abdullah has a unique chance for reform. He needs to liberalize the relationship between church and state, while rebuilding his infrastructure and expanding the Arab American Oil Company's output. He needs to find a stable government form, somewhere between absolute monarchy and fundamentalist chaos, that can suit the people of his country.

But against this prospect is the threat of terrorism, so strong in the Arab Middle East. Iran's ayatollahs and the U.S. war in Iraq certainly do not help. Nor does the putatively irresolvable clash between Palestinians and Israelis. If peace is not improved in the region and if Abdullah is unable to reform his political economy soon, then fundamentalist pressures could grow beyond control. I think most westerners are holding up on direct investment—and probably with good reason.

Western Europe in general and Italy in particular face some hard choices in the next few years. Global competition seems to be passing by their rigid work rules and welfare state. If Europe is to become more integrated and more competitive in the world economy, it needs to pursue some hard reforms—soon—especially in Germany, France, and Italy. But if Europeans take too long, they will lose out—to Japan and the United States on the high end, and to China and India in lower value-added competition.

In Japan, we looked at stagnation after decades of miracle growth. Here the focus was not only on deficits and debt but on the aging of the population—a problem facing Italy, Germany, France, the United States, and eventually, developing countries as well. We also focused on institutions—on outdated employment institutions, outdated corporate governance, an outdated educational establishment, and a parliamentary organization that barely works.

One wonders whether Japan can ever restore its glory days. With the fiscal deficit at 7.2 percent and gross government debt of 169 percent, one knows with absolute certainty that this cannot continue for long. Add to that the effects of aging, both on the budget and on the national savings rate, and we know that interest rates will soon rise. Can Japan continue to fund U.S. deficits if its savings are insufficient to fund its own investments and debt?

The alternative for Japan is to raise taxes significantly to mitigate these deficits, and hasten its structural reforms, like privatization of the post office, while tolerating slow growth. Its biggest challenge will be its declining number of working-age people, and whether Japan can open itself up to an immigrant workforce. True, it's growing now—but that growth cannot be sustained if debt and debt service become overwhelming.

Finally, we looked at the United States' descent into deficits and debt. Despite high growth, low inflation, and outstanding improvements in productivity, the United States had developed massive fiscal and trade deficits, with no savings to support them. It borrowed more and more from foreign savers, who consequently owned more and more U.S. assets. By 2006, these problems were reaching crisis proportions.

Consider a scenario where the fiscal deficit and the trade deficit worsen, as the United States is utterly bogged down in Iraq. The budget deficit hits $460 billion; the current account deficit $1 trillion. Americans keep spending, for a while, and the administration refuses to raise taxes. Before the next election, China, Japan, or some smaller country might decide to divest U.S. bonds. If that became endemic, interest rates would spike, the dollar would collapse, and the United States would plunge into a prolonged recession. American living standards would decline significantly as a consequence of a collapsing dollar. Other exporting countries, moreover, would likewise suffer a pretty big shock.

Alternatively, one could envision a different president after 2008 who would choose to raise taxes on the rich and cut spending on agricultural and infrastructural pork, thus again reducing the deficit. To curtail our massive defense obligations, that new administration could help the United Nations take responsibility for Iraq, eventually extricating the United States from its ruinous involvement in the Middle East. The new administration might also drive down the value of the dollar and create some new institution, like the Central Provident Fund, to force Americans to save. Our trade balance would eventually improve sharply. And finally, this administration could begin making the necessary adjustments to non-fossil-fuel energy, both mitigating our dependence on the Middle East and reducing our massive contribution to global warming.

Responsible Executives

Thinking about trajectories and their alternatives has at least two beneficial objectives. By asking what course a state might follow over the next few years, a manager can identify the crucial elements that would affect whatever business he or she is in. These can be tracked by carefully following economic performance and perhaps tied to the firm's strategic decision making.

Thus, if I were an investor I'd be increasingly worried about U.S. deficits, Japanese debt, and fundamentalism in the Middle East. I'd be more optimistic about doing business in India or Singapore, carefully optimistic about South Africa and Russia, and just plain careful about China, Mexico, and Europe.

But as a business executive having read this entire work, I would think about my own responsibility—as a well-informed citizen—for good public policy. Every country faces crucial policy issues affecting growth, trade, education, living environment, and security. If informed citizens in Japan, South Africa, or America do not contribute to sound government policy, then how can they complain about ineptitude? Who else, besides committed, well-informed business managers, can have a significant, positive effect on the policy process?

It is our responsibility to manage the globalization process—and to make our countries compete.

Chapter One

1. The concept of strategy and structure, as applied to business, developed at the Harvard Business School in the 1960s. In the 1970s, a group led by Bruce Scott transferred this idea, adding context, to the performance of nation-states. Out of this came a required course and a department of the school called BGIE—Business, Government, and the International Economy. I am deeply indebted to Bruce Scott, among others, for the basic ideas that frame many of the chapters of this book.

2. David Moss, *When All Else Fails* (Cambridge, MA: Harvard University Press, 2002).

Chapter Two

1. Edwin O. Reischauer, *The United States and Japan*, 3rd ed. (New York: Viking, 1964), 50–51.

2. Bruce Scott, John Rosenblum, and Audry Sproat, *Case Studies in Political Economy, 1954–1977* (Boston: Harvard Business School Press, 1980), 24.

3. Hugh Patrick and Henry Rosovsky, "Japan's Economic Performance: An Overview," in *Asia's New Giant*, ed. H. Patrick and H. Rosovsky (Washington, DC: Brookings Institution, 1976), 12.

4. Edwin O. Reischauer, *The Japanese* (Cambridge, MA: Harvard University Press, 1982), 167–178.

5. Chalmers Johnson, *MITI and the Japanese Miracle* (Palo Alto, CA: Stanford University Press, 1982), 242–259.

6. Richard Vietor, "Energy Policy and Markets," in *America Versus Japan*, ed. Thomas K. McCraw (Boston: Harvard Business School Press, 1986).

7. Leon Hollerman, *Japan's Dependence on the World Economy: The Approach Toward Economic Liberalization* (Princeton, NJ: Princeton University Press, 1967), 224–233.

8. Richard Caves, "Industrial Organization," in Patrick and Rosovsky, *Asia's New Giant*, 482–487.

9. Ministry of Finance, *General Survey of the Japanese Economy* (Tokyo: Ministry of Finance, 1955), 5; quoted in Scott, Rosenblum, and Sproat, *Case Studies in Political Economy*, 137.

10. Organization of Economic Cooperation and Development, *The Industrial Policy of Japan* (Paris: OECD, 1972), 15–17.

11. James C. Abegglen, ed., *Business Strategies for Japan* (Tokyo: Boston Consulting Group, 1970).

Chapter Three

1. Richard Vietor and Emily Thompson, "Singapore, Inc.," Case 9-703-040 (Boston: Harvard Business School, 2003).

2. Lady Raffles, "Memoir of the Life and Public Services of Sir Thomas Raffles," in *The Economic Development of Singapore*, ed. W. G. Huff (Cambridge: Cambridge University Press, 1994), 8.

3. "Singapore Is Out," *Straits Times*, August 10, 1965.

4. Lee Kuan Yew, *From Third World to First: The Singapore Story, 1965–2000* (New York: Harper Collins, 2000), 3.

5. Rajendra Sisddia, "Singapore Invests in the Nation-Corporation," *Harvard Business Review*, May–June 1992, 45; "Singapore After Lee: The Under-Nannies Take Over," *Economist*, October 27, 1990, 20.

6. Library of Congress, "Singapore: A Country Study," Library of Congress Web site, http://www.sabb.com.sa/projects/web/webprod.nsf.

7. Lim Boon Heng, secretary general of National Trade Union Congress, interview by author, December 2002.

8. Standards, Productivity and Innovation Board, *Annual Report 2001–2002* (Singapore: Spring 2003).

9. Lim Boon Heng, interview.

10. Lee Suan Hiang, CEO, SPRING, interview by author, December 2002.

11. Chua Mui Hoong, "Judge My Government By Its Results, Says PM," *Straits Times*, June 1, 2002.

12. Chua Taik Him, Assistant Managing Director, Economic Development Board, interview by author, December 2002.

13. Tan Chin Nam, interview by author, December 2002

14. Transparency International Corruption Perceptions Index 2994, www.transparency.org/cpi/2005.

15. Cherian George, *Singapore: The Air-Conditioned Nation* (Singapore: Landmark Books, 2000), 21.

16. Goh Chok Tong, quoted in Forest Reinhardt, "Singapore," Case 9-793-096 (Boston: Harvard Business School, 1996).

17. Teo Ming Kian, Chairman, EBD, quoted in Vietor and Thompson, "Singapore, Inc."

18. Quotations in this section by Chua Taik Him are from an interview by the author, December 2002.

19. Economic Development Board, *Annual Report 2001* (Singapore, 2002).

20. Channel News, Asia Web site, http://www.channelnewsasia.com/cna/parliament/erc.report8.htm.

21. Lee Hsien Loong, "State of the Economy: Looking Back on 2001, What's Ahead in 2002, Singapore: A Monthly Update from the Singaporean Embassy," January 2002, 2.

Chapter Four

1. Tim Clissold, *Mr. China* (London: Robinson, 2004), ch. 4.

2. Debora Spar, "China (A): The Great Awakening," Case 9-794-019 (Boston: Harvard Business School, 1994).

3. Robert Kennedy, "China: Facing the 21st Century," Case 9-798-066 (Boston: Harvard Business School, 1998).

4. Qian Long Emperor, "Letter to King George III," September 14, 1793, in *Annals and Memoirs of the Court of Peking*, ed. E. Backhouse and J. D. Bland (Boston: Houghton Mifflin, 1914), 322–331.

5. R. H. Tawney, *Land and Labor in China* (Boston: Beacon Press, 1966), 11.

6. *China Statistical Yearbook*, cited in Kennedy, "China: Facing the 21st Century."

7. Bruce Scott and Jamie Matthews, "China's Rural Leap Forward," Case 9-703-024 (Boston: Harvard Business School, 2003).

8. World Bank, *China 2020: Development Challenges in the New Century* (Washington, DC: World Bank, 1997).

9. Eswar Prasad, ed., *China's Growth and Integration into the World Economy* (Washington, DC: International Monetary Fund, 2004), 37.

10. Stephen Green, "Privatization," *China Economic Quarterly*, April–June 2004, 30.

11. Stephen Harner, "Earthquake," *China Economic Quarterly*, July–September 2004, 42–48.

12. Regina Abrami, "China and the WTO: Doing the Right Thing?" Case 9-704-041 (Boston: Harvard Business School, 2004).

13. Transparency International, "Corruption Perceptions Index," http://www.transparency.org/policy_research/surveys_indices/cpi.

14. Douglas Zeng, "China's Employment Challenges and Strategies After the WTO Accession," policy research working paper, World Bank, Washington, DC, February 2005.

15. Prasad, *China's Growth*, 57.

16. Kristen A. Day, ed., *China's Environment and the Challenge of Sustainable Development* (Armonk, NY: M. E. Sharpe, 2004).

17. Deepak Bhattashali et al., eds., *China and the WTO: Accession, Policy Reform and Poverty Reduction Strategies* (Washington, DC: World Bank, 2004), ch. 1.

18. "WTO After Three Years: Has It Worked?" *China Economic Quarterly*, July–September, 2004, 20–22.

19. *Economist* Intelligence Unit, *China Country Profile 2005* (London: EIU, 2005), 6.

20. U.S. Department of Defense, *Annual Report on the Military Power of the People's Republic of China* (Washington, DC: GPO, 2004).

Chapter Five

1. Robert W. Stern, *Changing India*, 2nd ed. (Cambridge: Cambridge University Press, 2003), 138.

2. D. G. Tendulkar, *Mahatma*, vol. 2 (Delhi: Government of India, 1960), 236.

3. Both quotations in this paragraph are from Tendulkar, *Mahatma*, 25.

4. Office of the Registrar General of India, *Census of India 2001* (New Delhi: Government of India, 2002).

5. Edward Luce, "Hands-On Politics: Integrity Has Given Way to Greed and Criminality in India's Public Life," *Financial Times*, October 12, 2002.

6. WGBH, "Commanding Heights: Interview with Manmohan Singh," http://www.pbs.org/wgbh/commandingheights.

7. Much of this text comes from Richard Vietor and Emily Thompson, "India on the Move," Case 9-703-050 (Boston: Harvard Business School, 2003).

8. Jairam Ramesh, interview by author, November 2002.

9. Edward Luce, "Rowdies Lower the Tone in World's Most Populous Democracy," *Financial Times*, April 20, 2002.

10. Jagdish Bhagwati and T. N. Srinivasan, *Foreign Trade Regimes and Economic Development: India* (New York: Columbia University Press, 1975), 114.

11. Quoted in Thayer Watkins, "The Economic History and the Economy of India," www.sjgh.edu/faculty/watkins/india.htm.

12. Dani Rodrik and Arvind Subramanian, "From 'Hindu Growth' to Productivity Surge: The Mystery of the Indian Growth Transition," working paper WP/04/77, International Monetary Fund, Washington, DC, May 2004.

13. John Williamson, "What Washington Means by Policy Reform," in *Latin American Adjustment: How Much Has Happened?* (Washington, DC: Institute for International Economics, 1990), ch. 2.

14. Robert Kennedy and Tersita Ramos, "India in 1996," Case 9-798-065 (Boston: Harvard Business School, 1998).

15. WGBH, "Commanding Heights: Interview with P. Chidambaram," February 6, 2001, http://www.pbs.org/wgbh/commandingheights.

16. Quoted in Joanne Slater, "Outsourcing—GE Reinvents Itself in India," *Far Eastern Economic Review*, March 27, 2003.

17. Sharda Cherwoo, CEO of shared services, Ernst & Young, interview by author, Bangalore, 2002.

18. Quoted in Vietor and Thompson, "India on the Move."

19. Aroon Purie, chief editor of *India Today*, interview by author, 2002.

20. Quoted in Lok Sabha, "Predentation on Disinvestment to Committee on Petitions," Congressional working paper, 29.

21. Arun Shourie, minister of divestment, interview by author, 2002.

22. Rakesh Mohan, interview by author, 2002.

23. Yashwant Sinha, minister of external affairs, interview by author, 2002.

24. Peter Wonacott and P. R. Venkat, "Politics & Economics: India's Economic Growth Keeps Pace With China; Agriculture Production, Strong Consumer Spending Top Multiple Forecasts," *Wall Street Journal*, June 1, 2006, p. A6.

Chapter Six

1. Quoted in Julia Preston, "A Crowning Defeat: Mexico as the Victor," *New York Times*, July 4, 2000.

2. Quoted in Richard Vietor and Rebecca Evans, "Mexico: The Unfinished Agenda," Case 9-701-116 (Boston: Harvard Business School, 2001), 1.

3. The analysis of political developments in Mexico provided in this section relies heavily on Julia Preston and Samuel Dillon, *Opening Mexico: The Making of a Democracy* (New York: Farrar, 2004), 32–84.

4. George W. Grayson, *The Politics of Mexican Oil* (Pittsburgh: University of Pittsburgh Press, 1980), 62–65.

5. World Bank, *World Bank Report* (Washington, DC: World Bank, 1987).

6. Quoted in Richard Vietor and Eilene Zimmerman, "Mexico in Debt," Case 9-797-110 (Boston: Harvard Business School, 1997), 3.

7. Helen Shapiro, "Mexico: Escaping from Debt Crisis?" Case 9-390-174 (Boston: Harvard Business School, 1990).

8. Miguel de la Madrid, interview by Helen Shapiro, January 1990.

9. Vietor and Zimmerman, "Mexico in Debt," 5.

10. De la Madrid interview.

11. Donald E. Schulz, *Mexico in Crisis* (Washington, DC: Strategic Studies Institute at the U.S. Army War College, 1995).

12. Richard Vietor and Rebecca Evans, "Mexico: The Unfinished Agenda," Case 9-701-116 (Boston: Harvard Business School, 2001), 5.

13. *Economist* Intelligence Unit, *Mexico Country Report 1990* (London: EIU, 1990).

14. Huw Pill, "Mexico (A): From Stabilized Development to Debt Crisis," Case 9-797-096 (Boston: Harvard Business School, 1997).

15. Carlos Salinas, interview by author, August 1994.

16. Donald E. Schulz and Stephen J. Wager, *The Awakening: The Zapatista Revolt and Its Implications for Civil-Military Relations and the Future of Mexico* (Washington, DC: Strategic Studies Institute, U.S. Army War College, 1994).

17. Preston and Dillon, *Opening Mexico*, 260.

18. Transparency International, "2005 Corruption Perceptions Index," http://www.transparancy.org/policy_research/surveys_indices/cpi.

19. Luis Rubio, "Democratic Politics in Mexico: New Complexities," in *Mexico Under Fox*, ed. Luis Rubio and Susan Purcell (London: Lyn Rienner Publishers, 2004).

20. Luis Rubio and Victor Lichtinger, interviews by author, October 2004.

21. Inter-American Development Bank, *Facing Up to Inequality in Latin America, 1998–1999 Report* (New York: IADB, 1998).

22. Organisation for Economic Co-operation and Development, *Economic Survey of Mexico* (Paris: OECD, 2004), 75–88.

23. Carlos Abascal, interview by author, October 2004.

Chapter Seven

1. Leonard Thompson, *A History of South Africa* (New Haven: Yale University Press, 1995), ch. 1.

2. Monica Wilson, "The Nguni People," in *The Oxford History of South Africa*, vol. 1, ed. Monica Wilson and Leonard Thompson (New York: Oxford University Press, 1971), 120.

3. Geoffrey Wheatcroft, *The Randlords* (New York: Simon & Schuster, 1985).

4. Quoted in Thompson, *A History of South Africa*, 144.

5. South African Foundation, *Growth for All: An Economic Strategy for South Africa* (Johannesburg: South African Foundation, February 1996).

6. Thompson, *A History of South Africa*, 190.

7. Quoted in Fatima Meer, *Higher Than Hope* (New York: Harper & Row, 1988), 67.

8. Allister Sparks, *The Mind of South Africa* (Jeppestown, South Africa: Jonathan Ball Publishers, 1990), ch. 15.

9. Richard Vietor, "South Africa: Getting in GEAR," Case 9-798-012 (Boston: Harvard Business School, 1998).

10. South African Police Service Criminal Information Management Center, "Report on Crime 1996," http://196.33.209.55/mious.html.

11. Office of the Presidency, *Towards a Ten-Year Review* (Pretoria, South Africa: 2003).

12. Lisa Garbus, "HIV/AIDS in South Africa," Country AIDS Policy Analysis Project, University of California at San Francisco, October 2003, http://hivinsite.ucsf.edu/insite?page=cr-ari.

13. Department of Finance, *Growth, Employment and Redistribution: A Macroeconomic Strategy* (Pretoria: Government of South Africa, June 14, 1996).

14. Thabo Mbeki, State of the Union Address to Parliament, Capetown, February 9, 2001.

15. South African Financial Community, "Financial Sector Charter," draft, 2004.

16. Jabu Molaketi, interview by author, September 2004.

Chapter Eight

1. Royal Embassy of Saudi Arabia, "Crown Prince Abdullah's Foreign Affairs Advisor Answers Questions on U.S.-Saudi Relations," July 13, 2005, www.saudiembassy.net/2005news/newsdetail.asp?cindo=5410.

2. This early history relies heavily on James Wynbrandt, *A Brief History of Saudi Arabia* (New York: Checkmark Books, 2004), ch. 1.

3. Alfred Guillaume, *The Life of Muhammad: A Translation of Ishaq's "Sirat Rasul Allah"* (New York: Oxford University Press, 1955).

4. *The Holy Quran,* translated to English by Amatul Rahman Omar, explained by Allamah Nooruddin (Korea: Noor Foundation-International, 1997), 69.

5. Abu Hakima, *The Brilliance of the Meteor in the Life of Muhammad ibn Abd al-Wahhab*; quoted in Madawi al-Rasheed, *A History of Saudi Arabia* (Cambridge: Cambridge University Press, 2002), 17.

6. Richard Vietor, *Energy Policy in America Since 1945* (New York: Cambridge University Press, 1984), ch. 1.

7. Ibid., ch. 9.

8. Significant passages of this chapter are taken directly from Richard Vietor and Rebecca Evans, "Saudi Arabia: Getting the House in Order," Case 9-702-031 (Boston: Harvard Business School, 2002).

9. Osama Bin Laden, "Declaration of War," August 23, 1996.

10. Saudi American Bank, *The Saudi Economy in 2002* (Riyadh: SAMBA, 2003).

11. Joshua Teitelbaum, *Holier Than Thou: Saudi Arabia's Islamic Opposition* (Washington, DC: Washington Institute for Near Eastern Policy, 2000).

12. Ministry of Economy and Planning, "Seventh Development Plan," http://www.planning.gov.sa/planning/introe.htm.

13. Interviews with business leaders, Jeddah and Riyadh, January 2002.

14. Richard Vietor and Rebecca Evans, "World Oil Markets," Case 9-702-030 (Boston: Harvard Business School, 2002).

15. Quoted in "Regal Reformer," *Financial Times,* June 25, 2001.

16. Kingdom of Saudi Arabia Supreme Commission for Tourism, *Sustainable Tourism Development Plan,* draft version 7 (Riyadh: Commission for Tourism, 2002).

17. Brad Bourland, *The Saudi Economy: 2004 Performance, 2005 Forecast* (Riyadh: SAMBA Financial Group, 2005).

18. K. S. Ramkumar and Michel Cousins, "Saudization: The Battle Ahead," *Arab News,* January 2002.

19. Interview by author, Jeddah, January 2002.

20. Center for Monitoring the Impact of Peace and the American Jewish Committee, *The West, Christians, and Jews in Saudi Arabian Schoolbooks,* http://www.edume.org/reports/10/toc.htm.

21. Hani A. Z. Yamani, author of *To Be a Saudi,* interview by author, January 2002.

22. Hani A. Z. Yamani, *To Be a Saudi* (London: Janus Publishing Co., 1997), 125.

23. Elaine Sciolino, "Riyadh Journal: Taking a Rare Peek Inside the Royal House of Saud," *New York Times,* January 28, 2002, 4.

24. National Public Radio, *Morning Edition: Saudi Women,* February 25, 2002.

25. Nazih Ayubi, quoted in Teitelbaum, *Holier Than Thou.*

26. Ralph Peters, "The Saudi Threat," *Wall Street Journal,* October 29, 2001.

27. Nawaf Obaid, "In Al-Saud We Trust," *Foreign Policy,* February 2002, 72–74.

28. Matthew Simmons, *Twilight in the Desert* (Hoboken, NJ: John Wiley & Sons, 2005).

29. CNN.com, "Excerpts from Saudi Crown Prince's Speech," March 28, 2002.

30. PBS, "Frontline: Interview with Prince Bandar Bin Sultan," September 2001, www.pbs.org/wgbh/pages/frontline/shows/terrorism/interviews/Bandar.html

Chapter Nine

1. This chapter was drafted with considerable help from Alexander Veytsman, an economics graduate student at Harvard University and my research assistant.

2. Boris Yeltsin, *The Presidential Marathon* (Moscow: AST, 2000).

3. Joseph Stalin, *The Problem of Leninism* (Moscow: Foreign Languages Publishing House, 1953), 454.

4. Alexander Dyck, "The USSR 1988: The Search for Growth," Case 9-795-060 (Boston: Harvard Business School, 1995).

5. Marshall Goldman, *The Privatization of Russia* (London: Routledge, 2003), 62.

6. David Hoffman, *The Oligarchs* (New York: Public Affairs, 2002), 14–15.

7. Quoted in John Lloyd, "Yeltsin Deputy Attacks Government," *Financial Times*, December 18, 1996.

8. Andrei Schleifer and Robert Vishny, *The Grabbing Hand: Government Pathologies and Their Cures* (Cambridge, MA: Harvard University Press, 1998), 11; quoted in Rawi Abdelal, "Russia: The End of a Time of Troubles," Case 9-701-076 (Boston: Harvard Business School, 2001), 5.

9. Quoted in Abdelal, "Russia," 4.

10. Alan Greenspan, speech to the Woodrow Wilson International Center for Scholars, New York, June 10, 1997, 5; quoted in Goldman, *The Privatization of Russia*, 30.

11. Abdelal, "Russia," 8–11.

12. Ibid.

13. Quoted in Lilia Shevtsova, *Putin's Russia* (Washington, DC: Carnegie Foundation, 2003), 30–32.

14. Quoted in Abdelal, "Russia," 12.

15. Ibid., 12.

16. Ibid., 13.

17. Rawi Abdelel, "The State," Case 9-701-077 (Boston: Harvard Business School, 2001).

Chapter Ten

1. Commission of the European Communities Directorate General Economic and Financial Affairs, *The EU Economy: 2004 Review*, ECFIN (2004) REP 50455-EN, 8.

2. Michael Calingaert, *The Challenge from Europe: Development of the European Community's Internal Market* (Washington, DC: National Planning Association, 1988), and Pascal Fontaine, *Europe in 10 Points* (Luxembourg: European Commission, 1998).

3. Much of this section is taken from Richard Vietor and Sabina Ciminero, "European Monetary Union," Case 9-799-131 (Boston: Harvard Business School, 1999).

4. "A Survey of Europe's Internal Market," *Economist*, July 8, 1988, 8.

5. Commission of the European Communities, *Completing the Internal Market: White Paper from the Commission to the European Council* (Brussels: European Commission, June 14, 1985).

6. Interview by author in Amsterdam, April 7, 1999.

7. Ibid.

8. European Commission, *Economic Reform: Report on the Function of Community Product and Capital Markets* (Brussels: European Commission, 1998), 6.

9. European Commission, *The Single Market Review: Impact on Services—Credit Institutions and Banking*, vol. 3 (Brussels: European Commission, 1997), 19–23.

10. In the summer of 2005, for example, ABN AMRO of the Netherlands tried to buy Banca Antonveneta of Italy. Antonio Fazio, head of the Bank of Italy, intervened to redirect the merger to Banca Popolare Italiana. See Rawi Abdelal and Christopher Bruner, "Politics and Prudential Supervision: ABN AMRO's Bid for Antonveneta," Case 9-706-009 (Boston: Harvard Business School, 2005).

11. Interview by author, Deutsche Bank, April 8, 1999.

12. European Union, *The EU Economy: 2004 Review*, 115–119.

13. Organization of Economic Cooperation and Development, *Benefit Systems and Work Incentives, 1998* (Paris: OECD, 1999); and European Commission, *Economic Reform*.

14. Organization of Economic Cooperation and Development, *Employment Outlook, 2004* (Paris: OECD, 2004).

15. Tito Boeri, "Reforming Labor and Product Markets: Some Lessons from Two Decades of Experiments in Europe," working paper WP/05/97, International Monetary Fund, Washington, DC, May 2005.

16. Interview by author at the European Central Bank, April 19, 1999.

17. Much of this portion of text is taken from Richard Vietor and Rebecca Evans, "Italy: A New Commitment to Growth," Case 9-703-007 (Boston: Harvard Business School, 2003).

18. Kristien Michoel of NOMISMA, interview by author, February 2000.

19. Hilary Partridge, *Italian Politics Today* (Manchester: Manchester University Press, 1998), 81.

20. Mario Mignone, *Italy Today: At the Crossroads of the New Millennium* (New York: Peter Lang Publishing, 1999), 149.

21. Italian Institute of Foreign Trade, "Spotlighting Italy: Focus on Clusters," *Economist*, February 5, 2000, quoted in Vietor and Evans, "Italy: A New Commitment to Growth."

22. Michael E. Porter, *The Competitive Advantage of Nations* (New York: Free Press, 1980).

23. Giuseppe Bussolari, Industria Macchine Automatiche director, interview by author, February 2000.

24. Europa, "The Lisbon Special European Council (March 2000): Toward a Europe of Innovation and Knowledge" (Brussels: Europa, 2000).

25. European Union, *The EU Economy: 2004 Review*, 160–164.

26. Marian Tupy, "EU Enlargement: Costs, Benefits, and Strategies for Central and Eastern European Countries," *Policy Analysis*, September 18, 2003.

27. Silvio Berlusconi, interview by author, June 2002.

28. Banca D'Italia, *Economic Bulletin*, no. 40, March 2005.

Chapter Eleven

1. Heizo Takenaka, minister of economy and fiscal policy, interview by author, June 3, 2005.

2. Junichiro Koizumi, quoted in Richard Vietor and Rebecca Evans, "Japan: Beyond the Bubble," Case 9-702-004 (Boston: Harvard Business School, 2002).

3. Parts of this chapter are taken from three Harvard Business School cases: Richard Vietor, "Japan: Free, Fair and Global," Case 9-798-083 (Boston: Harvard Business School, 1998); Vietor and Evans, "Japan: Beyond the Bubble"; and Richard Vietor, "Japan: Deficits, Demography and Deflation," Case 9-706-004 (Boston: Harvard Business School, 2005).

4. Takatoshi Ito, *The Japanese Economy* (Cambridge, MA: MIT Press, 1992).

5. Eisuke Sakakibara and Robert Alan Feldman, "The Japanese Financial System in Comparative Perspective," *Journal of Comparative Economics* 7 (1983): 1–24.

6. Minoru Makihara, president of Mitsubishi, interview by author, 1998.

7. National Institute of Population and Social Security Research, *Population Projections for Japan: 2001–2050* (Tokyo, January 2002).

8. Japanese Ministry of Finance, "Ministry of Finance Seminar on the Japanese Economy and Japanese Government Bonds" (Tokyo, January 2005), 24, 27–28.

9. Paul Krugman, "It's Baaack! Japan's Slump and the Return of the Liquidity Trap," Brookings Paper on Economic Activity, February 1998, 137–187.

10. Nobuyuko Takakura, senior policy coordinator, policy planning and evaluation division, minister's secretariat, Ministry of Health and Welfare, interview by author, 1998.

11. CNN.com, "Short on Detail, Koizumi Pledges Deep Reforms," May 7, 2001, http://archives.cnn.com/2001/world/ascapcf/east/05/07/japan/koizumi.03.

12. General Affairs Divisions, Pension Bureau, *Brief Overview of 2004 Pension Revision* (Tokyo: Pension Bureau, December 2004).

13. Hiroshi Yoshikawa, Council on Economic and Fiscal Policy, interview by author, June 2005.

14. *Economist* Intelligence Unit, *Japan Country Report 2005* (London: EIU, March 2005).

15. Hiromitsu Ishi, chairman, Tax System Council, interview by author, June 2005.

16. Kakutaro Kitashiro, chairman of IBM and chairman of Keizai Doyukai, interview by author, June 2005.

Chapter Twelve

1. Gavin Wright, "Natural Resources," in *Encyclopedia of the United States in the Twentieth Century*, vol. 3, ed. Stanley Kutler et al. (New York: Charles Scribner's Sons, 1996), 1383–1406.

2. Thomas McCraw, "American Capitalism," in *Creating Modern Capitalism*, ed. McCraw (Cambridge, MA: Harvard University Press, 1997), 303–350.

3. Alfred D. Chandler Jr., *The Visible Hand: The Managerial Revolution in American Business* (Cambridge, MA: Harvard University Press, 1977).

4. Richard Vietor, *Contrived Competition: Regulation and Deregulation in America* (Cambridge, MA: Harvard University Press, 1994).

5. John Maynard Keynes, *The General Theory of Employment, Interest and Money* (London: MacMillian, 1936).

6. Stephen Bailey, *Congress Makes a Law: The Story Behind the Employment Act of 1946* (New York: Columbia University Press, 1950).

7. Michael G. Rukstad, "The Tax Cut of 1964," Case 9-382-078 (Boston: Harvard Business School, 1982).

8. Richard Nixon, "Message on Extension of Surtax," March 26, 1969.

9. Pete Peterson, *The United States in the Changing World Economy* (Washington, DC: GPO, 1971).

10. William Safire, *Before the Fall* (New York: Doubleday, 1975), 510.

11. Richard Vietor, *Energy Policy in America Since 1945* (New York: Cambridge University Press, 1984), ch. 10.

12. Vietor, *Contrived Competition*.

13. Michael G. Rukstad, "The Decline of the Dollar: 1978," Case 9-384-116 (Boston: Harvard Business School, 1984).

14. Jack Kemp and David Stockman, "Avoiding a GOP Economic Dunkirk," reprinted in George Lodge, "The Reagan Plan," Case 9-381-173 (Boston: Harvard Business School, 1981).

15. *New York Times*, February 20, 1981.

16. Jay Kim, "The Energizer Bunny President," *Harvard Crimson*, December 15, 1993.

17. Walter Dean Burnham, "The Politics of Repudiation," *The American Prospect* 4, no. 12 (January 1993).

18. Ibid.

19. Robert E. Rubin, *In an Uncertain World* (New York: Random House, 2003), 119.

20. William Clinton, *A Vision of Change for America* (Washington, DC: Office of Management and the Budget, February 17, 1993), 5.

21. George W. Bush, *A Blueprint for New Beginnings* (Washington, DC: Office of Management and Budget, February 28, 2001), 3.

22. Donald Marron, Acting Director, Congressional Budget Office, testimony before the House Subcommittee on National Security, July 18, 2006.

ACKNOWLEDGMENTS

OVER THE PAST TEN YEARS, I have taught Business, Government, and the International Economy to more than twenty-four hundred executives attending the Advanced Management Program at the Harvard Business School. The opportunity to discuss international political economy with these smart managers has overwhelmingly shaped this book. In each of these countries, interviews with senior executives, bureaucrats, presidents, and prime ministers were arranged by my enthusiastic students, determined to help me learn. For this, I am immensely grateful.

The Harvard Business School has unstintingly supported this expensive research. The school financed my travel and my research assistants, never turning down a single request. And indeed, I have had some wonderful research assistants. Sabina Ciminero, Rebecca Evans, Emily Thompson, Alex Veytsman, and Eilene Zimmerman have done the basic research on these countries, arranged interviews, traveled to distant places, and drafted the cases on which this manuscript draws. My friend Ben Wechsler patiently helped with proofreading; Juliana Seminerio, my assistant, has helped with research, produced tables and charts, patiently edited my faulty prose, and got the manuscript together. Jeff Kehoe, my editor at Harvard Business School Press, and the rest of the staff there have been immensely helpful. I can't thank these individuals enough.

Special thanks go to my colleague Professor Rawi Abdelal, who allowed me to use his work on Russia. And I have long been grateful to Professor Bruce Scott, who created the underlying analytical concepts of Business, Government, and the International Economy—the application of strategy, structure, and context to the nation-state.

While I have been traveling seventy to eighty days a year for the past several years, my wife, Cindy, has patiently managed our home and raised our children. Without her love and commitment, there would be no book.

RICHARD H. K. VIETOR is the Senator John Heinz Professor of Environmental Management at the Harvard Graduate School of Business Administration. Professor Vietor received a BA from Union College, an MA from Hofstra University, and a PhD from the University of Pittsburgh. He taught history at the University of Missouri before coming to the Harvard Business School. At Harvard, he teaches courses in regulation and in international political economy.

Professor Vietor's research on business and government policy has been published in numerous journals and books. His books include *Environmental Politics and the Coal Coalition* (1980), *Energy Policy in America Since 1945* (1984), *Telecommunications in Transition* (1986), *Strategic Management in the Regulated Environment* (1989), *Contrived Competition: Regulation and Deregulation in America* (1994), *Business Management and the Natural Environment* (1996), and *Globalization and Growth: Case Studies in National Economic Strategies* (2004). Vietor has written more than eighty-five cases, on environmental and economic regulation and on national development strategy.

He serves on the board of the *Business History Review* and the Luigi Gerardo Napolitano Society, and the advisory boards of Airtricity, IESE (Spain), IPADE (Mexico), and INALDE (Colombia). He is consultant to several corporations and to the Prime Minister of Malaysia.

Professor Vietor and his wife, Cindy, have three adult children—Nicholas, Christopher, and Meredith.